Democracy, Market Economics, and Development

An Asian Perspective

Farrukh Iqbal and Jong-Il You
Editors

The World Bank
Washington, D.C.

Cover design by UltraDesigns

Library of Congress Cataloging-in-Publication Data

Democracy, market economics, and development / edited by Farrukh Iqbal, Jong-Il You.
        p. cm.
    Includes bibliographical references.
    ISBN 0-8213-4862-0
        1. Capitalism. 2. Democracy. 3. Economic development. I. Iqbal, Farrukh. II. You,
Jong-Il, 1958-

HB501 .D423 2001
338.9—dc21   2001017950

CONTENTS

FOREWORD

This book contains a selection of papers which were originally presented at a conference held in Seoul, Korea in February 1999. The idea for the conference arose the year before in a meeting between Mr. Kim Dae-jung, President of the Republic of Korea and Mr. James Wolfensohn, President of the World Bank Group. Recognizing that the recent travails of the East Asian region provided an opportunity to review the links between styles of political governance, economic strategies and development, they agreed to sponsor a conference at which these issues could be discussed among development practitioners, political leaders, and members of civil society. This book is being published to bring some of this thinking to a larger audience.

The conference revealed some common patterns in views and experiences. There was broad agreement on the need to conceive of development as a multi-faceted objective rather than one comprising solely of changes in income per capita. Regarding governance, it was noted that civil and political liberties were important in their own right as well as effective instruments with which to attack corruption and poverty. The need to achieve social consensus and support through participatory means was highlighted in discussions about the design and implementation of market-oriented economic reforms. Good corporate governance, supported by sound and prudential regulations, was also thought necessary for markets to operate in the public interest. Finally, there was a broad consensus that developments in Asia reveal complex links running from values and culture through institutions to economic performance which suggest that it is inappropriate to ascribe the 1997-98 crisis in East Asia to a simple-minded conception of so-called Asian values. These ideas and others are discussed at length in the papers that have been selected for this book.

The perspectives discussed in these papers were shaped in part by the comments and suggestions of several persons who served as moderators, discussants and panelists at the conference. In this connection, we gratefully acknowledge the contributions of Sri-Ram Aiyer, Walden Bello,

Mark Malloch Brown, Yung Hee Choi, Yul Choi, Soo Bok Chung, Peter Geithner, Carolina Hernandez, Chul Kyu Kang, Moon Kyu Kang, Daniel Kaufmann, Il Soo Kim, Choongsoo Kim, Keum Soo Kim, Robert Klitgaard, Duk Seung Lee, Jin Soon Lee, Gill-Chin Lim, Ronald Maclean-Abaroa, Kamal Malhotra, Don Oberdorfer, Mari Pangestu, Funkoo Park, Won Soon Park, Young Hye Park, Hak-Yong Rhee, Shaha Riza, Jean-Michel Severino, Gunnar Stalsett, Laksamana Sukardi, Kari Tapiola, Vinod Thomas, Lisa Veneklasen, Vivienne Wee, Lynn Williams, William Witherell and Jung Sook Yoon. In addition, we would like to thank the following persons who rendered invaluable help in making the conference a success: Byung-Goo Cho, Hun Choi, Kwang-Hai Choi, Ha-Won Jang, Mun-Soo Kang, Choon-Sun Kim, Ho-Shik Kim, Jin-Pyo Kim, Tae-Dong Kim, Joyce Rompass and Haruyuki Shimada. Migara de Silva rendered able assistance in preparing the manuscript for publication.

Finally, we would like to acknowledge the financial support of the Government of Japan, the Government of Korea and the World Bank, and the organizational support of the Korea Development Institute and the World Bank Institute which enabled the conference to be held.

Farrukh Iqbal
Jong-Il You

CONTRIBUTORS

William A. Douglas
Adjunct Professorial Lecturer, School of Advanced International Studies, Johns Hopkins University, Washington, DC, USA

Francis Fukuyama
Omer L. and Nancy Hirst Professor of Public Policy, George Mason University, Virginia, USA

Stephan M. Haggard
Professor, Graduate School of International Relations & Pacific Studies, University of California, San Diego, California, USA

Kuniko Inoguchi
Professor, Faculty of Law, Sophia University, Tokyo, Japan

Farrukh Iqbal
Lead Economist, World Bank Institute, The World Bank, Washington, DC, USA

Ha-sung Jang
Professor, College of Business Administration, Korea University, Seoul, Republic of Korea

Kim Dae-jung
Nobel Laureate and President, Republic of Korea

Minxin Pei
Senior Fellow, Carnegie Endowment for International Peace, Washington, DC, USA

Amartya Sen
Nobel Laureate and Master of Trinity College, University of Cambridge, Cambridge, UK.

Joseph Stiglitz
Professor, Department of Economics, Stanford University, Palo Alto, California, USA

Jong-Il You
Professor, School of Public Policy and Management, Korean Development Institute, Seoul, Republic of Korea

Jong-keun You
Governor, North Cholla Province, Republic of Korea

OVERVIEW

Farrukh Iqbal and Jong-Il You

This book presents a selection from papers originally presented at a conference entitled Democracy, Market Economy and Development that was held in Seoul, Republic of Korea, in February 1999. The main objective of the conference was to examine the extent to which democracy is important to the achievement of sustainable development. While it is widely accepted that economic freedom, as ensured broadly by the operation of the economy according to market or laissez-faire principles, is a critical determinant of development, the role of political freedom, as ensured broadly by the practice of democracy, is less well understood. The scope of this overview is limited to the ideas, references, and cases covered by the selected papers. The papers focus largely on the experience of East Asia in recent years. Thus, other experiences, such as those of Eastern European countries and Russia, while certainly relevant to the understanding of the links between political governance and economic outcomes, are not covered here.

Five common themes are prominent in the papers published here, as encapsulated in the following propositions:

- Democracy and markets are "two wheels of a cart." This metaphor is offered by Kim Dae-jung, President of the Republic of Korea, to emphasize that both democratic politics and market economics are needed to improve the lives of citizens. This proposition is discussed at length by several papers here.
- Democracy is intrinsic to development. This proposition is at the core of the paper by Amartya Sen. Sen argues that development, by definition, should include a component of civil and human rights and liberties, and that those rights and liberties are best conveyed by the democratic system of governance.
- Participation is fundamental to democracy and development. A democratic system is a necessary condition for sustainable development, but not a sufficient one. Rather than its mere mechanics, it is the practice of democracy, as demonstrated by the scope for voice and by the openness and transparency of the system, that is most critical to the long-term sustainability of development. This idea is most prominently espoused in the paper by Joseph Stiglitz.

- Liberal participatory democracy promotes sustainable economic reforms by ensuring the legitimacy of reform efforts. In the absence of "buy-in" from affected groups, reforms are often blocked at the implementation stage and sometimes reversed. Several papers in this volume address various aspects of this proposition. Notably, the preconditions that participatory democracy requires in order to fully support reforms are discussed, with supporting evidence from the experiences of countries in Latin America and Asia.
- The political and economic institutions of Asia and the West are set to converge. The debate about "Asian values" has been inconclusive. In general, it appears likely, as Francis Fukuyama puts it, that the "distinctive institutions and practices fostered by Asia's cultural systems will converge over time with the patterns seen in the West."

COMPLEMENTARITY OF DEMOCRACY AND MARKETS

In the first paper, which is distilled from his opening address at the conference, President Kim Dae-jung introduces a metaphor that anticipates much of the discussion to follow, by comparing democracy and the market economy to "two wheels of a cart" that must move together and that depend on each other for forward motion. Market-friendly economic policies can by themselves produce prolonged income growth, but the sustainability of such growth is enhanced by democratic policies and institutions. Operation of the market process in an authoritarian rather than in a democratic environment typically has two serious shortcomings: namely, that it concentrates wealth and economic power (an "equity" issue) and that it is prone to corruption and regulatory failures (a "governance" issue). These shortcomings, their probable causes, and the most promising remedies are widely discussed in other papers.

President Kim supports his metaphor with references to the case of Korea, where rapid economic growth came at the costs of rampant cronyism and of inequality between regions and income groups. He argues that the lack of fair and transparent rules of competition produced a financial system riddled with cronyism; unchecked by democratic institutions, the resulting inefficiencies ultimately caused a full-fledged financial crisis. He concludes:

> If Korea had pursued a parallel development of democracy and a market economy from the start, it would have been possible to check the collusive relationship between government and big business that developed within the government-controlled financial sector. It would even have been possible to avoid the destructive storm of the currency crisis.

The complementarity argument for democracy is also advanced by Amartya Sen, who argues that democracy can help markets function better by providing political incentives for good governance. The recent crisis in the region, he argues, is "the penalty of undemocratic governance." Sen identifies a link between the crisis and the lack of transparency in corporate and financial matters, observing that "the absence of democratic process meant that influential families and organizations were able to conduct their business essentially unchallenged."

You Jong-keun also refers to the complementarity of democracy and markets. He connects the two concepts via the rule of law, noting that "rule of law is the foundation of a market economy" and that "democracy promotes the rule of law through checks and balances on the exercise of power." You illustrates this connection with the example of the Korean financial sector: The proliferation of moral hazard and the evaporation of discipline in the Korean financial sector was, he argues, "not for want of prudential regulations but because of the government's inability to enforce them." The lack of enforcement in turn stemmed from the long entrenchment in power of a single political party, a situation that only changed with the onset of a financial crisis in 1997.

Evidence that the relationship between democracy and markets also works the other way—for example, that societies that achieve certain threshold levels of prosperity typically become politically freer—is provided by several papers, including those of Pei Minxin and Stephan Haggard. Sustained prosperity is typically associated with a rise in education levels, growth of the middle class, and an increase in economic and cultural linkages with the outside world. These factors in turn help to create greater demand for political and civil liberties, and provide a solid structural foundation for the responsible exercise of, and support for, such liberties.

CONTRIBUTIONS OF DEMOCRACY TO DEVELOPMENT

To fully appreciate the connection between development and democracy it is important to be clear about the meanings of these terms. Amartya Sen makes a strong case that development should be broadly understood to mean the process by which society's ability to enjoy various freedoms—including civil and political rights, income security, and the right to transact in the market—is enhanced.

Sen identifies three ways in which democracy can contribute to this broad goal of development. First, intrinsically, by enriching the lives of citizens through providing more political and civil freedoms. Second, instrumentally, by providing political incentives for responsive and good governance. And third, constructively, by providing the opportunity for the debate and discussion that helps formulate a system of values and priorities. The first point is self-evident: Political and civil rights are ends in themselves, and democracy provides the best means to achieve these ends. The second point suggests that the checks and balances inherent in a democratic system contribute to good governance. The third point is more complex and is based on two propositions: that social preferences cannot be merely inferred but must be established through public discussion; and that it is the democratic process that is best able to elicit, describe, and modulate such preferences.

Sen's famous assertion that famine cannot occur in a liberal democracy illustrates the point he makes about the positive contribution of democracy. In this example, the constructive role of democracy helps to define a strongly anti-famine social preference, regardless of ethnic and class considerations, and its instrumental role helps to ensure that government moves swiftly to prevent or mitigate famine. Democracy's intrinsic contribution to society's freedom from hunger is self-evident. Nevertheless, some paradoxes remain. As Sen notes, democratic governance in countries such as India has for long periods of time coexisted with "social ills" like mass illiteracy, malnutrition, and gender bias.

The discussion of the contribution of democracy to development has so far been largely at the conceptual level. It is possible to add an empirical perspective as well since a substantial body of empirical work, including several items referenced by Pei Minxin in this volume, is now available. In general, the literature finds no statistically significant relationship between measures of democracy and measures of income growth. Some studies report a weak positive correlation and others a weak negative one. The relationship may in reality be nonlinear, with improvements in political rights and civil liberties resulting in significant growth for countries with initially high levels of repression, and lesser growth for those that already enjoy some degree of democracy. A much stronger connection is found between corruption and democracy. Corruption tends to be lowest in countries with the highest degree of civil and political liberties, suggesting that the checks and balances inherent in a democratic political system are effective in reducing corruption. Among democracies, the older and better established countries tend to have much lower corruption than the newer, fledgling ones. Corruption is also generally found to have an adverse effect on the quantity and quality of investment. To the extent that investment promotes income growth, this result may be taken to provide indirect support for the assertion that democracy has a positive impact on growth. An interesting nuance is reported by Pei Minxin based on his own empirical analysis. He shows that while both economic freedom and democracy are related to income growth, policies that affect the former have a much more powerful effect on reducing corruption than policies that aim primarily at the latter. This leads him to conclude that, where a choice must be made, it would be better to promote economic freedoms initially while leaving political reform to a later stage. Of course, where a choice need not be made, it would be best to pursue both sets of reforms simultaneously.

DEMOCRACY, PARTICIPATION, AND DEVELOPMENT

Just as it is important to be clear about the meaning of development, so should the meaning and content of democracy be understood. The consensus of these papers is that democracy is more than just votes, elections, and majority rule. Amartya Sen, for example, argues that democracy "requires the protection of liberties and freedoms, respect for legal entitlements, and the guarantee of free discussion and uncensored distribution of news." This is consistent with the view expressed by Joseph Stiglitz, who notes that "participation does not refer simply to voting . . . [but] must entail open dialogue and broadly active civic engagement." Stiglitz argues that the participatory process must extend through national government to local and provincial government, to the workplace, and to the capital markets.

Why is participation so important? Stiglitz offers several reasons. To begin with, participation helps mitigate the "agency problem," in which the interests of the agent are not necessarily those of the owners. Agency problems are most likely to occur in a situation where there is concentrated economic and political power, such as is typically observed under a politically authoritarian regime. In such situations, the lack of transparency in the decision-making process creates a risk that the agent (for example, the national government or a company manager) will act in a way that is contrary to the best interests of the owners (citizens or shareholders). A typical example of agency abuse would be the diversion of public resources to special groups. Participatory processes can reduce this risk by strengthening civil society as a means of countervailing cronyism, by mandating the "right to know" for the average citizen, and providing the mechanisms to enforce this right. In the United States, for example, such mechanisms include the Freedom of Information Act, and the right to sue for information about the use of public resources.

Participatory processes can facilitate social development, specifically the ability of a society to reconcile competing interests in a nonviolent, noncoercive fashion. They do so by helping to create a sense of community and trust—or in academic parlance, by building social capital. Social capital can in turn support the establishment of the credit culture that is necessary to strengthen the underpinnings of a financial system. It can also enable the establishment of civic norms and practices that reduce crime, corruption, and violence, thereby allowing markets to work both more efficiently and more equitably.

Participatory processes are also important to the conduct and governance of business corporations, which are often significant consumers of public resources and, through their impact on employment and credit flows, can have a significant effect on public welfare. Joint-stock limited companies obtain certain privileges from the public, in return for which they are expected to operate within laws and guidelines consistent with the public interest. The quality of corporate governance and performance may have significant negative externalities. For example, the bankruptcy of a large corporation can have a serious effect on the economy, imposing costs on stakeholder groups other than those with a direct interest in the bankrupt corporation itself—including the average taxpayer. As Stiglitz puts it:

> These are issues that involve both economics and participatory processes. If citizens fail to participate in the decision-making process, and by so doing allow businesses to delay the building or implementation of the necessary legal and regulatory framework, those same citizens will face adverse consequences that clearly are not of their own direct making.

The Korean *chaebols* provide a case in point, as described by Jang Ha-sung:

> [The] *chaebols* do not have any corporate governance mechanisms, either internal or external. All decisions are made by the chairman, who exercises absolute and unquestioned authority. No chairman of a *chaebol* has ever taken responsibility for a failed investment or for an illegal activity. Accounting manipulation and improprieties are standard practice . . . and legal protection of shareholder's rights . . . extremely limited.

Jang argues that poor corporate governance was at the root of *chaebol* infringements of investors' rights, and is the explanation for their ubiquitous involvement in seemingly all cases of political corruption and large-scale bribery. It was this corporate misgovernance that enabled the over-borrowing and over-investment by Korea's giant corporations that ultimately brought down the economy.

Jang makes an interesting point about the role of public participation in ensuring proper functioning of the market. He argues that, to foster sustainable and equitable development, it is necessary to protect the rights of the individual as worker, consumer, investor, and taxpayer. Competitive markets help to protect the first three rights, and competitive politics the fourth. Where competition is unequal, the state must set new rules, assisted by external forces "in areas where government cannot or should not intervene." Those external forces include the general public. By scoring some landmark successes against the largest *chaebols*, Jang argues that recent minority shareholder activism has made important advances in the protection of investors' rights in Korea, and has shown that the active participation of the concerned public can enhance the rights of all stakeholders.

A final point concerns the connection between participatory processes and the effectiveness and sustainability of economic policies and reforms. Two observations are appropriate here. First, although it has been reasonably argued that participatory processes—which require that the public be informed, their opinion sought, and their interests reconciled—can be slow, there are also occasions when such processes can expedite decision-making. Where an authoritarian government might delay a decision in order to protect the vested interests of its cronies, a democratic, participatory government would not be hobbled by the same constraints. In its waning months, the Suharto regime in Indonesia notoriously avoided taking decisions on bank closures and mergers to protect the financial interests of certain well-connected families, for example. Second, participatory processes enhance the legitimacy of reforms, and thereby promote their sustainability. This point is discussed below.

DEMOCRACY, LEGITIMACY, AND REFORMS

One of the most persuasive arguments for participatory democracy rests in its potential to help attain and sustain difficult economic reforms. The open discussion that is at the core of participatory democracy makes possible the reconciliation of different interests, and broad agreement on reform. This in turn makes possible the creation of a sense that the burden of change and adjustment will be shared fairly across society, thus giving the reform measures a degree of legitimacy and of public ownership.

William Douglas provides here a discussion of how inclusion and transparency can help the cause of reform. Douglas notes that for adjustment programs to be acceptable to labor—a critical stakeholder group—they must be shown to be effective, necessary, desirable, fair, and consensual. A participatory approach is essential for the realization of the last three conditions. Douglas argues that authoritarian governments typically proceed without regard to the need for desirable, fair, and consensual reform, focusing instead on those measures recommended by technocrats as being necessary and likely to be effective. Little thought is given to which groups are likely to bear the brunt of the reform measures, nor to how they might react: it should not be surprising, therefore, that reform programs that are not constructed through a participatory and inclusive process often fail to take root. As Douglas puts it, "Adjustment programs designed behind closed doors by finance ministers and International Financial Institution (IFI) representatives and then handed down as *diktats* to the public have little hope of gaining the acceptance that is so important to their chances of success."

An Asian example of how an inclusive process can expedite reforms is provided by Korea. Labor market rigidity was among the key structural problems obstructing Korean efforts to recover from the financial crisis of 1997. To break down this rigidity, the newly elected government of President Kim Dae-jung organized a Tripartite Commission of representatives of government, business, and labor to discuss and negotiate reform strategies. This was the first time in Korea that labor had been formally included in policy discussions. Despite the contentious nature of the underlying issues, the commission was able to produce an accord containing detailed measures for restructuring the Korean corporate sector, and labor concessions on issues such as redundancies, retraining, and severance. The failure of employment to keep pace with improvements in the corporate sector has since put pressure on the accord, but it has held.

The Korean experience, and the Latin American experience with structural adjustment in the 1980s, suggest that adjustment can be "facilitated under democratic auspices through corporatist institutions that provide a consultative forum between political leaders and . . . major interest groups" (Haggard). For corporatist solutions to be effective, these interest groups must be significant stakeholders with the internal cohesiveness to ensure that they deliver the necessary compliance with any agreements reached. For the new or re-energized democracies of Asia, Haggard notes:

> Corporatist arrangements along the lines of the small European democracies are not likely to constitute an option for most developing countries in Asia because of the weakness of interest groups; other representative institutions and a more fragmented nongovernmental institution (NGO) sector will have to play this role.

Haggard draws attention to another, somewhat paradoxical, aspect of the Asian situation. He notes that regulatory failure was at the heart of the financial crisis in Asia, and that regulatory reforms to strengthen and give greater autonomy to technocratic groups within the bureaucracy are the preferred solution to problems of financial and corporate governance. One such technocratic group is the Financial Restructuring Agency of Thailand, an independent body set up and charged by the Thai government to pass judgment on the insolvency or illiquidity of Thai finance companies, and to manage the assets of the insolvent ones. Similar agencies are also in operation in Korea and Indonesia. The paradox lies in the idea of an elected group (parliament) strengthening the powers of a nonelected group (technocrats) to achieve reform and recovery, a process that would appear to run contrary to the policy of enhancing public participation in reform, and that would seemingly also reduce the policy space over which democracy might be exercised in the future. The antidemocratic tendency of this delegation of power can be mitigated by the use of parliamentary oversight mechanisms to allow for public comment and review, however, and, given the limitations of representative democracy in some countries, these mechanisms could also exercise a disciplining effect on technocratic groups. The minority shareholder movement discussed by Jang Ha-sung appears to be playing such a role in Korea.

The case of Japan provides insight into the practicalities—or otherwise—of attempting the technocratic/corporatist solution. Policy-making in Japan has for decades been strongly influenced by two groups, bureaucrats and well-organized interest groups such as the construction and banking lobbies. But according to Kuniko Inoguchi, this arrangement has become increasingly dysfunctional over the last decade, with administrative and economic reforms in Japan moving too slowly to revive the economy. While Japanese society is ready to become more closely integrated with the rest of the world, Japanese bureaucracy continues to stubbornly adhere to its now redundant role as a "transmitter and gatekeeper of global standards and values." Compounding the problem, the business lobbies obstruct policy adjustments that would benefit the consumer if it appears that they would impose even short-term costs on business and labor.

Inoguchi argues that Japan's interests would be best served by a truly inclusive democratic system. She claims that the dominance of middle-aged men in positions of power in government, business, the labor unions, and the universities has limited the range of reforms that are considered feasible, and has produced a preponderance of construction-based reflation plans in every reform attempt. Insufficient attention is given to social reforms that would improve housing, child-care services, and services for the elderly; reforms that would provide more variety in education; business reforms that would assist nontraditional businesses such as software development; and finance reforms that would provide venture capital. Inoguchi notes that "if Japanese institutions were to appoint more women to higher positions, it is likely that the Japanese economy would be more resilient, more flexible, and more creative—in fact, more reform-oriented."

ASIAN VALUES AND DEMOCRATIC DEVELOPMENT

There has been much discussion in recent years about the connection between "Asian values" and development. For convenience, the issues may be framed by two questions: Do Asian values provide an edge or a handicap in economic development? And are they antithetical to liberal democracy? These questions need to be addressed both at the conceptual and at the empirical level.

At the conceptual level, many argue that the term "Asian values" is so general as to be meaningless. Where attempts have been made to define the term, it is often taken to imply a supposed Confucian value system of paternalistic authoritarianism that rates order and hierarchy higher than individual rights and competition. This definition immediately invites four questions. First, in what sense can Confucian values be taken to represent the cultures of non-Sinic Asia: for example, of countries like Malaysia and Indonesia, where Islam is the dominant religion? Second, is Confucianism the only important influence in countries like Korea, Japan, and China? Amartya Sen argues, for example, that Christianity and Buddhism have also been important in shaping the value systems that prevail in northern Asia, and both of these traditions are generally supportive of the notion of individual freedoms and rights. Third, can Confucianism be equated with paternalistic authoritarianism? Sen again notes the existence of different schools within Confucianism and remarks that "Confucianism does not speak with one voice." Fourth, one must question the implied link between values and behavior. As Francis Fukuyama notes, "values almost never have a direct impact on behavior; they must be mediated through a variety of institutions to make themselves manifest." The explanations for Asia's economic growth and for the nature of democracy in the region are more likely to be found in the institutions that have grown up in recent decades than in a supposed singular and ancient value system.

Other arguments also challenge the presumed link between Asian values and economic development. While some extol Asian values for having engendered the remarkable economic development of various Asian countries, others blame those same values for causing the current economic crisis. If there is a link, it is clearly a complex one. Some Asian economic institutions—notably the Japanese and Korean systems of state-led capitalism directed by a technocratic elite, the Japanese system of lifetime employment, and the Korean *chaebol* system—do exhibit an apparent preference for a paternalistic hierarchy and discipline. It is also likely that these institutions supported growth in Japan and Korea at early stages of development. However, these institutions are not common elsewhere in Asia and therefore cannot be said to have contributed to high growth rates in Malaysia and Indonesia, for example. And finally, if they are to be credited with promoting economic growth, how are they to be assessed in the wake of economic collapse?

Another practice that is common across business in Asia, and which has therefore been ascribed as an Asian cultural value, is the use of personal relationships to influence business decisions. This famously includes the *guanxi* arrangements favored by Chinese-owned businesses in Southeast Asia, Hong Kong, and China, and the "crony" arrangements in Indonesia and Malaysia. These long-standing practices have come in for sweeping condemnation for engendering a level of corruption that ultimately undermined the economies of the region, but as Fukuyama points out, levels of corruption in fact vary widely throughout Asia. Given the enormous discretionary power of bureaucrats in Japan and Korea, it is even arguable that cultural factors have suppressed corruption rather than nurtured it. Corruption, where it has existed in Asia, may be due less to cultural characteristics than to a lack of the institutional checks and balances of a mature democracy. This view is supported by You Jong-keun, who argues that the crisis in Korea was the product of institutional weaknesses rather than cultural ones. In You's view, "in terms of the basic values that Western and Eastern societies have sought to realize, there is . . . no fundamental difference." It is not that democracy and market orientation were not part of the Korean value system, but that the institutions in place to achieve them were flawed.

The second question, of whether Asian values are complementary or antithetical to liberal democracy, is fortunately made a little clearer by empirical evidence. First, it is clear that most Asian countries have become increasingly democratic as they have become increasingly prosperous. This applies in particular to Japan, Korea, Taiwan, and Thailand. There are also exceptions, but the point remains that Asian countries have behaved more or less like Western countries in this regard—their underlying value system, whatever it was, cannot have been of decisive importance. Second, it should be noted that the supposed attractions of the authoritarian brand of democracy practiced in countries like Singapore and Malaysia no longer seem as compelling in the wake of the economic crisis. With the possible exception of China, a more liberal and participatory form of democracy is increasingly being seen in Asia as a way out of the crisis, offering both a means of reforming corporate governance and of building consensus around reforms.

The move toward liberal and participatory democracy in Asia supports the idea of a convergence of values. It should be understood, however, that this convergence is not happening purely as a response to the crisis; it also reflects deeper underlying trends that have been obscured by the sensationalization of the Asian values debate. As Fukuyama notes, "there are good reasons for thinking that the distinctive institutions and practices fostered by Asia's cultural systems will converge over time with the patterns seen in the West." You Jong-keun concurs broadly with this view in his prognosis for Korea, arguing that Korea accepted democracy as a desirable value more than a decade ago but has not yet developed the institutions to support democracy. Convergence with the mechanisms commonly used in the West to achieve participatory democracy and the rule of law will follow. Pei Minxin has a more nuanced view of the notion of convergence. He agrees that political and economic freedoms should both be enhanced, but at different rates. As a practical matter, Pei argues that economic institutions should be strengthened first, and political institutions later. Convergence will come in both cases, just a little faster in one than in the other.

1

DEMOCRACY AND THE MARKET ECONOMY: TWO WHEELS OF A CART*

Kim Dae-jung

THE REPUBLIC OF KOREA AND OTHER COUNTRIES affected by the global economic crisis have struggled to cope with the economic problems and social repercussions of the crisis that started in 1997. Many people have lost their jobs and are facing the threats of poverty, insecurity, and even despair.

This great pain and suffering has not been in vain. We have learned an invaluable lesson from the crisis. We have learned that the solution to our problems requires much more than the piecemeal reform measures attempted in the past. It demands nothing less than a fundamental change in our approach to the idea of development—a paradigm shift toward a parallel pursuit of democracy and a market economy. Neglected during our rapid economic development, the intrinsically important issues of economic justice and social security are now earning much more widespread attention.

For more than 30 years, Korea enjoyed a period of stunning economic growth. But when the economic crisis hit at the end of 1997, the distorted structure of the Korean economy was exposed. Although hidden from the outsider, these weaknesses were not entirely unknown to us.

The most serious of the problems lay in our failure to pursue democratic development alongside economic development. Without democracy, we cannot expect development of a genuine market economy under fair and transparent rules of competition. Economic growth achieved under conditions of political repression and market distortion is neither sound nor sustainable. Democracy and a market economy are like two wheels of a cart: both must move together, and each depends on the other for forward motion.

Upon assuming the presidency in 1998, I presented the concept of the parallel development of democracy and a market economy as the gov-

---

* Extracted from the opening address made by President Kim Dae-jung at the International Conference on Democracy, Market Economy and Development, February 26–27, 1999, Seoul, Republic of Korea.

erning philosophy of my administration. I advocated a transition to a truly open economy and emphasized that, in order to improve our economic fundamentals, it was necessary to open our market to foreign products and foreign investment. I insisted that it was crucial to scrap the protective system of a government-controlled economy that favored a few *chaebol* firms. I also called on the government to provide genuine opportunities for small and medium-sized companies.

When Korea launched its industrialization drive in the early 1960s, the Korean government set about pursuing rapid growth. By mobilizing resources and influencing investment and distribution decisions, it was able to achieve a great deal in a short period. The cost of this growth, however, was the suppression of democracy and the perpetuation of authoritarian rule. Other Asian developmental states also followed this path.

By channeling scarce resources into a few targeted areas and suppressing social conflict, authoritarian rule can appear very effective in the short run, but hidden behind the facade of rapid growth are the increasing problems of moral hazard, bureaucratic rigidity, and political cronyism. The problem of inequality—between regions, classes, and industries—also becomes more serious. Due to the lack of fair and transparent rules of competition, the concentration of economic power increased in Korea. The cozy relationship between government, big business, and banks resulted in an inefficient financial sector, and in the absence of an institutionalized system of checks and balances, these problems grew into crisis.

If Korea had pursued a parallel development of democracy and a market economy from the start, it would have been possible to check the collusive relationship between government and big business that developed within the government-controlled financial sector. It would even have been possible to avoid the destructive storm of the currency crisis.

We are now applying the important lessons we have learned from these past mistakes. Korea has been carrying out fundamental reforms in four major areas: the financial, corporate, and public sectors; and the labor market.

The reforms in the financial sector are designed to put an end to the previous system of governmental control, and to guarantee the greatest possible degree of autonomy for the management of financial institutions. The government has limited its role in this area to prudential regulation.

The restructuring process has entailed much pain and sacrifice, but I believe it was necessary for the long-term health of the financial industry. The old practice of government-controlled finance has disappeared, and efforts are underway to enhance the autonomy of our financial institutions. Uncompetitive financial institutions have been closed down or taken over through mergers and acquisitions, and we hope our financial industry will soon become competitive in the new environment of open financial markets.

In the corporate sector, important measures are underway to overhaul the previous and much-abused system of corporate governance. *Chaebol* owners have promised to enhance their transparency of management; to stop their subsidiaries from giving financial cross-guarantees; to build up healthy financial structures; to narrow their focus to core businesses; and to assume legal responsibility for the management of their companies. These fundamental reforms and related legal measures are already being put into effect.

These measures are designed to protect the interests of shareholders, reward efficient management, and lower the entry barriers to start-ups with new ideas. These measures also address the endemic problem of major corruption and the collusive relationship between government and big business.

In addition to these restructuring efforts, we have taken a variety of measures to enhance public sector performance. Examples include an annual salary system, a performance-based bonus system, a target management system, and an incentive program for budget saving. The government will also continue its efforts to improve customer orientation and to introduce competitive elements into the public sector.

We have also carried out a bold program of deregulation, reducing the number of government regulations to half the previous level of 11,000. Deregulation will reduce corruption, improve social welfare, promote the development of a market economy, and enhance the climate for foreign investment.

In the labor market, reform has also made much progress, thanks to a tripartite agreement by representatives of labor, management, and government—a rare example for Korea of reform through democratic consensus. In return for accepting layoffs, workers have gained increased rights for labor activities and political participation, and have won backpay guarantees and the consolidation of health care provisions. The government has also set aside considerable funds for the unemployed, and is providing food, clothes, health care, and secondary education for their children. Retraining and reemployment programs have been set up for unemployed workers.

The reform process has by no means been easy or perfect. While nearly everyone agreed with the general objectives for reform, people had different ideas about how to achieve those objectives. Some resisted when faced with the threat of painful restructuring; others expressed disappointment when the actual reform measures failed to meet their expectations.

Reform, by its very nature, is a difficult and drawn-out process. It is not possible to immediately overcome resistance from anti-reform groups, nor to fix the habits and practices formed over many decades. Reform is a gradual process through which we overcome the limitations of the old order and find a new mode of life.

Looking back, I draw one important conclusion: Introducing new laws and institutions alone is not enough. Reform can succeed only when institutional changes are accompanied by changes in people's attitudes. This is the real challenge.

For example, the liberalization of foreign investment by law will have little effect if the closed nationalistic sentiment of the past continues to dominate our thinking. The legal measures taken to enhance labor market flexibility will meet serious resistance if workers continue to believe in the notion of lifetime employment. The same goes for entrepreneurs. It will be difficult to establish transparent and accountable management practices by legal coercion alone; nor will it be easy to cultivate a corporate culture that relies on technical know-how and innovative ideas to compete in the global market.

In response to these challenges, Korea has started the Second Nation-Building Movement. This movement invites all citizens to become active agents of national reform, under the slogan: "Let us participate, live right, work hard again." We aim to shake off the unfavorable legacies of the twentieth century as we move forward into the twenty-first century. Every citizen should strive to be a global citizen and a "new intellectual"—not necessarily a person of impressive academic credentials, but one who makes full creative use of his or her intellectual potential.

We believe this national movement will encourage a positive attitude as Korea faces its future. It is imperative that private citizens and public officials work as one, so the movement aims to build on private initiative and public involvement. Public involvement is also essential to create an efficient and customer-oriented government. It goes without saying that democracy and a market economy provide the philosophical basis for this movement.

The twenty-first century will be the century of the sixth and greatest revolution in human history.

The first revolution was the birth of the human species. The second was the emergence of settled, agrarian civilization about 10,000 years ago. The third revolution saw the development of four great civilizations around the valleys of the Tigris-Euphrates, the Nile, the Indus, and the Yellow River, about 5,000 to 6,000 years ago.

The fourth revolution occurred in the history of thought approximately 2,500 years ago. This revolution was led by the great philoso-

note long view   Neolib ideas

phers, including Lao Tzu, Confucius, and Mencius in China; the Buddha and his disciples in India; Thales, Socrates, Plato, and Aristotle in Greece; and Isaiah, Amos, and Haggai in Israel. How we think and live today is deeply rooted in this revolution in thinking.

The fifth revolution is the Industrial Revolution, which started at the end of the eighteenth century. This revolution brought with it an era of fervent nationalism, which developed as a result of the fact that the new economic structure born out of the Industrial Revolution could be organized most effectively with the nation as the basic unit. Strong nations emerged through this revolution that did not hesitate to commit aggression against other nations. Weaker nations struggled to defend themselves. The fervency of aggressive nationalism led to two world wars.

The days of such narrow-minded nationalism are now passing away. The scale of the world economy has now become too great to be dominated by individual nations—in many ways, there are no longer national boundaries when it comes to economic issues.

The World Trade Organization (WTO) symbolizes this transition from a system of national economies to a single, global economy. The recent financial crisis that originated locally in a few countries, then spread quickly to surrounding regions hence to the whole world is a case in point. No single nation can be safe or free from the vicissitudes of the world economy. A globalized economy has emerged, in which nations must cooperate as well as compete.

Globalization has been made possible through revolutionary developments in communication and transportation technologies. Of particular significance is the sharing of knowledge and ideas the world over, facilitated by the capability for the almost instantaneous exchange of information. The nearly 6 billion inhabitants of this world are now walking out from old national boundaries into a new world of "universal globalism." This is the sixth revolution. Globalization is not only happening in the economy: it also happening in transportation, communications, and culture. It is happening everywhere.

Korea, for its part, must not shy away from the challenge of adapting to this trend. At the end of the nineteenth century, Korea fell behind in industrializing and modernizing its economy—we failed to respond to the changing world situation. As a result, Korea suffered colonial occupation and against its own will became a divided nation. Such tragedies should never be repeated.

The only way for our nation to move forward is to participate in the trend toward globalization, and to embrace the challenges of the new millennium.

I believe that, in the twenty-first century, all nations of the world will enjoy the benefits of democracy. To participate fully in globalization, I believe it is necessary to practice genuine democracy, and to allow a free exchange of ideas and information. Korea will follow this path. We will also practice genuine market economics, competing and cooperating with the world. This is the only way to provide equality of opportunity and a fair chance for all.

2

DEMOCRACY AND SOCIAL JUSTICE*

Amartya Sen

SOME TIME AGO, IN THE SUMMER OF 1997, a leading Japanese newspaper (*Nihon Keizai Shimbun*) wanted me to identify the most important thing that has happened in the twentieth century. I found this to be a thought-provoking question; so many things of gravity have happened over the last hundred years. The European empires—mostly British and French—that had so dominated the nineteenth century came to an end. We witnessed two world wars. We saw the rise and fall of fascism and Nazism. The century also witnessed the rise of communism and a mixture of a fall (as in the former Soviet Union) and a radical transformation (as in China). It also saw a shift from the economic dominance of the West, to a new economic balance, which is much more dominated by Japan and east and southeast Asia. Even though that region is going through some financial and economic problems right now, this is not going to nullify the shift in the balance of the world economy that has occurred through many decades (in the case of Japan, through nearly the entire century). There is no lack of major events to focus on.

But I ended up arguing that the pre-eminent development of the period is the rise of democracy. Indeed, in the distant future when people look back at what happened in this century, they would find it difficult not to accept the pre-eminence of the emergence of democracy as the most striking development of this period.

This is not to deny that democracy has evolved gradually over a very long period, advanced by many developments: from early Greek theorizing and ephemeral practice (and other early writings on political and civil governance in different societies), to the Magna Carta in 1215, to the French and the American Revolutions in the eighteenth century, to the spread of adult franchise in Europe and north America in the nineteenth century. But it is in the twentieth century that the idea of democracy got established as the "normal" form of government to which any nation is

---

* Keynote Address at the International Conference on Democracy, Market Economy and Development, February 26-27, 1999, Seoul, Republic of Korea.

entitled—whether in Europe, or America, or Asia, or Africa. We do not have to establish afresh, each time, whether such and such country (South Africa, or Chile, or Congo, or Cambodia) is "ready" for democracy (the type of question that was prominent in discourses in the nineteenth century); we now take that for granted.

In earlier times, there were lengthy discussions on whether one country or another was yet "fit for democracy" (for example, the British discussed it regularly in denying India independence). That changed only quite recently, with the recognition that the question itself was wrongheaded: a country does not have to be judged to be fit for democracy, rather it has to become fit *through* democracy. This is a truly momentous change.

In discussing the significance of the issue of democracy as a constituent of development—indeed as an integral part of a good society in the contemporary world—I shall argue that democracy has three distinctly positive contributions. First, it enriches individual lives through more freedom (involving political and civil rights). Second, it provides political incentives to the rulers to respond positively to the needs and demands of the people. Third, the process of open dialogues and debates that democracy allows helps in the formation of values and priorities, and this constructive function of democracy can be very important for equity and justice, as well as efficiency.

Markets too have a major function in the process of development—a role that has been much discussed and applauded over the last few decades. The world has benefited plentifully from the increase in productivity and prosperity that the market mechanism has made possible. The economic advantages of the use of markets, which Adam Smith discussed with exceptional clarity more than two hundred years ago, do not have to be freshly acknowledged in the contemporary world. They are part of the standard understanding that economic analysis generates, and this lesson has been widely recognized.

However, while democracy is important—indeed crucial—for development and for social justice, the success of democracy depends not only on the institutional forms that are adopted (important as they are), but also on the vigor of practice. The opportunities created by political and civil rights have to be seized and used in line with our understanding of fairness and justice. The functioning of democracy depends to a great extent on its constructive role, since its achievements depend on the actions of citizens, influenced by values and norms. The success of democracy depends ultimately on the emergence, sustaining and strengthening of values that make responsible democratic practice effective and consequential. We have to discuss the conditions that may be complementary to democratic institutions.

IDEAS OF JUSTICE

In this context I must discuss the exact relevance of ideas of justice in influencing the operation and development of societies, and in swaying the making of public policies. Ideas of justice can influence not only our political preferences and our public actions, but also our day-to-day behaviors as they impact on others. Our sense of justice works powerfully, but typically implicitly, in our minds, even if—like M. Jourdain in Moliere's play who was unaware of the fact that he "spoke prose"—we may not fully recognize that we do invoke implicit concepts of justice when we judge and decide what is to be done. Our general concerns and values have implications for the acceptability of different social arrangements, and of the distinct sets of predicaments and achievements that may emerge from them.

Policy makers, in particular, have two distinct reasons for taking an interest in the ideas of social justice. The first—and the more direct—reason is that justice is a central concept in identifying the aims and objectives of public policy, and also in deciding on the instruments that are appropriate in pursuing the chosen ends. This can be important both in consolidating already established lines of policy, or—more strikingly—in providing a point of departure for another outlook, another approach, another set of articulated concerns. I take the liberty of quoting from the moving as well as tightly reasoned diagnosis of injustice in James Wolfensohn's address to the Board of Governors in 1998:

> But today I have other memories: Dark, searing images of desperation, hopelessness, and decline. Of people who once had hope, but have it no more. The mother in Mindanao, pulling her child out of school, haunted by the fear that he will never return. The family in Korea with a mid-sized scrap metal business, made destitute through lack of credit. The father in Jakarta, paying a money lender three times in interest what he can make that day, falling deeper and deeper into debt. Not knowing how he will ever work himself free. The child in Bangkok, now condemned to work the streets, a child no longer.

Concepts of justice are crucially relevant for cogent analysis and reasoned selection of ends and means of public policy. This includes, *inter alia*, the particular use to which the market mechanism is placed, and also the ways in which the general mandates of democratic decisions are to be translated into actual policies.

The second—more indirect—reason is that all public policies are dependent on how individuals and groups in the society behave. Their behavior cannot but be influenced by, among other things, their own

understanding and interpretation of what behavior is proper and what
outcomes are acceptable. This can influence a whole range of behavioral
regularities, varying from proneness or resistance to financial corruption,
to judgments about how many children to have, or about the relative
claims of girls vis-a-vis boys.

For the making of public policy, it is extremely important to understand the functional role of the values and concepts of justice of the general public. Indeed, the pursuit of justice in public policy cannot be
divorced from the nature and changeability—indeed the dynamic—of
the understanding of justice by the citizens themselves.

CONTRIBUTIONS OF DEMOCRACY

What exactly is democracy? We must not identify democracy with majority rule alone. Democracy has complex demands, which certainly include
voting and respect for election results, but it also requires the protection
of liberties and freedoms, respect for legal entitlements, and the guaranteeing of free discussions and uncensored distribution of news and fair
comment. Indeed, even elections can be deeply defective if they occur
without giving the different sides adequate opportunity to present their
respective cases, or without giving the electorate the freedom to obtain
news and to consider the views of the competing protagonists. Democracy is a demanding system, and not just a mechanical condition (like
majority rule), seen in isolation.

We can distinguish between three different ways in which democracy
enriches the lives of the citizens, as was briefly identified earlier. First,
political freedom is a part of human freedom in general, and civil and
political rights are crucial for good living of individuals as social beings.
Political and social participation has intrinsic value in human life and
well-being. To be prevented from participation in the political life of the
community cannot but be a major deprivation, even if leaders of authoritarian governments try to persuade us that governing is best left to efficient bureaucrats.

Second, democracy has an important instrumental value in enhancing
the hearing that people get in expressing and supporting their claims to
political attention (including the claims of economic needs). It gives political incentives to ruling governments to respond to the demands of people, and it makes the governors more responsible and accountable.

Third, the practice of democracy gives the citizens an opportunity to
learn from each other, and to re-examine their own values and priorities,
along with those of others. Even the idea of "needs" (including the
understanding of "economic needs") requires public discussion and
exchange of information, views and analyses. In this sense, democracy

has constructive importance, in addition to the intrinsic value it has in the lives of the citizens and its instrumental role in political decisions.

The conceptualization—even comprehension—of what are to count as "needs," including "economic needs" may itself require the exercise of such rights. Indeed, an adequate understanding of what economic needs are—their content and their force—requires discussion and exchange. Political and civil rights, especially those related to the guaranteeing of open discussion, debate, criticism and dissent, are central to the process of generating informed and reflected choices. These processes are crucial to the formation of values and priorities, and we cannot, in general, take preferences as given independently of public discussion, that is, irrespective of whether open debates and interchanges are permitted or not.

Miseries and deprivations can be of various kinds—some more amenable to social remedying than others. The totality of the human predicament is not discriminating enough to identify our "needs." For example, there are many things that we might have good reason to value. We could even want immortality, or being altogether free from all ailments. However, we do not see immortality or total freedom from all illnesses as a "need" since neither is, in fact, feasible. Our conception of needs relates to our ideas of the preventable nature of some deprivations, and to our understanding of what can or cannot be done about them. In the formation of these understandings and beliefs, public discussions play a crucial role. Political rights, including freedom of expression and discussion, are not only pivotal in inducing social responses to economic needs, they are also central to the conceptualization of economic needs themselves.

In evaluating the role of democracy we also have to examine the claim of some commentators that non-democratic systems are better in bringing about economic development. This belief sometimes goes by the name of "the Lee hypothesis," after the presentation of this point of view by Lee Kuan Yew, the distinguished leader and former president of Singapore. He is certainly right that some relatively disciplinarian states (such as a pre-democratic South Korea, his own Singapore, and post-reform China) have had faster rates of economic growth than many less authoritarian ones (including Costa Rica, or Jamaica, or India). But a general relation of this kind cannot be established on the basis of purposefully selective evidence. For example, we cannot really take the high economic growth of Singapore or China as "definitive proof" that authoritarianism does better in promoting economic growth, any more than we can draw the opposite conclusion on the basis of the fact that the best record of economic growth in Africa (in fact, one of the finest records of economic growth in the whole world) can be seen in Botswana, which has been a oasis of democracy in that continent, over the decades. We need more systematic empirical studies to sort out the claims and counterclaims.

There is, in fact, no convincingly general evidence that authoritarian governance and the suppression of political and civil rights are really beneficial in encouraging economic development, even if we identify development merely with economic growth (which we should not—I shall have more to say on this presently). Indeed, the general statistical picture does not permit any such induction. Systematic empirical studies based on inter-country comparisons (for example, by Robert Barro or by Adam Przeworski) firmly contradict the thesis of any general conflict between political rights and economic performance.[1] Taking into account all the comparative studies that are now available, the hypothesis that there is no relation between economic growth and democracy—in either direction—remains extremely plausible. Since democracy and political liberty have *importance of their own*, the case for them, therefore, remains untarnished.

DEMOCRACY AND SECURITY

In this context, we must also go beyond the narrow confines of economic growth and scrutinize the broader demands of economic development, including the need for economic and social security. In that context, we have to look at the connection between political and civil rights, on the one hand, and the prevention of major economic disasters, on the other. Political and civil rights give people the opportunity to draw attention forcefully to general needs, and to demand appropriate public action. The governmental response to the acute suffering of people often depends on the pressure that is put on it. The exercise of political rights (through voting, protesting, criticizing, and so on) can make a real difference to the political incentives that operate on a ruling government.

I have discussed elsewhere the remarkable fact that in the terrible history of famines in the world, no substantial famine has ever occurred in any independent and democratic country with a relatively free press.[2]

[1] Adam Przeworski et al., *Sustainable Democracy* (Cambridge: Cambridge University Press, 1995); Robert J. Barro, *Getting It Right: Markets and Choices in a Free Society* (Cambridge, MA: MIT Press, 1996).

[2] On this see my "Development: Which Way Now?" *Economic Journal,* vol. 93 (December 1983); *Resources, Values and Development* (Cambridge, MA: Harvard University Press, 1984); "Rationality and Social Choice," *American Economic Review,* Presidential Address to the American Economic Association, March 1995. See also Jean Dreze and Amartya Sen, *Hunger and Public Action* (Oxford: Clarendon Press, 1987); Frances D'Souza, ed., "Starving in Silence: A Report on Famine and Censorship" (London: Article 19 International Centre on Censorship, 1990), with articles by Frances D'Souza, Alex de Waal, and an anonymous Chinese scholar; *Human Rights Watch, Indivisible Human Rights: The Relationship between Political and Civil Rights to Survival, Subsistence and Poverty* (New York: Human Rights Watch, 1992); International Federation of Red Cross and Red Crescent Societies, *World Disaster Report 1994* (Geneva: Red Cross, 1994).

We cannot find exceptions to this rule, no matter whether we look at the current starvation in Sudan and North Korea, or the recent famines in Ethiopia, Somalia or in other dictatorial regimes, or earlier famines in the Soviet Union in the 1930s, or in China during 1958-61 with the failure of the Great Leap Forward, or earlier still the famines in Ireland or India under alien rule. It is remarkable also that China which was doing, in many ways, much better economically than India, still managed to have the largest recorded famine in history when nearly 30 million died of the famine of 1958–61, with the faulty governmental policies remaining uncorrected for full three years while millions and millions died each year. The policies were also uncriticized, since there were no opposition parties in parliament, no free press, and no multi-party elections; indeed it is precisely this lack of challenge that allowed the deeply defective policies to continue even when they were killing millions each year. The same can be said about contemporary famines in North Korea and Sudan.

Famines are often associated with what look like natural disasters, and the commentators on famines often settle for the simplicity of explaining famines by pointing to these events: the floods in China during the failure of the Great Leap Forward, the droughts in Ethiopia, or crop failures in North Korea. But the fact is that many countries with similar natural problems—often worse—manage perfectly well, because a responsive government intervenes to help alleviate hunger. Since the primary victims of a famine are the indigent, famine deaths can be prevented by recreating incomes (for example, through employment programs), which makes the available food accessible to the potential famine victims. Indeed, even the poorest democratic countries that have faced terrible droughts or floods or other natural disasters (such as India in 1973, or Zimbabwe and Botswana in the early 1980s) have been able to feed their people without experiencing a famine.

Famines are easy to prevent if there is a serious effort to prevent them, and a government of a democratic country—facing elections, and criticisms from opposition parties and independent newspapers—cannot but make a serious effort to prevent famines. Not surprisingly, while India continued to have famines under British rule right up to independence (the last famine was in 1943, four years before independence, which I witnessed as a child), they disappeared suddenly, after independence, with the establishment of a multi-party democracy with a free press.

The occurrence of famines is only one example of the reach of democracy. The positive roles of political and civil rights apply to the prevention of economic and social disasters in general. When things go fine and everything is routinely good, this instrumental role of democracy may not be particularly missed. But it comes into its own when things get fouled up, for one reason or another. And then the political incentives provided by democratic governance acquire great practical significance.

There are important lessons here. Many economic technocrats recommend the use of economic incentives (which the market system provides) while ignoring political incentives (which democratic systems could guarantee). But to ignore political incentives by concentrating only on economic incentives is to opt for a deeply unbalanced set of ground rules. Indeed, the security provided by democracy may not be much missed when a country is lucky enough to be facing no serious calamity, when everything is running along smoothly. But the danger of insecurity, arising from changes in the economic or other circumstances or from uncorrected mistakes of policy, can lurk behind what looks like a healthy state.

ASIAN ECONOMIC CRISIS

The recent problems of East and Southeast Asia bring out, among other things, the penalty of undemocratic governance in two striking respects. First, the development of the financial crisis in some of these economies has been closely linked with the lack of transparency in business, in particular the lack of public participation in reviewing financial and business arrangements. The absence of an effective democratic forum has been consequential in this failing. The opportunity that would have been provided by democratic processes to challenge the hold of selected families or groups could have made a big difference.

Second, once the financial crisis led to a general economic recession, the protective power of democracy—not unlike that which prevents famines in democratic countries—was badly missed in some countries, such as Indonesia and Thailand. The newly dispossessed did not have the hearing they needed. A fall of total Gross National Product of, say, even 10 percent may not look like much, if it follows the experience of past economic growth of 5 or 10 percent every year for some decades, and yet that decline can decimate lives and create misery for millions, if the burden of contraction is not shared together but allowed to be heaped on those—the unemployed or those newly made economically redundant—who can least bear it. The vulnerable in Indonesia or Thailand may not have missed democracy when things went up and up, but that very lacuna kept their voice muffled and ineffective as the unequally shared crisis developed. The protective role of democracy is strongly missed when it is most needed.

ASIAN VALUES AND POLITICAL AND CIVIL RIGHTS

In arguing for democracy in Asia, we must also examine a cultural argument that has been used against the appropriateness of political and civil

rights in this part of the world. It has been claimed that Asians traditionally value discipline—not political freedom, and thus the attitudes to full
democracy (including political and civil rights) cannot but be much more
skeptical in these countries.

Is this line of reasoning sound? I would argue that it is not at all
sound.[3] It is very hard to find any real historical basis for this intellectual
claim in the actual history of Asian cultures. For example, one of the ear-
liest—and most emphatic—advocates of individual rights and of the tolerance of pluralism and focused articulation on the duty of the state to
protect minorities can be found in the forceful inscriptions of Ashoka, the
Buddhist emperor in India, in the third century B.C. Other examples can
be plentifully found in the classical traditions in India, the Middle East,
Iran, China, east and southeast Asia, and other parts of Asian civilizations.

Asia is, of course, a very large area, with 60 percent of the world's population, and generalizations about such a vast group are not easy. Sometimes the advocates of "Asian values" have tended to look primarily at
east Asia as the region of particular applicability. However, even east Asia
itself has much diversity, and there are many variations to be found
between Japan and China and Korea and other parts of east Asia, and
even *within* each particular country: Japan or China or Korea. Confucius
is the standard author quoted in interpreting Asian values, but he is not
the only intellectual influence in any of these countries (for example,
there are very old and very widespread Buddhist traditions as well, in
each of them, powerful for over a millennium and a half, and also considerable presence of Christianity).

Take Korea, for example. Confucianism has indeed been a major cultural influence in this country, but there have been many different interpretations of Confucianism. For example, in the fifteenth century
onwards, the "Neo-Confucian literati" (*Sarim*) challenged the earlier
readings of Confucianism, and interpretational disputes were powerfully
pursued by the different sides. Neo-Confucians themselves divide into
different schools, according to different lines of division, including the
classic Chinese distinction between *li* and *ch'i* (called *i* and *ki* in Korea). In
the seventeenth and early eighteenth century, the contest between the
"Old Doctrine" (*Noron*), led by Song Si-yol, and the "Young Doctrine"
(*Soron*), led by Yun Chung, related in part to different views of good
behavior and of good social arrangements. Confucianism does not speak

---

[3] I have discussed this thesis in some detail in my Morgenthau Memorial Lecture at the
Carnegie Council on Ethics and International Affairs: "Human Rights and Asian Values,"
(1997); published in a shortened form in *The New Republic*, July 14 & 21, 1997.

in one voice, and the particular emphasis on *li* in the authoritarian interpretations of Confucius is by no means the only claim that obtains loyalty.

There are also influences other than Confucianism. Buddhism has
been a major force here, as it has been in China and Japan, and from the
seventh century when Buddhism became the state religion, it has had
political ups and downs, but a constant cultural presence in this country.
As is widely known, freedom is an extremely important concept in Buddhism (indeed the language of freedom is used even to explain such crucial notions as *Nirvana* and *Moksha*), and this applies to East and
Southeast Asian Buddhist schools as well as to the original Indian Buddhism. Christianity too has had a major presence in Korea, and from the
eighteenth century, regular intellectual confrontations can be seen
between the creed of so-called "Western learning" which disputed Confucian orthodoxy, along with other challengers, such as the individualist
doctrines of the Wang Yang-ming school of Neo-Confucianism, and of
course various theorists of Buddhism. No monolithic reading of "Asian
values" can possibly be drawn on the basis of a serious reading of the history of Korea. Similar remarks can be made about China, Japan and the
rest of East Asia. While politicians often criticize academics for being
somewhat impractical about politics, perhaps some political leaders can
also be questioned for being somewhat impractical about academic matters, including the reading of history and its bearing on contemporary
political philosophy. Dubious history does nothing to vindicate dubious
politics.

There is no real evidence of a homogeneous worship of order over
freedom in Asian cultures. It is not, of course, hard to find authoritarian
writings within the Asian traditions. But nor is it in Western classics, and
one has to reflect only on the writings of Plato or Aquinas to see that
devotion to discipline is not a special Asian taste. To dismiss the plausibility of democracy as a universal value on the ground of the presence of
some Asian writings on discipline and order would be similar to reject-
ing the plausibility of democracy as a natural form of government in
Europe or America today on the basis of the writings of Aquinas or Plato
(not to mention the vast medieval literature in support of the inquisi-
tions).

Diversity is a feature of most cultures in the world. The Western civilization is not an exception to this. The practice of democracy that has
won out in the *contemporary* West is largely a result of a consensus that
has emerged since the Enlightenment and the Industrial Revolution, and
particularly in the last century or so. To read in this an allegedly millen-
nia-old historical commitment of the West to democracy, to be contrasted
with authoritarian non-Western traditions (treating each as monolithic)
would be a great intellectual mistake.

There is also a point about international political relations that I want to make in this context. Western discussion of non-Western societies is often too respectful of authority—the governor, the Minister, the military junta, the religious leader. This "authoritarian bias" receives support from the fact that Western countries themselves are often represented, in international gatherings, by governmental officials and spokesmen, and they in turn seek the views of their "opposite numbers" from other countries. An adequate approach of development cannot really be so centered only on those in power. The reach has to be broader, and the need for popular participation is not just sanctimonious rubbish. Indeed, the idea of development cannot be dissociated from the recognition of political diversity.

THE PRACTICE OF DEMOCRACY AND THE ROLE OF OPPOSITION

Diversity is also important for the effectiveness of democracy. The achievements of democracy depend not only on the rules and procedures that are adopted and safeguarded, but also on the way the opportunities are used by the citizens. Fidel Valdez Ramos, the former President of the Philippines, put the point with great clarity in a speech at the Australian National University:

"Under dictatorial rule, people need not think—need not choose—need not make up their minds or give their consent. All they need to do is to follow. This has been a bitter lesson learned from Philippine political experience of not so long ago. By contrast, a democracy cannot survive without civic virtue. The political challenges for people around the world today is not just to replace authoritarian regimes by democratic ones. Beyond this, it is to make democracy work for ordinary people."[4]

Democracy does create this opportunity, which relates both to its "instrumental importance" and its "constructive role," as discussed earlier. But with what strength these opportunities are seized depends on a variety of factors, including the vigor of multi-party politics as well as the dynamism of value formation. For example, in India the priority of preventing starvation and famine was fully gripped already at the time of independence (as it had been in Ireland as well, with its own experience of famine under British rule). There was much effectiveness in the activism of political participants in preventing famines, and in sharply condemning governments for open starvation, and the quickness and force of this process made the prevention of such calamities an

---

[4] Fidel Valdez Ramos, "Democracy and the East Asian Crisis," Inaugural Address at the Centre for Democratic Institutions, Australian National University, Canberra, vol. 26 (November 1998), p. 2.

inescapable priority of every government. And yet successive opposition parties have been quite docile in not condemning widespread illiteracy, or the prevalence of non-extreme but serious undernourishment (especially among the children), or the lack of completion of land reform programs legislated earlier. This docility of opposition has permitted successive governments to get away with unconscionable neglect of these vital matters for public policy.

Another such area is the persistence of gender inequality, which too requires forceful engagement, involving critique as well as pointers to reform. Indeed, as these neglected issues come into public debates and confrontations (for example, both women's movements and pressure groups in favor of elementary education have gathered force in India over the last decade or so), the authorities are beginning to respond. In a democracy, people tend to get what they demand, and more crucially, do not typically get what they do not demand.

VALUE FORMATION AND THE CONSTRUCTIVE OPERATION OF DEMOCRACY

All this does, of course, relate directly to ideas of social justice—what is tolerable and what is not in the contemporary world. I made the point earlier that ideas of justice influence individual behavior as well, which are not governed (as claimed in some economic textbooks) only by the pursuit of narrowly defined self-interest. Indeed, the point can be illustrated even with the role of democracy in the prevention of famines. The economic analysis of famines across the world indicates that only a small proportion of the population tends to be stricken by it—rarely more than 5 percent or so. Since the share of income and food of these poor groups tend normally to be no more than 3 percent of the total for the nation, it is not hard to rebuild their lost share of income and food, even in very poor countries, if a serious effort is made in that direction.[5] Famines are thus easily preventable, and while rulers never starve, the need to face public criticism and to encounter the electorate provides the government with the political incentive to take preventive action with some urgency.

But the question that does arise is this. Since only a very small proportion of the population is struck by a famine (rarely more than 5 or 10 percent), how does it become such a serious concern—and effective issue—in majority-rule elections and in general public criticism? This would be in some tension with the assumption of universal self-cen-

---

[5] See my *Poverty and Famine* (Oxford: Clarendon Press, 1981); and jointly with Jean Dreze, *Hunger and Public Action* (Oxford: Clarendon Press, 1989).

teredness. Presumably, we do have the capacity—and often the inclination—to understand and respond to the predicament of others.[6] This example, like many others, draws attention forcefully to the fact that as human beings we are not forever imprisoned in a world of universal self-centeredness, and ideas of good and the right, the fair and the just, do influence our priorities, commitments and actions.

All this also draws attention to the role of public discussion and open dialogue in value formation—what was called the "constructive" role of democracy. There is also a deep complementarity between the institutions of democracy and the nature of civil society and social opportunities that can make them more effective. In this respect, the prevalence of illiteracy has tended to hinder the full flowering of democracy in India. This has hampered the articulation of the points of view of the underdogs: the socially excluded poor, the economically precarious landless laborers, the mute and suppressed illiterate, and the doubly deprived women from the lower classes. That loss is only slowly being remedied with the slow emergence of neglected voices.

The reach and effectiveness of open and articulate dialogue is often underestimated in assessing social and political problems. For example, public discussion has an important role to play in reducing high rates of fertility that characterize many developing countries. There is, in fact, much evidence that the sharp decline in fertility rates that has taken place in the more literate states in India has been crucially influenced by public discussion of the bad effects of high fertility rates especially on the lives of young women, and also for the community at large. If the view has emerged in, say, Kerala or Tamil Nadu that a happy family in the modern age is a small family, much discussion and debating have gone into the formation of these perspectives. Kerala now has a fertility rate of 1.7 (similar to that in Britain and France, and well below China's 1.9), and this has been achieved with no coercion, but mainly through the emergence of new values—a process in which political and social dialogues have played a major part. The high level of female literacy of the Kerala population (much higher than China's—indeed higher than every province of China) combined with an open political climate, has greatly contributed to making such social and political dialogues possible and effective.

BUSINESS ETHICS, TRUST, AND CONTRACTS

Even the effective operation of an exchange economy depends on mutual trust and the use of norms—explicit and implicit. For example, values are

---

[6] I have discussed this issue in my Presidential Address to the American Economic Association, "Rationality and Social Choice," March 1995.

crucial in preventing a climate of corruption, which may drown attempts at marketization, or in the development of a culture of justifiable trust, the absence of which may make business deals that much more difficult.[7] When these behavioral modes are plentifully there, it is easy to overlook their role. But when they have to be cultivated, that lacuna can be a major barrier to economic success.

Capitalism's need for motivational structures that are more complex than pure profit maximization has been acknowledged in various forms, over a long time, by many leading social scientists, such as Marx, Weber, Tawney, and others.[8] The role of non-profit motives in the success of capitalism is not a new point, even though the wealth of historical evidence and conceptual arguments in that direction is often neglected in contemporary professional economics.[9]

A basic code of good business behavior is a bit like oxygen—we take an interest in its presence only when it is absent. Adam Smith had noted this general tendency in an interesting remark in his *History of Astronomy*:

> ... an object with which we are quite familiar, and which we see every day, procedures, though both great and beautiful, has but a small effect upon us; because our admiration is not supported either by Wonder or by Surprise.[10]

What may not cause wonder or surprise in Zurich or London or Paris may, however, be quite problematic in Cairo or Bombay or Lagos (or

---

[7] I have addressed these issues in *On Ethics and Economics* (Oxford: Blackwell, 1987); also in "Adam Smith's Prudence," in S. Lall and F. Stewart, eds., *Theory and Reality in Development* (London: Macmillan, 1986); "Does Business Ethics Make Economic Sense?", *Journal of Business Ethics*, 1993; "On Corruption and Organized Crime, " address to the Italian Parliament's Anti-Mafia Commission, Rome, 1993; Italian translation in Luciano Violante, ed., *Economia e criminalita* (Roma: Camera dei deputati, 1993); *Economic Wealth and Moral Sentiments* (Zurich: Bank Hofmann, 1994); "Moral Codes and Economic Success," in Samuel Brittan and Alan Hamlin, eds., *Market Capitalism and Moral Values* (Aldershot: Elgar, 1995); French Version, *Libre*, 1993; Italian translation, *Il Mulino*, 1994.

[8] Karl Marx (with F. Engels), *The German Ideology* (1845–46, English translation, New York: International Publishers, 1947); Richard Henry Tawney, *Religion and the Rise of Capitalism* (London: Murray, 1926); Max Weber, *The Protestant Ethic and the Spirit of Capitalism* (London: Allen Unwin, 1930).

[9] A central issue is the importance of what Professor Bruno Frey has called "intrinsic motivation": tertium dater, which goes well beyond the reach of narrowly defined self-interest. See his "Tertium Dater: Pricing, Regulating and Intrinsic Motivation," *Kyklos*, vol. 45 (1992).

[10] Adam Smith, "History of Astronomy, " in his *Essays on Philosophical Subjects* (London: Cadell and Davies, 1795); republished, edited by W.P.D. Wightman and J.C. Bryce (Oxford: Clarendon Press, 1980), p. 34.

Moscow), in their challenging struggle to establish the norms and institutions of a functioning market economy.

In the economic difficulties experienced in the former Soviet Union and countries in east Europe, the absence of behavioral codes that, along with institutional structures, are central to successful capitalism has been particularly problematic. There is need for the development of behavioral norms and codes which may be quite standard in the evolved capitalist economies, but which are relatively hard to install suddenly as a part of "planned capitalism." These changes can take quite some time to function—a lesson that is currently being learned rather painfully in these countries in east Europe and the former Soviet Union. The importance of institutions and behavioral experiences was rather eclipsed there in the first flush of enthusiasm about the magic of allegedly automatic market processes.

These issues require recognition and analysis as well as public discussion and debates. Just as there is need for institutional arrangements that make corruption and other failings have punitive implications, there is also the need for the development of a culture of trust and trustworthiness in economic dealings. The norm of pure profit maximization is not adequate for business success. We need the development of business ethics as well, and in the context of other social problems, also the emergence of values that are friendly to the environment and to the demands of fairness to groups other than fellow businessmen.[11] All this calls for dialogues and openness in a way the strong silent men who populate the economic textbooks may not be able to instantly comprehend.

CONCLUDING REMARKS

In this paper, I have tried to discuss the role of democracy in the contemporary world, especially in Asia. I have argued that developing and strengthening a democratic system is an essential component of the process of development. The significance of democracy lies, I have argued, in three distinct virtues: (1) its intrinsic importance, (2) its instrumental contributions, and (3) its constructive role in the creation of values and norms. No evaluation of a democratic form of governance can be complete without considering each.

However, while we must acknowledge the importance of democratic institutions, they cannot be viewed as mechanical devices for development. Their use is conditioned by our values and priorities, and ulti-

---

[11] I have discussed these issues in *On Ethics and Economics* (1987), and "Environmental Evaluation and Social Choice: Contingent Valuation and the Market Analogy," *Japanese Economic Review*, vol. 46 (1995).

mately by our sense of justice. Some serious harm has resulted, in the past, from taking the market mechanism to be itself—on its own—a solution to many problems, whereas it is an instrument that can be used in different ways—with or without vision, with or without social responsibility. Indeed, a social commitment to norms and priorities is essential not only for equity, but also for the efficiency of the market mechanism itself.

Public debates and discussions can play a major part in the formation of values. In this sense, the openness associated with democracy is part of the solution of the problems of value failures that hinder the effectiveness of markets. The force of public discussion is not only one of the correlates of democracy, with an extensive reach, its cultivation can also make democracy itself function better.

Just as it is important to emphasize the need for democracy, it is also crucial to safeguard the conditions and circumstances that ensure the range and reach of the democratic process. Valuable as democracy is as a major source of social opportunity (a recognition that calls for vigorous defense—not least in Asia), there is also the need to examine ways and means of making it function well, to realize its potentials. The achievement of social justice depends not only on institutional forms (including democratic rules and regulations), but also on effective practice. I have tried to present reasons for taking this issue to be of central importance. This is the major agenda that we face today.

REFERENCES

Barro, Robert J. 1996. *Getting It Right: Markets and Choices in a Free Society.* Cambridge, MA: MIT Press.

Dreze, Jean. and Amartya Sen. 1987. *Hunger and Public Action.* Oxford: Clarendon Press.

D'Souza, Frances, ed.. 1990. *Starving in Silence: A Report on Famine and Censorship.* London: Article 19, International Centre on Censorship.

D'Souza, Frances, Waal, Alex de., and an anonymous Chinese scholar. 1992. *Indivisible Human Rights: The Relationship between Political and Civil Rights to Survival, Subsistence and Poverty.* New York: Human Rights Watch.

Frey, Bruno. 1992. "Tertium Dater: Pricing, Regulating and Intrinsic Motivation." *Kyklos* 45.

International Federation of Red Cross and Red Crescent Societies. 1994. *World Disaster Report 1994*. Geneva: Red Cross.

Marx, Karl (with F. Engels). 1947. *The German Ideology*, 1845–46. New York: International Publishers. English translation.

Przeworski, Adam, et al. 1995. *Sustainable Democracy*. Cambridge: Cambridge University Press.

Ramos, Fidel Valdez. 1998. "Democracy and the East Asian Crisis." Inaugural Address at the Centre for Democratic Institutions, Australian National University, Canberra.

Sen, Amartya. 1981. *Poverty and Famine*. Oxford: Clarendon Press.

———. 1983. "Development: Which Way Now?" *Economic Journal* 93. December.

———. 1984. *Resources, Values and Development*. Cambridge, MA: Harvard University Press.

———. 1986. "Adam Smith's Prudence." In S. Lall and F. Stewart, eds., *Theory and Reality in Development*. London: Macmillan.

———. 1987. *On Ethics and Economics*. Oxford: Blackwell.

———. 1993a. "Does Business Ethics Make Economic Sense?" *Journal of Business Ethics*.

———. 1993b. "Markets and Freedom." *Oxford Economic Papers*.

———. 1993c. "On Corruption and Organized Crime." address to the Italian Parliament's AntiMafia Commission. Rome. In Luciano Violante, ed. 1993. *Economia e criminalit*. Roma: Camera dei deputati. Italian translation.

———. 1994. *Economic Wealth and Moral Sentiments*. Zurich: Bank Hofmann.

———. 1995. "Environmental Evaluation and Social Choice: Contingent Valuation and the Market Analogy." *Japanese Economic Review*. 46.

————. 1995. "Moral Codes and Economic Success." in Samuel Brittan and Alan Hamlin, eds., *Market Capitalism and Moral Values*. Aldershot: Elgar. French Version, *Libre*, 1993; Italian translation, *Il Mulino*. 1994.

————. 1995. "Rationality and Social Choice." *American Economic Review*. Presidential Address to the American Economic Association, March.

————. 1997. "Human Rights and Asian Values." Morganthau Memorial Lecture, New York: Carnegie Council on Ethics and International Affairs. Published in a shortened form in *The New Republic*.

————. 2000. *Development as Freedom*. New York: Anchor Books, a division of Random House, Inc.

Sen, Amartya, and Jean Dreze. 1989. *Hunger and Public Action*. Oxford: Clarendon Press.

Smith, Adam. 1795. "History of Astronomy." *Essays on Philosophical Subjects*. London: Cadell and Davies. Republished, edited by W. P. D. Wightman and J. C. Bryce, Oxford: Clarendon Press, 1980.

Tawney, Richard Henry. 1926. *Religion and the Rise of Capitalism* London: Murray.

Weber, Max. 1930. *The Protestant Ethic and the Spirit of Capitalism*. London: Allen Unwin.

Wolfensohn, James D. 1998. "The Other Crisis, Address to the Board of Governors." Washington, DC: The World Bank. October 6.

3

POLITICAL INSTITUTIONS, DEMOCRACY, AND DEVELOPMENT

Minxin Pei

THE COMPLEX RELATIONSHIP BETWEEN government, economic development, and underlying political and cultural values has been the subject of scholarly research for more than 100 years. In recent years, questions related to this triangular relationship have attracted the attention of policymakers, as there is a growing awareness that problems of governance, public policy, and economic performance are interconnected: the solution to one set of problems may often be found in the solution to another set. This paper addresses two questions that are at the heart of the relationship: How do democracy and development influence each other, and what policy and institutional reforms have the most immediate and measurable effects on improving governance?

The first section of the paper reviews the theoretical literature on the relationship between democracy and development, and discusses the claims therein. The second section analyzes recent data on the correlation between democracy, wealth, economic freedom, and corruption, and explores the relationship between these variables. The third section applies some of the insights from these findings to the Chinese development experience since 1979. And finally, the fourth section offers an approach to solving the dilemma of balancing democracy and development.

DEMOCRACY AND DEVELOPMENT

Numerous thinkers and scholars have written on this relationship. This paper concentrates on the narrow discussion of how political systems and economic development affect each other. With the unavoidable exception of common issues, it does not address the question of the relationship between markets and democracy.

Does Wealth Lead to Democracy?

The impact of economic development on the transformation of political systems has long been thought to be both direct and positive.[1] It has been widely assumed that sustained economic development leads to the emergence of democratic institutions and ultimately to democracy itself, as follows:

- Economic development transforms the social structure and creates a middle class that provides the social basis for democracy. This is the most important process.
- Economic development may, as its by-product, lead to the emergence of new political values (such as an enhanced sense of individuality, personal autonomy, and belief in the rights of personal freedom and choice) that support democratic institutions and practices.
- A direct effect of economic development is an increase in the level of education. An educated citizenry is likely to be both more knowledgeable about the political process and more aware of its rights. It is also more vigilant in defending those rights, and possesses more effective means of doing so.
- Successful development generates economic wealth, enabling private sector actors to accumulate the resources that enhance their independence from the state, thus strengthening civil society as a counterweight to the state. Another beneficial effect of wealth is its ability to resolve redistributional conflicts (the bigger the pie, the more likely it is that everyone will get a piece).
- Because successful development is more likely to occur in an open economy, it may also promote social, cultural, and political linkages with the international community. These linkages act to facilitate the flow of information, and therefore to undermine the possibility of authoritarian rule; and by opening the economy to external influences, to constrain autocratic rulers.

Academic research in the last few years has begun to shed light on how economic development may affect the emergence and durability of

---

[1] Classics on this topic include Seymour Martin Lipset, "Some Social Requisites of Democracy: Economic Development and Political Legitimacy," *American Political Science Review*, vol. 53 (March 1959); Robert Dahl, *Polyarchy* (Yale University Press, 1971); Samuel P. Huntington, *The Third Wave: Democratization in the Late Twentieth Century* (Oklahoma University Press, 1991); Dietrich Rueschemeyer, Evelyne Stephens, and John Stephens, *Capitalist Development and Democracy* (University of Chicago Press, 1992).

democracy. In a groundbreaking statistical study of the relationship between wealth and democracy, Adam Przeworski and Fernando Limongi disputed the notion that rising economic wealth leads to democracy,[2] arguing that wealth has a measurable effect on the survival rate of democracy, but not on its rate of emergence. In other words, to the extent that wealth is an independent variable, poor democracies are more likely to collapse than wealthy democracies. More specifically, Przeworski and Limongi's analysis shows that rising wealth does not increase democracy; in certain cases, for example, wealthy autocracies have remained autocratic despite rising wealth. But the effect of wealth above a certain level on the durability of democracy is powerful and unambiguous: the probability of a democracy's survival rises with wealth measured in per capita income. When per capita income is $1,000 (measured in purchasing power parity, or PPP), a democracy's life expectancy is eight years. When per capita income is between $2,001 and $3,000, the life expectancy of a democracy rises to 26 years; and when per capita income rises above $6,000, democracy acquires immortality. Statistical evidence shows that autocracy can persist above these wealth thresholds, from which Przeworski and Limongi conclude that the notion of linearity between wealth and democracy must be rejected.

Research by other political scientists, in contrast, has concluded that wealth produces a measurable, though modest, effect on democracy. A statistical analysis performed by John Londregan and Keith Poole reports that a doubling of per capita income has an especially large effect on moderately authoritarian countries; typically, a doubling of per capita income would increase the degree of democracy in a moderately authoritarian country by 30 percent. The effects of rising wealth on extremely authoritarian countries are small, however, a doubling of per capita income leading to a 5 to 15 percent increase in the level of democracy in the most repressive regimes. The law of diminishing returns also applies: a doubling of per capita income only marginally increases the degree of democracy in relatively open societies.[3]

These two studies may differ in their conclusions about the exact effects of economic development on democracy, but their disagreement in detail should not obscure the central fact of their agreement in general: Development is beneficial to democracy.

---

[2] Adam Przeworski and Fernando Limongi, "Modernization: Theories and Facts," *World Politics*, vol. 49 (January 1997).

[3] John Londregan and Keith Poole, "Does High Income Promote Democracy?" *World Politics*, vol. 49 (October 1996).

Do Political Regimes Matter?

The converse relationship—that of the impact of democracy on development—is far more contentious. The once-fashionable idea that autocratic regimes have an advantage in economic development has been largely discredited, but the question of whether or not political regimes affect economic growth nonetheless remains unanswered.[4]

The advantages of autocratic regimes were not intrinsically derived. Rather, these regimes were supposed to have an edge in development mainly because they were said to lack the disadvantages often associated with democracy, specifically:

- insecure property rights of the wealthy, resulting from the enfranchisement of the poor, who are presumed to use their voting power to seek the redistribution of wealth;
- high propensity to consume, resulting from the pressure on politicians within an electoral system to appease the short-term demands of voters;
- rent-seeking by special interest groups that penetrate the open political process and use their influence to produce socially inefficient policies.

The theory that autocracy is good for development is extremely weak. Open political processes under democracy may indeed lead to the problems outlined above, but there is nothing intrinsic to autocracy that suggests that the same problems would not exist under autocratic rule. Property rights are by no means secure in an autocracy whose rulers are immune from institutional constraints such as an independent judiciary or parliamentary competition. Quite the opposite: autocratic rulers have the capacity to impose confiscatory rates of taxation, or even to refuse to honor their financial obligations. Autocrats have historically been known also to plunder their societies for personal gain, exhibiting predatory behavior that is partly motivated by an insecurity that greatly reduces their time-horizon. The vice of rent-seeking is also familiar within autocracies—even the most absolutist rulers must rely on their supporters to keep them in power. To maintain their support, autocratic rulers must constantly reward their constituents with favors, such as monopolies, subsidies, tax privileges, and licenses. All of these can greatly reduce economic efficiency.

---

[4] For a survey on this topic, see Alberto Alesina and Roberto Perotti, "The Political Economy of Growth: A Critical Survey of the Recent Literature," *The World Bank Economic Review*, vol. 8, no. 3 (1994); Adam Przeworski and Fernando Limongi, "Political Regimes and Economic Growth," *Journal of Economic Perspectives*, vol. 7, no. 3 (Summer 1993).

The case that democracy promotes development rests on the central idea that the political institutions critical to economic development are more likely to exist and function effectively under democratic rule. These institutions include the rule of law, which protects property rights; individual liberties that foster creativity and entrepreneurship; freedom of expression, which ensures the production and unimpeded flow of information; and institutional checks and balances that prevent the massive theft of public wealth often observed in autocracies.[5] One statistical study of growth data for 115 countries from 1960 to 1980 claims that countries with high degrees of political openness achieved an average annual real per capita growth rate of 2.53 percent, compared with 1.41 percent in more closed political systems. This implies that democratic countries grow 80 percent faster than less democratic ones.[6]

Other statistical studies, however, have yielded more ambiguous conclusions.[7] One study examining Gross National Product (GNP) growth data from 94 countries for 1960–1979 (excluding centrally planned economies, colonies, and capital-surplus oil-exporting countries) reported that democracy has a weak negative overall effect on economic growth.[8] A statistical analysis of growth data for 100 countries from 1960 to 1990 by Robert Barro reached a similar conclusion.[9] Barro's study, however, also suggests that the relationship between democracy and growth may be nonlinear, and may take an inverted U-form. According to his analysis, economic growth is likely to be slowest in the most politically repressed societies; but his analysis also shows that the improvement of political rights and civil liberties in such societies tends to produce much higher growth. His data show that growth rates tend to peak when the level of democracy is in the mid-range, and that they gradually taper off as the level of democracy rises.

These theoretical and empirical explorations may have advanced our understanding of the relationship between democracy and development, but they leave several important puzzles unresolved. The most important is the relationship between the rule of law and political regimes. This issue is central to the puzzle because economic historians have persuasively demonstrated that secure property rights constitute the institu-

---

[5] See Gerald Scully, "The Institutional Framework and Economic Development," *Journal of Political Economy*, vol. 96, no. 3 (1988); Mancur Olson, "Dictatorship, Democracy, and Development," *American Political Science Review*, vol. 87, no. 3 (September 1993); Jagdish Bhagwati, "Democracy and Development," *Journal of Democracy*, vol. 3, no. 3 (July 1992).

[6] Scully, p. 657.

[7] These results were reported in Przeworski and Limongi, "Political Regimes and Economic Growth."

[8] Erich Weede, "The Impact of Democracy on Economic Growth," *Kyklos*, vol. 36 (1983).

[9] Robert Barro, "Democracy and Growth," NBER Working Paper no. 4909 (October 1994).

tional foundations of sustained economic development.[10] The rule of law—generally understood to mean the supremacy of legal norms and codes, enforced by an independent judiciary—has proven to be the institution most important to the protection of property rights. The relationship between the rule of law and property rights is now so uncontroversial that the two concepts have almost become interchangeable when used in the context of economic development.

The relationship between the rule of law and political regimes is far more complex. Intuitively, democracy in general and democratic institutions in particular—including multi-party systems, competitive elections, and a free press—should be viewed as part of the political foundations of the rule of law, for the reason that the functioning of these institutions ensures that the rule of law will have its defenders (parties, candidates, and the media). More importantly, the competitive nature of democracy ensures that no single individual or political force will acquire so much political power as to overwhelm all other forces, and this in turn means that no individual or entity can rise above the law or threaten the rule of law. The return relationship is also thought to hold true: The rule of law is now thought to be such an inseparable part of democracy that it is difficult to imagine a democracy without it.

The political foundations of the rule of law may be more complex and less thoroughly understood. Democratic institutions may strengthen or defend the rule of law; but the same institutions also have the capacity to undermine it. Electoral politics may be a double-edged sword, with the capacity also to undermine the rule of law. A government elected by majority vote, for example, conceivably has the franchise to make new laws that victimize the minority. Several recent, draconian U.S laws against illegal immigrants and convicted criminals would seem to support this point. Democratically elected leaders can also rig the judicial process through their own appointments; ultimately, the institutions that defend the autonomy of the judiciary are but the products of political decisions. Voters' preferences may change, and such a change can lead to a conscious decision, even in the form of constitutional amendments, to reduce the autonomy of the judiciary. Recent U.S. history is filled with examples of attempts to revise the Constitution to permit the passage of laws that were deemed unconstitutional by the Supreme Court (such as the law banning the burning of the American flag). That most attempts have failed is an indication of the resilience of the U.S. democracy, but they also warn of the potential of democracy to weaken the rule of law.

---

[10] See Douglass North and Robert Paul Thomas, *The Rise of the Western World* (Cambridge University Press, 1973); North, *Institutions, Institutional Change and Economic Performance* (Cambridge University Press 1990).

The existence of this potential, of a coalition's ability to build a democratically formed majority to change the law, makes property rights insecure. Admittedly, a complete redistribution of wealth under democracy has not taken place, but this does not disprove the existence of such a possibility. Instead, it may say something about the type of democracy that the United States has in place—one whose embedded institutions, for example, are designed to protect property rights rather than to promote mass sovereignty.

Second, it is unclear whether or not democracy is a precondition to the rule of law (it seems indisputable that the converse is true, that the rule of law is a precondition to democracy). Historical evidence shows that many nondemocratic regimes—such as the Kaiser's Germany, pre-1945 Japan, Pinochet's Chile, Hong Kong under colonial rule, Singapore, Franco's Spain, and nearly all Western European countries before they became democratic in the mid-1800s—had the capacity to maintain the rule of law. The claim that only popular sovereignty can guarantee the rule of law is thus questionable on empirical ground as well as on theoretical ground. Of course, the political factors that help defend the rule of law may be different in democracies from those in autocracies. But one central similarity is that the rule of law can maintain its effectiveness only when the rulers, whether democratically elected or not, are placed under certain political constraints. These need be neither formal nor constitutional. The autocracies that were able to maintain the rule of law—primarily those of Western Europe—were nearly all subject to powerful political constraints that defended property rights. These constraints included the power of an independent aristocracy, the church, the rising urban capitalist class, and ever-present external threats, and obliged rulers to exercise political moderation.

It may in fact be more accurate to say that it is political and institutional pluralism, rather than formal democracy, that has proved to be the ultimate defender of property rights. This gives rise to a conclusion that is counter to the post-Cold War doctrine of democratic enlargement: The first priority of the international community is not to promote formal democracy, but to promote political and institutional pluralism as an intermediate step to democracy.

DEMOCRACY, DEVELOPMENT, ECONOMIC FREEDOM, AND CORRUPTION: SOME RECENT EVIDENCE

Democracies generally have many embedded institutional advantages that support economic development, but for poor countries these advantages may be neither apparent nor real. A simple analysis of recent data on per capita income, political rights and civil liberties, economic freedom, and perceived corruption illustrates this point. This exercise assumes a direct relationship between good governance and sustained economic development. Since it is difficult to establish measures of governance, the corruption perceptions index compiled by Transparency International, a well-known nongovernmental organization, has been used as a substitute, on the assumption that less corrupt countries have better governance.

Wealth, Regimes, and Economic Freedom

The data (see Appendix Table 3.A.1) contains information on per capita Gross Domestic Product (GDP) income (measured in $PPP), combined measures of political rights, civil liberties, and economic freedom for 159 countries and show a close relationship between wealth and democracy, as measured by the combined scores of political rights and civil liberties. Regression analysis (equation No. 1 in Table 3.1) demonstrates a statistically significant and positive effect of per capita income on democracy (as proxied by index of political and civil liberties). Each increase of PPP $1,000 raises the measured degree of democracy by 0.287.[11]

Regression results also indicate that wealth (as proxied by PPP) has a small but positive effect on economic freedom. Each per capita GDP increase of PPP $1,000 leads to an increase of 0.0775 in the economic freedom index. Political regimes, in comparison, have a bigger impact on economic freedom. Regression results show that an increase of 1 in the index of autocracy (for example, from 10 to 11 in the Freedom House index) would result in a reduction of economic freedom by 0.125. This implies that, everything else being equal, the effect of increasing political rights and civil liberties by 1 (on a scale of 2 to 14) would produce almost twice as large an effect on economic freedom.

Wealth, Regimes, Economic Freedom, and Governance

To understand the complex relationship between per capita income, political regimes, economic freedom, and corruption perceptions (a proxy for governance), a multivariate regression analysis was performed on data from 83 countries (equation No. 1). The statistically significant results show that wealth, democracy, and economic freedom, as expected,

---

[11] Technically speaking, because the smaller the combined measure of political rights and civil liberties in the Freedom House survey, the more democratic the country is. The sign of the coefficient of $PPP in the regression is negative, which means that a unit increase in wealth reduces the freedom index score (thus increasing democracy).

Table 3.1. Selected Determinants of Corruption, Economic Freedom and Civil Liberties

Independent Variables	Dependent Variables			
	(Equation 1) Political Rights & Civil Liberties	(Equation 2) Economic Freedom	(Equation 3) Economic Freedom	(Equation 4) Perceived Corruption Index
Per Capita Income ($PPP)	–.0002872 (9.77)	–.0000775	—	.0001878 (6.57)
Political Rights & Civil Liberties	—	—	0.125407 (8.69)	–0.0923626 (1.74)
Economic Freedom	—	—	—	–0.6975913 (1.95)
C	—	3.69 (48.058)	2.26 (18.78)	5.647138 (4.88)
N	159	159	159	83
R^2	0.25	0.38	0.32	0.72
Adjustable R^2	0.25	0.37	0.32	0.71

Note: The variables in this table are defined in Appendix Table 3.A.1. T-statistics are in parentheses.

all contribute to good governance, as reflected in the perceived corruption index. Of the three independent variables, economic freedom has the most powerful effect on corruption. After adjustment (because the range in the economic freedom index is 1.25 to 5.0 and that in the freedom index is 2 to 14), a unit increase in economic freedom has about three times the effect on governance that a unit increase in political freedom generates. By comparison, increase in wealth has the smallest impact. A rise of per capita GDP of PPP $1,000 leads to an increase of 0.187 on the corruption perceptions index (a rise in the index indicates less corruption).

These statistical findings reconfirm our intuitive understanding of the relationship of wealth, economic freedom, political regimes, and governance. In countries with greater economic freedom, fewer opportunities for rent-seeking exist; there should therefore be less corruption in these countries. Of course, the relationship can also work in reverse: more corrupt countries would have less economic freedom because groups or individuals benefiting from corruption would use their influence to limit economic freedom.

Nor is the finding that political regimes have a positive, although modest, effect on governance surprising, as it fits with the conclusion that there is a stronger case to be made for sustained economic development under democracy than under autocracy. But one should be cautious not to read too much into this finding, as many democratic countries are known to have relatively poor governance. This can be explained as follows:

In the sample of 83 countries for which the data on corruption perceptions were available, 63 countries returned median and above-median scores for political rights and civil liberties. (The freest countries score 2 and the least free countries 14. The median score is 8.)[12] Twenty countries in the sample have scores of 9–14, and are considered "not free." Given the assumption that freer countries should be less corrupt, a country with a median freedom score but an above-median score of corruption perception (more corrupt) appears anomalous. Additionally, of the 63 countries with median and better freedom scores, 40 (63 percent) have above-median (i.e., worse than median) scores on the corruption perceptions index, and are ranked at 27 and above.[13] A closer examination of these "anomalous" countries shows that nearly all of them are relatively new democracies or are semiauthoritarian regimes in transition, and have scores for political rights and civil liberties that suggest they are not yet consolidated democracies. Moreover, their income is low compared to that of established democracies; most have per capita GDP income of less than PPP$10,000. Of the 37 countries with above-median freedom scores but per capita GDP income of less than PPP$10,000, only three have better-than-median corruption perception scores (i.e., are considered less corrupt).[14] This shows that (1) although democracies may not be able to eliminate corruption, established and consolidated democracies have less corruption than new democracies; and (2) the likelihood that a new democracy or a transitioning semiauthoritarian regime with a per capita GDP income of less than PPP$10,000 will have a worse-than-median corruption score is high (almost 92 percent).

Autocracies do not fare better in this area. The analysis shows that they may in fact do considerably worse—although the small sample size weakens the validity of this conclusion. The first sign that autocracies may be more corrupt (as measured by the simple method used here) is that, of the 20 autocracies in the sample, as identified by freedom scores

[12] The Freedom House classifies those countries with scores of 2–5 as free; 6–10 as partly free; and 11–14 as not free.

[13] These countries are: Malawi, India, Nicaragua, Honduras, Ghana, Bolivia, El Salvador, Philippines, Latvia, Jamaica, Romania, Ecuador, Bulgaria, Thailand, the Slovak Republic, Venezuela, Uruguay, Argentina, South Korea, Uganda, Senegal, Ukraine, Guatemala, Paraguay, Russia, Colombia, Brazil, Mexico, Jordan, South Africa, Poland, Costa Rica, Uruguay, Czech Republic, Greece, Mauritius, Taiwan, Italy, and Belgium.

[14] They are Chile, Estonia, and Botswana.

of 9–14, 18 (90 percent) have worse-than-median corruption scores (i.e., are ranked higher than 27).[15] Two have better-than-median corruption scores.[16] Controlled for income, autocracies are thus shown to have a greater likelihood of being more corrupt (90 percent vs. 63 percent) than democracies. All 18 of the autocracies with per capita income of less than PPP$10,000 have worse-than-median corruption scores. This is marginally higher than the 92 percent of countries with better-than-median freedom scores that have worse-than-median corruption scores.

The findings of this statistical analysis echo the widely held view that institutions play an important role in maintaining good governance. As far as governance, as measured by corruption, is concerned, countries with more political rights and civil liberties have a slight edge over those with fewer political rights and civil liberties. But the advantage enjoyed by economically more free countries over economically less free countries is much greater. This conclusion supports the view that, to the extent that political and economic institutions influence economic development, the top priority of the international community is not to promote democratic reforms immediately (although such reforms are beneficial), but to promote the reform of the key economic institutions that have a direct impact on economic freedom.

In reality, of course, democratic political reforms and economic institutional reforms may be closely interrelated. In some cases, economic institutional reforms cannot proceed without the implementation of democratic reforms to dislodge rent-seeking groups from power. But when considering the promotion of democracy as a means of economic development, one must be wary of raising expectations and cautious in devising policies. The finding here that new and unconsolidated democracies tend to have above-median corruption scores cautions that the positive effects of democratic reforms may not be immediate. In practice, while democratic reforms can quickly yield visible improvements in political rights and civil liberties, their benefits in the area of economic reform are generally much slower in coming.

GOVERNANCE AND DEVELOPMENT: WILL THE CHINESE MIRACLE TURN INTO MIRAGE?

There is a widely shared belief that China's economic development in the last two decades has been extremely successful: the country has achieved

---

[15] These countries are: Tanzania, Zambia, Nigeria, Vietnam, Kenya, Ivory Coast, Cameroon, Zimbabwe, China, Morocco, Indonesia, Egypt, Belarus, Turkey, Pakistan, Peru, Tunisia, and Malaysia.

[16] They are Hong Kong and Singapore.

sustained high growth rates, it has quadrupled its GDP per capita income, raised millions of people out of poverty, increased efficiency, and established broad links with the world economy.[17] There is much less consensus on whether or not governance in China has improved correspondingly—and there is even less agreement on whether or not China's economic gains can be sustained without important reforms in its political institutions and improvement in its governance.

On the surface, it is tempting to cite the East Asian miracle in general, and China's developmental success in the last two decades in particular, as evidence that governance-enhancing institutional reforms are not necessary for sustained economic development. China has obtained its remarkable gains without undertaking many of the critical reforms that are generally considered to be the necessary foundations for long-term growth, such as the rule of law, financial regulatory regimes, transparency, and a system of accountability.

This reading of the East Asian miracle and the Chinese reform experience misses several important points. In the Chinese case, one may even argue that China's experience actually supports the argument for a link between good governance and sustainable development. Although the country has undeniably made real and rapid advances in its economic development, its growth in the last two decades has benefited from many one-off factors that cannot be counted on to sustain the country's development momentum.

Compared to the preceding 140 years of foreign invasion, national disintegration, civil war, and domestic turmoil, China has enjoyed relative political stability since 1979. The country's most important institutional reform—the dismantling of the commune system in rural areas—produced huge one-off efficiency gains and freed up rural labor. China's gradual economic liberalization, however limited, was also a positive contributing factor, and unlike many of the transition economies of the former Soviet bloc, the Chinese economy had better economic fundamentals, including high savings rates; a young and relatively well-educated and healthy labor force; a relatively small socialist state; and a flexible central-local political structure conducive to local initiatives. The combination of enlightened government policy and the lure of its huge potential market additionally attracted enormous foreign direct investment, mostly from the Chinese diaspora. However, the benefits produced by most of these factors have been diminishing in recent years, and at the same time, more deeply embedded problems have been surfacing.

---

[17] The best summary of the Chinese reform experience is The World Bank, *China 2020* (1997).

China's late leader Deng Xiaoping called his economic reform the "second revolution;" his successor, Jiang Zemin, now faces the prospect of leading the "third revolution" if China is to sustain its progress. Unlike Deng's reforms, which focused on economic liberalization, Jiang's reform must focus on building the institutional foundations of development.

This third revolution is essential for several reasons. First, China's past success is no guarantee for its future success. Second, China's success has been built up almost from nowhere. When overall conditions are so poor, a small improvement can produce huge one-off gains. Third, in addition to delaying tackling its most difficult economic problems—especially the crisis of the state-owned enterprises—the Chinese government has only made minor progress in improving the institutions of governance. For instance, China's legal system remains rudimentary and poorly equipped to enforce contracts and to protect property rights. The country's unitary state institutions are also seriously at odds with its federalist political reality, creating serious friction between the central government and local governments. China's civil society remains weak and heavily controlled by the state, resulting in poor social cohesion and rising social anomie (or normless behavior). The government is fearful of the political consequences of democratization, and there are therefore few open participatory channels, such as the electoral and legislative processes, through which popular discontent and needs may be expressed. This is directly causing increasing social unrest, expressed in more violent forms.

All of these institutional weaknesses will likely cause governance to deteriorate. If this were to be the case, it would inevitably jeopardize China's economic performance by producing higher levels of political instability and by increasing the economic costs of poor governance through corruption, prohibitive transaction costs due to a weak legal system, and opportunistic behavior by local governments. Conservative estimates put the direct economic costs of official corruption in China at around $10 billion, or about 1 percent of GDP, in 1998.[18]

The indirect costs could be much higher, as demonstrated by the case of the government's financial losses in its grain procurement fund. Through a combination of interventionist policies, direct theft, and misappropriation of funds, government agents and grain brokers contributed to the loss of more than $25 billion of public funds budgeted for the purchase of grain over a six-year period. Government auditors found that $10 billion of the lost funds lost were either stolen or diverted to sideline businesses operated by the government officials in charge of the funds.[19] Another area

---

[18] *The Wall Street Journal*, January 11, 1999, A10.
[19] *The Wall Street Journal*, January 26, 1999, A1.

plagued by corruption is public works: Official reports suggest that about $12 billion a year is wasted on low-quality public works projects.[20]

The dilemma facing the Chinese government today is that it is under tremendous external pressure—and increasing internal demand—to liberalize its political system, but at the same time elite resistance to democratizing remains strong. Moreover, China's current governance institutions, such as the legal system, quasi-federalist institutions, and civic organizations, are perhaps too poorly developed to withstand the political shock of full democratization. The last thing the Chinese leaders want to do is effect a premature political opening resulting in a Soviet-style collapse.

Refusal to reform for fear of instability will only delay, but not remove, the day of reckoning. If anything, delay will further complicate the problem and increase the eventual costs of reaching a solution. If social science research is any guide for policy, Chinese leaders would be well advised to expend their limited political capital on improving governance institutions that have a direct impact on economic efficiency, rather than to attempt dramatic democratizing reform. Recent events in China, such as the reform of the central bank and the fiscal system, suggest that this may be the route the country's leaders have chosen. This is also suggested by the willingness to discuss certain reforms in international fora, and to make international commitments as is happening, for example, in the context of China's negotiations to enter the World Trade Organization (WTO).

CONCLUSION: PUTTING ECONOMIC INSTITUTIONS FIRST

The findings of this paper have several implications for policy. First and foremost, if, as shown, increases in wealth have only a modest effect on improving governance, it would be naïve to count on accelerating economic development alone as a means of achieving good governance. Such a strategy would surely fail because sustained development is impossible without good governance. Second, it is also naïve to believe that democratization alone can immediately improve governance. Countries scoring higher on the index of political rights and civil liberties may have a slight edge in governance, but most young democracies have relatively poor governance records. The most effective means of achieving good governance is the joint development of institutions governing economic activities, and the implementation of reforms that increase economic freedom.

---

[20] *South China Morning Post*, February 12, 1999.

Economic historians such as North have made a strong case that institutions are vital to the long-term economic development of any society. Recent empirical studies of the East Asian development experience have reached similar conclusions.[21] However, an appreciation of the role of institutions in economic development is not enough. There is little doubt that such appreciation, differing only in the degree of sophistication, exists today at the elite level in most countries, but the most serious challenge is political: how to build economic institutions in the inhospitable political environment characteristic of many undemocratic countries, and newly democratized countries.

The theoretical discussion of why the rule of law may not function fully under democracy, and empirical examples showing the coexistence of democracy and serious corruption in many developing countries illustrate that democratization, despite its long-term promise, is not a panacea for development. A two-pronged approach must therefore be considered.

First, in countries where democratization has already occurred, the top priority must be given to the establishment and consolidation of those institutions that have the most immediate, direct, and powerful impact on macroeconomic stability, security of property rights, and free trade. These steps necessarily involve the strengthening of the independence of the central bank, the regulatory regime of the financial system, the courts, and competition regimes. This institutional reform process may encounter political difficulties created by the new democratic institutions and processes. There is no conclusive evidence on whether the democratization process itself would aid or hinder these steps.

Second, in countries where democratization has yet to occur, the emphasis of change should be placed more on the establishment and strengthening of existing economic institutions than on the direct promotion of democracy (or more crudely, elections). The strategy of direct democratic promotion in these societies, however desirable, faces enormous odds, including strong resistance from the ruling elite and weak socioeconomic and institutional foundations. The success of direct democratic promotion is highly uncertain; the beneficial effects of democratization on economic development, even if one assumes the success of democratic promotion, may not be immediately substantial.

A strategy emphasizing institution-building without regime change may be more practical and yield more immediate results. Such a strategy aims at finding allies within the ruling autocratic regime who (for complex reasons) have a long-term interest in the development of these insti-

---

[21] See for example, The World Bank, *The East Asian Miracle*; Robert Wade, *Governing the Market*; Stephan Haggard, *Pathways from the Periphery*.

tutions. Moreover, this step poses less threat to the regime than does the democratic promotion strategy, and is likely to encounter less resistance. Given that reformers, both domestic and international, tend to have limited political capital, this strategy may also be the most cost-effective, since it makes the building of a reform coalition (with critical participation from elite members inside the regime) more achievable.

The long-term benefits of this indirect approach—building economic institutions ahead of democratic institutions—may be twofold. Economically, such institutions would undoubtedly contribute to sustained long-term growth. Politically, these institutions would not only promote the eventual development of democracy through sustained growth, but would help insulate future democratic institutions and processes from the temptation of rent-seeking, as the rents available would be greatly diminished by the operation of strong economic institutions. A final advantage of having strong economic institutions before democratization is that the existence and operation of these institutions would increase the likelihood of democratic survival and consolidation during the post-transition phase. As the statistical analyses performed by some political scientists show, poor democracies tend to die of economic crisis.[22] Such crises would perhaps not have the same devastating impact if those countries have strong economic institutions capable of containing them.

There are, however, several serious political risks for advocating and implementing this strategy. Despite the convergence of the long-term objectives of this economic-institutions-first strategy and of the democracy promotion strategy, the former is likely to attract less political support from leading industrial democracies because the pay-off of the strategy is long-term and uncertain, and pressures for short-term results are considerable. The strategy is especially vulnerable to criticisms from human rights groups if it is applied in authoritarian countries with unacceptable rights records.

Finally, such a strategy does not guarantee success. Since it is predicated upon finding elite-level allies inside the ruling hierarchy, its fate is closely tied with that of the indigenous reformers—a highly unpredictable factor over which external actors have little control. The challenge for the international development community is therefore primarily political: how to build domestic political coalitions to support the strategy, and how to find allies within the ruling political regime of the target nation to implement it.

---

[22] Adam Przeworski, Michael Alvarez, Jose Antonio Cheibub, and Fernando Limongi, "What Makes Democracies Endure?", *Journal of Democracy*, vol. 7, no. 1 (January 1996).

Appendix Table 3.A.1. Wealth, Democracy, Economic Freedom, and Corruption

Country	Per capita GDP in $PPP (1994–95)	Index of Freedom (1997–98)	Economic Freedom (1999)	Index of Ranking of Corruption (1998)
Albania	2,850	8	129	—
Algeria	5,620	12	90	—
Angola	1,840	12	149	—
Arab Rep. of Egypt	3,720	12	97	66
Argentina	8,720	5	34	61
Armenia	2,160	9	106	—
Australia	18,120	2	14	11
Austria	19,560	2	18	17
Azerbaijan	1,510	10	143	—
Bahamas	15,470	3	11	—
Bahrain	13,220	13	3	—
Bangladesh	1,330	6	129	—
Barbados	11,210	2	41	—
Belarus	4,320	12	140	47
Belgium	20,270	3	14	28
Belize	5,600	2	54	—
Benin	1,630	4	75	—
Bolivia	2,400	4	43	69
Botswana	5,210	4	48	23
Brazil	5,400	7	90	46
Bulgaria	4,380	5	106	66
Burkina Faso	800	9	111	—
Burundi	700	14	133	—
Cambodia	1,110	13	97	—
Cameroon	1,950	12	111	85
Canada	19,960	2	14	6
Cape Verde	1,920	3	119	—
Chad	720	11	124	—
Chile	8,890	4	18	20
China	2,510	14	124	52
Colombia	5,330	8	81	79
Costa Rica	6,000	3	54	27
Côte d'Ivoire	1,370	10	97	59
Croatia	3,970	8	116	—
Cuba	3,100	14	160	—

(Continued on the following page.)

Appendix Table 3.A.1. (continued)

Country	Per capita GDP in $PPP (1994–95)	Index of Freedom (1997–98)	Economic Freedom (1999)	Index of Ranking of Corruption (1998)
Cyprus	14,800	2	45	—
Czech Republic	8,900	3	12	37
Dem. Rep. of Congo	350	13	153	—
Dem. Rep. of Korea	4,060	14	160	—
Denmark	19,880	2	22	1
Djibouti	1,300	11	88	—
Dominican Republic	3,760	6	97	—
Ecuador	4,190	6	65	77
El Salvador	2,410	5	22	51
Equatorial Guinea	1,710	14	143	—
Estonia	4,510	3	18	26
Ethiopia	430	9	120	—
Fiji	5,940	7	81	—
Finland	16,150	2	22	2
France	19,670	3	34	21
Gabon	3,760	9	65	—
Gambia	1,100	13	115	—
Georgia	1,390	7	116	—
Germany	19,480	3	25	15
Ghana	2,050	6	72	55
Greece	10,930	4	62	36
Guatemala	3,440	7	48	59
Guinea	1,140	11	97	—
Guinea-Bissau	820	7	151	—
Guyana	2,750	2	111	—
Haiti	930	9	135	—
Honduras	1,940	5	85	83
Hong Kong	22,950	9	1	16
Hungary	6,080	3	62	33
Iceland	19,210	2	25	—
India	1,280	6	120	66
Indonesia	3,600	12	65	80
Iran	5,480	13	153	—
Iraq	3,170	14	157	—
Ireland	13,550	2	7	14
Israel	15,300	4	54	19
Italy	18,460	3	34	39

Appendix Table 3.A.1. (continued)

Country	Per capita GDP in $PPP (1994–95)	Index of Freedom (1997–98)	Economic Freedom (1999)	Index of Ranking of Corruption (1998)
Jamaica	3,400	5	45	49
Japan	21,140	3	12	25
Jordan	4,100	8	48	38
Kazakhstan	2,810	11	137	—
Kenya	1,310	12	75	74
Kuwait	24,730	10	28	—
Kyrgyz Republic	1,730	8	135	—
Laos	2,570	13	157	—
Latvia	3,220	3	61	71
Lebanon	4,980	11	90	—
Lesotho	1,730	8	106	—
Libya	6,310	14	157	—
Lithuania	3,290	3	72	—
Luxembourg	35,860	2	7	11
Madagascar	640	6	106	—
Malawi	650	5	116	45
Malaysia	8,440	9	28	29
Mali	520	6	81	—
Malta	13,300	2	65	—
Mauritania	1,570	12	124	—
Mauritius	12,720	3	43	33
Mexico	7,040	7	85	5
Moldova	1,550	7	97	—
Mongolia	3,910	5	8	—
Morocco	3,470	10	65	50
Mozambique	860	7	129	—
Myanmar	1,130	14	143	—
Namibia	4,320	5	48	29
Nepal	1,230	7	104	—
Netherlands	18,750	2	18	6
New Zealand	15,870	2	4	4
Nicaragua	1,800	6	111	61
Niger	770	12	120	—
Nigeria	1,190	13	95	81
Norway	20,210	2	27	8
Oman	8,590	12	48	—
Pakistan	2,130	9	97	71

(Continued on the following page.)

Appendix Table 3.A.1. (continued)

Country	Per capita GDP in $PPP (1994–95)	Index of Freedom (1997–98)	Economic Freedom (1999)	Index of Ranking of Corruption (1998)
Panama	5,730	5	28	—
Papua New Guinea	2,680	6	85	—
Paraguay	3,550	7	75	84
Peru	3,610	9	41	41
Philippines	2,740	5	48	55
Poland	5,480	3	65	39
Portugal	11,970	2	38	22
Qatar	19,100	13	75	—
Rep. of Congo	1,900	12	123	—
Rep. of Korea	10,330	4	28	43
Romania	4,090	4	95	61
Russian Federation	4,610	7	106	76
Rwanda	330	13	143	—
Saudi Arabia	9,480	14	72	—
Senegal	1,580	8	90	55
Sierra Leone	700	13	137	—
Singapore	21,900	10	2	7
Slovak Rep.	7,320	6	75	47
Slovenia	6,230	3	81	—
South Africa	5,130	3	62	32
Spain	13,740	3	34	23
Sri Lanka	3,160	7	38	—
Sudan	1,110	14	141	—
Suriname	2,470	6	129	—
Swaziland	3,010	11	54	—
Sweden	17,130	2	33	3
Switzerland	25,150	2	5	10
Syria	5,370	14	141	—
Taiwan	16,610	2	7	—
Tajikistan	970	12	147	—
Tanzania	620	10	90	—
Thailand	6,970	6	28	61
Togo	1,130	11	134	—
Trinidad and Tobago	8,670	3	38	—
Tunisia	5,020	11	65	33
Turkey	4,710	9	54	54
Turkmenistan	2,340	14	149	—

Appendix Table 3.A.1. (continued)

Country	Per capita GDP in $PPP (1994–95)	Index of Freedom (1997–98)	Economic Freedom (1999)	Index of Ranking of Corruption (1998)
Uganda	1,410	8	54	73
Ukraine	2,620	7	124	69
United Arab Emirates	18,000	11	14	—
United Kingdom	17,970	3	7	11
United States	25,880	2	6	17
Uruguay	7,710	3	45	42
Uzbekistan	2,370	13	147	—
Venezuela	7,770	5	104	77
Vietnam	1,240	14	152	74
Western Samoa	2,060	4	54	—
Yemen	870	11	139	—
Zambia	860	9	75	52
Zimbabwe	2,040	10	124	43

Notes:
1. Measures of Freedom consist of two separate indicators: political rights and civil liberties. The combined score of political rights and civil liberties is between 2 and 14, 2 being the most free and 14 being the least free. Freedom House considers countries with scores of between 2 and 5 "free"; those scoring between 6 and 10 as "partly free"; and those scoring between 11 and 14 as "unfree." The median score is 8.
2. Measures of Economic Freedom consist of one index in which the freest economy (Hong Kong) scores 1.25 and the least free economy (the Democratic Republic of Korea) scores 5.0. The median is 3.125. Countries with scores near the median (such as Mexico, with a score of 3.15) are ranked 85th.
3. Ranking of corruption is based on data provided by Transparency International (1998). The score for the least corrupt country is 10, and for the most corrupt, 1.4; the median score is 5.7. The country with the median score is Estonia, ranked 26th.
Sources: United Nations, Human Development Report 1998; World Bank, World Development Report 1996; Freedom House, Freedom in the World 1997/98; Bryan Johnson et al., Index of Economic Freedom 1999; Transparency International, "Corruption Perceptions Index 1998."

REFERENCES:

Alesina, Alberto, and Roberto Perotti. 1994. "The Political Economy of Growth: A Critical Survey of the Recent Literature." The World Bank Economic Review 8(3).

Barro, Robert. 1994. "Democracy and Growth." NBER Working Paper No. 4909. October.

Bhagwati, Jagdish. 1992. "Democracy and Development." *Journal of Democracy* 3(3). July.

Dahl, Robert. 1971. *Polyarchy.* New Haven: Yale University Press.

Freedom House. *Freedom in the World 1997/98.*

Huntington, Samuel P. 1991. *The Third Wave: Democratization in the Late Twentieth Century.* Oklahoma University Press.

Johnson, Bryan, et al. 1999. *Index of Economic Freedom.*

Lipset, Seymour Martin. 1959. "Some Social Requisites of Democracy: Economic Development and Political Legitimacy." *American Political Science Review* 53 (March).

Londregan, John, and Keith Poole. 1996. "Does High Income Promote Democracy?" *World Politics* 49 (October).

North, Douglass. 1990. *Institutions, Institutional Change and Economic Performance.* Cambridge: Cambridge University Press.

North, Douglass, and Robert Paul Thomas. 1973. *The Rise of the Western World.* Cambridge: Cambridge University Press.

Olson, Mancur. 1993. "Dictatorship, Democracy, and Development." *American Political Science Review* 87(3). September.

Przeworski, Adam, and Fernando Limongi. 1993. "Political Regimes and Economic Growth." *Journal of Economic Perspectives* 7(3). Summer.

———. 1997. "Modernization: Theories and Facts." *World Politics* 49 (January).

Przeworski, Adam, Michael Alvarez, Jose Cheibub Antonio, and Fernando Limongi. 1996. "What Makes Democracies Endure?" *Journal of Democracy* 7(1). January.

Rueschemeyer, Dietrich, Evelyne Stephens, and John Stephens. 1992. *Capitalist Development and Democracy.* Chicago: University of Chicago Press.

Scully, Gerald. 1988. "The Institutional Framework and Economic Development." *Journal of Political Economy* 96(3).

South China Morning Post. 1999. February 12.

Transparency International. 1998. "Corruption Perceptions Index 1998."

United Nations. 1998. *Human Development Report 1998*.

The Wall Street Journal. 1999. January 11, A10.

———. 1999. January 26, A1.

Weede, Erich. 1983. "The Impact of Democracy on Economic Growth." *Kyklos* 36.

World Bank. 1994. *The East Asian Miracle*. Washington, D.C.

———. 1996. *World Development Report 1996*. Washington, D.C.

———. 1996. *World Development Report 1996*. Washington, D.C.

———. 1997. *China 2020*. Washington, D.C.

4

PARTICIPATION AND DEVELOPMENT: PERSPECTIVES FROM THE COMPREHENSIVE DEVELOPMENT PARADIGM

Joseph Stiglitz

THE RELATIONSHIP BETWEEN DEMOCRACY and development has long been debated. In the years immediately following World War II, there was a belief (articulated in Paul Samuelson's classic textbook) in a tradeoff between democracy and growth. The Soviet Union, it was argued, had grown faster than the countries of the West, but in order to do so had jettisoned basic democratic rights. The lack of full participatory democracy in many of the most successful countries during the subsequent East and Southeast Asian economic boom was seen once again as reflecting these tradeoffs.

A subject of this importance has not escaped the statisticians' close scrutiny, but their scrutiny has been conducted with the kind of ambiguity that we have come to expect from cross-sectional and time series analysis and has been compounded by severe measurement problems.[1] The host of factors that affect growth and that interact with each other make it difficult to identify with clarity the precise role of any one factor. Even if we could establish a positive correlation, it would be necessary to ascertain causality: Does democracy promote growth or does growth promote democracy?

While the data may leave open the question of the relationship between the variables, it is clear that the tradeoff once envisioned is not a necessary condition of economic growth. Countries can strive for openness and participation without fear that they will hamper development. Furthermore, research at both the macroeconomic and microeconomic levels has provided strong evidence to identify some of the ingredients that contribute to successful long-term growth. But while it is clear that open and transparent participatory processes can promote long-term development, they do not guarantee success.

---

[1] For an earlier review, see "Symposia: Democracy and Development," *Journal of Economic Perspectives* (1993), including the article by Przeworski and Limongi.

Participation and the Transformation of Society

A comprehensive paradigm is emerging that sees development as a trans-
formative movement from the traditional to the modern. Where traditional societies accept the world as it is, modern society seeks change and
recognizes that individuals and societies can affect that change, reducing
infant mortality, raising life expectancy, and increasing productivity.

This new paradigm contrasts with the dominant paradigm of the past
50 years, which focused narrowly on specific economic or allocative
issues. The earlier perspective argued that if the supply of capital
increased and the efficiency of resource allocation improved, development would occur. We have since come to see this perspective as too narrow: while these two conditions are arguably necessary for development,
they are far from sufficient. It may be possible to raise productivity and
even change attitudes within an enclave of the economy without achieving a development transformation of the society as a whole.

The inadequacy of the traditional, narrowly economic approach has
been highlighted by the experience of Russia and of many of the other
economies in transition. The practices of the socialist regime of the former
Soviet Union saw central planning (which was informationally inefficient), distorted prices, and attenuated incentives lead to outputs that
were below the economy's potential. Reforms introduced since the collapse of communism—privatization, free market prices, and decentral-
ization—even if not perfectly implemented, should have moved the
economy far closer to its potential. Since at the same time defense expenditures were cut back drastically, consumption should also have
increased (unless savings increased—which did not happen). In reality,
output and consumption in most of the former socialist countries remain
below the levels of a decade ago, when the transition began. Part of the
explanation for this lies in the destruction of organizational capital, and
part lies in the fact that privatization alone is insufficient to make an effective market economy. A further significant part of the explanation lies in
the destruction of the already weak social capital, manifested in the
growth of criminal organizations.

If development therefore requires a change of mindset, it is clear that
attention needs to focus on how to affect that change.[2] The change cannot

---

[2] "All [vicious development] circles result from the two-way dependence between development and some other factor, be it capital or entrepreneurship, education, public administration, etc. But the circle to which our analysis has led us may perhaps lay claim to a
privileged place in the hierarchy of these circles inasmuch as it alone places the difficulties
of development back where all difficulties of human action begin and belong: in the mind."
(Hirschman 1958, 11)

be ordered or forced from the outside: it has to come from within;[3] and the most effective way of ensuring that it reaches deep down in society is arguably through the kinds of open and extensive discussion that are central to participatory processes. Indeed, there is a whole tradition that identifies "government by discussion" as key.[4]

The Broad Range of Participation

For the purposes of this paper, the term "participation" is used in its broadest sense to encompass transparency, openness, and voice in both public and corporate settings. There are a variety of institutional arrangements that are consistent with participation in this sense. Additionally, the term "participatory processes" refers not just to those processes by which decisions are made in national governments, but also to processes used at local and provincial levels, at the workplace, and in capital markets. Participation does not refer simply to voting:[5] Participatory processes must entail open dialogue and broadly active civic engagement, and must give individuals a voice in the decisions that effect them.[6]

Processes, not just outcomes, are key to this broader interpretation of participation. The stress on processes is a natural outgrowth not only of the increasing emphasis on equity, but also of our greater recognition of agency problems. That is to say, we now recognize the importance of potential discrepancies between the actions taken by a party (the government, for example) and the interests of those whom the party is supposed to serve.[7] A government that engages in secrecy, making it impossible for

---

[3] In the West, the clear recognition of the inability to externally force a change in mindset dates from the Reformation. "As little as another can go to hell or heaven for me, so little can he believe or disbelieve for me; and as little as he can open or shut heaven or hell for me, so little can he drive me to faith or unbelief." See Luther (1942 [1523]). This insight was basic to the liberty of conscience and the attitudes of religious tolerance fostered in Europe after the Reformation.

[4] See, for example, John Stuart Mill (1972 [1859]), Walter Bagehot (1948 [1869]), James Bryce (1959 [1888]), John Dewey (1927, 1939), Ernest Barker (1967 [1942]), Frank Knight (1947), and Charles Lindblom (1990).

[5] "In theory, the democratic method is persuasion through public discussion carried on not only in legislative halls but in the press, private conversations, and public assemblies. The substitution of ballots for bullets, of the right to vote for the lash, is an expression of the will to substitute the method of discussion for the method of coercion." (Dewey 1939, 128)

[6] See Hirschman (1970) for a discussion of "voice."

[7] Agency theory is one of the principal strands in the modern theory of the economics of information. See, for example, Ross (1973), Stiglitz (1974), and the huge literature that followed. The essential point is that because of imperfections of information, actions of agents are not perfectly observable, and one cannot infer whether the agent took the "appropriate" action from observing outputs alone.

citizens to develop informed opinions about policies that are critical to their lives and to the well-being of their country, weakens accountability and the quality of decision-making.[8] A government that controls television broadcasting or that allows an oligarchy to control the media also undermines accountability. Over the short term, a country may be able to engage in a meaningful national dialogue on its future evolution without free elections, but in the long run, the dissonance may become too great. The legitimacy of those in decision-making positions depends not only on their actions being in accord with popular sentiment, but also on their having attained such positions through open electoral processes.

In many countries, an absence of rule of law and a lack of transparency both weaken the economy and undermine the participatory processes. In some countries, for instance, the rich and powerful are able to use their influence to gain access to the seats of political power, hence to obtain for themselves special favors and exemptions from the rules that otherwise seek to ensure equal opportunity for all. They may also buy access to the legislative and executive branches of government, and once again thereby to obtain rules and regulations that favor them.

The adverse impact on economic growth of practices such as these has been well documented. Research shows a direct relationship between secure property rights and the rule of law, and higher levels of investment and growth.[9] It has also shown that countries with policies that embrace open, transparent governance earn multiple benefits: growth is faster, and foreign aid is both more forthcoming and more effective.[10] It is a truism, however, that concentrations of economic power and wealth almost inevitably translate into attempts to gain political influence. The question is, what can be done about this?

Part of any strategy should be to limit these concentrations of wealth and economic power. This provides part of the justification for redistributive taxation, and especially inheritance taxation, and also provides part of the motivation for the anti-trust laws enacted in the United States at the end of the last century. More broadly, Thomas Jefferson, the third President of the United States and author of the American Declaration of Independence, argued for the importance of smallholder agriculture to the future of the newly founded American democracy. Jefferson's view translates today into government support of small and medium-sized enterprises.

In the Republic of Korea, the corporate restructuring currently underway is similarly designed in part to limit the economic power of the *chae-*

---

[8] See Stiglitz (1999c).

[9] Knack and Keefer (1995), Clague et al. (1996).

[10] World Bank (1998).

bols (although concerns exist that this process of rationalization may actually increase concentrations of power in certain industries). The restructuring may reduce the economy of scale achieved by the largest corporations, but any loss in efficiency should be more than offset by the overall efficiency gained by curbing their excessive market power. Even should this prove not to be the case, the issue of the adverse effect of a few dominant corporations on participation and openness should not be forgotten.

There is a second strategy to limit concentrations of wealth and economic power: the strengthening of checks on abuses of this power. There are at least three elements to this strategy. The first is to strengthen civil society as a source of countervailing power, to include political parties, unions, consumer groups, think tanks, and NGOs. In the parlance of modern economics, ensuring participatory processes and promoting the public good is itself a public good. Active public support is essential to this element of the strategy, and is critical to the implementation of meaningful democratic reforms.

Second, governments should not only increase transparency, but should also recognize that there exists the basic "right to know." Citizens have a right to know what their government is doing, and why, and they have a right to know when exceptions are made to rules and regulations. In the United States, the Freedom of Information Act is an example of a measure taken in support of a citizen's right to know.

Third, societies should extend their citizens' rights to legal recourse—i.e., to sue. The United States has recognized that there are potential political pressures that might dissuade governments from acting to break up monopolies or prevent anticompetitive practices, and as a result has passed antitrust laws that enable any injured party to sue for damages. Although in the United States these laws have been interpreted too narrowly and occasionally abused, civil remedies of this sort have a role to play in economies burdened by large enterprises exercising excessive political influence.

Corporate Governance and Economic Efficiency

Many of the above issues are relevant not only to governments, but also to the governance of corporations. Corporations are public institutions: they collect funds from the "public" and invest them in productive assets. Workers are stakeholders, often with a great deal invested in the corporation: given the constraints on labor mobility, a worker who is mistreated or fired cannot costlessly turn to other options, as he or she might in the idealized, neoclassical model. The managers of the corporation are in a fiduciary position of trust. Delimited by the contractual arrangement they hold with the company, their actions affect others, from minority shareholders to bondholders to workers.

Laws and the implementation of laws affecting governance have implications for both equity and efficiency. If minority shareholders or bondholders are not ensured fair treatment, they will not turn funds over to the corporation. The corporation therefore faces the choice of settling for limited growth or of turning to the bank for additional finance. As leverage increases, the risk of bankruptcy increases. As more firms struggle with high leverage, the economy as a whole may be threatened; and the costs of financial crisis are borne by taxpayers and workers, not just the firm and its lenders. A strong legal system providing for corporate governance is therefore essential to an effective capital market. And a strong bank regulatory system is essential if banks are not to provide the high levels of leverage that put the entire economy at risk.

These are issues that involve both economics and participatory processes. If citizens fail to participate in the decision-making process, and by so doing allow businesses to delay the building or implementation of the necessary legal and regulatory framework, those same citizens will face adverse consequences that clearly are not of their own direct making.

The legal system must provide for the strong protection of minority shareholders and must furnish the kinds of fair trading provisions incorporated in typical securities and exchange regulations, and it must also ensure transparency and accountability. There should be the possibility of both civil and criminal redress in, for instance, cases of fraud. Civil action, and the threat of it, can help make up for weaknesses or corruption in state supervision and law enforcement: and where civil action is possible, there are far more actors in the economy who have an incentive and the right to ensure enforcement of the law.

These issues are recognized to be central to the success of an economy, even one operating under the narrow objective of maximizing economic growth. As the 1997 World Development Report showed, if governments are not transparent, countries will fail to attract investment and growth will slow. A recent World Bank report on aid effectiveness[11] reinforced the conclusions drawn here about public governance as a contributor to growth. Recent events have also provided evidence to support claims that without transparency and accountability in the corporate sector, investment and growth may lag. As James Wolfensohn recently remarked: "Free markets cannot work behind closed doors."

---

[11] World Bank (1998).

Making Change Acceptable, and the Acceptance of Change

Development requires a change in mindset, and specifically, an acceptance of change. Change is often threatening, to the point where individuals may be willing to forgo promised opportunities in favor of the status quo. The concerns of such individuals are valid and should be heard; the participatory process ensures that not only are they heard, but they are also addressed. Much of the resistance to change can be dissipated in this way.

Consider the example of the free-trade advocate who cavalierly dismisses his opponents as "special interests" trying to protect their "rents." Among those effected by trade reforms will be many who will lose their jobs, and if the economy is suffering unemployment of 10 percent or more, there is a serious risk of extended unemployment. Further, if the society lacks an adequate safety net, the unemployed worker may also risk true impoverishment, with potentially disastrous effects on the lives of all family members. The concern of the worker is not just his loss of "rents," but the loss of his family's livelihood, and those experts who are not disciplined by accountability to the citizenry too often ignore this fact. The use of participatory processes makes it more likely that the concerns of the worker will be understood and addressed, and greater equality ensured. Acting with the worker's interests in mind may even generate a more efficient outcome; for example, by trading off the potential gain of more efficient use of resources against the potential loss associated with an extended period of unemployment.

Participation is thus essential to affect the systemic change in mindset required by the development transformation, and to engender the policies that make change acceptable. And because participation gives individuals a voice in shaping the changes, those changes have a better chance of being accepted or embraced, and a smaller likelihood of being reversed at the first opportunity.

Participation and Project Effectiveness

Recent research has begun to provide evidence at the grass-roots level that participation is necessary for a fully effective, society-wide development transformation.[12] Public participation in development projects has been shown to bring to the project information that outside agencies are unlikely to have. It also brings commitment, and commitment in turn brings greater effort—the kind of effort that is required to make a project

---

[12] See Isham, Narayan, and Pritchett (1995) and Isham, Kaufmann, and Pritchett (1997).

successful.[13] For example, schools in which parents have a voice may be more successful partly because this participation also encourages greater parental involvement with their children's work. Water projects in which there has been community participation are more likely to be successful because participation engenders the kind of long-term commitment that is required to keep the project effective.

The Knowledge Economy and Participation

One of the major changes facing the world is the growth of the "knowledge economy," which promises to enable the greater participation of individuals in the decision-making process. Success in the knowledge economy, both in the business world and in society generally, will in fact depend on this participation. The organization of knowledge-based work requires recognition of the autonomy and self-direction of the mind, and must encourage the active involvement of the learner. Learning is best achieved by doing, not by watching or memorizing, as described in John Dewey's pragmatic philosophy of education.[14]

The active involvement of the learner should ideally be encouraged through motivation that is intrinsic to the activity. External incentives can modify short-term behavior, but they usually will only temporarily override the internal system of motivation—when the external incentives are removed, internal motivations again take over. All of these principles are fundamental for the knowledge-based transformation of a developing country. Best practices and reforms that are imposed on a country through conditionality ("carrots and sticks") will likely fail to produce lasting change. Worse, they tend also to undermine people's natural motivations and to weaken their confidence in their own abilities: There is a real danger that an external development agency, instead of acting as a catalyst for change, will create a sense of impotence.

Broad participation in the vital activities of a developing society, like shop-floor participation in a company, is both helpful to and perhaps even essential for a lasting transformation. Active involvement increases the commitment to practice the lessons learned and gives ownership of

---

[13] "But, over time, development experience has shown that when external experts *alone* acquire, analyze, and process information and then present this information in reports, social change usually does not take place; whereas the kind of "social learning" that stakeholders generate and internalize during the participatory planning and/or implementation of a development activity *does* enable social change." (World Bank, 1996).

[14] Dewey (1939, 53) recognized as well the connection between political and economic conditions. "If you wish to establish and maintain political self-government, you must see to it that conditions in industry and finance are not such as to militate automatically against your political aim."

the results. Participation and involvement needs to reach beyond managers and government officials to include those who are often excluded, and who are key to the strengthening of social and organizational capital.[15] While outside experts can encourage ownership of "best policies," the degree of ownership is likely to be much greater if those who carry out the policies are actively involved in the process of shaping, adapting, and even reinventing them.

Success in a knowledge-based economy will require a highly educated citizenry with strong higher-level cognitive skills, and it will require effective use of a decentralized communications network such as the Internet. These prerequisites will together enhance the possibilities of effective participation—and will make that participation difficult to suppress.

Participatory Processes and the Effectiveness of Decisions

Underlying the debate about the tradeoff between democracy and development is the hypothesis that participatory processes inhibit the kind of quick decision-making that is necessary for rapid economic growth. Supporters of this hypothesis sometimes make an analogy to the military—although few would posit the reverse analogy, that market mechanisms be applied to the allocation of military resources in time of war. The military analogy primarily advances the limited case that centralized control may be an effective organizational form for short periods of time and for well-defined objectives.[16]

The rapid industrialization of the early part of the twentieth century was viewed in much the same terms. Resources had to be marshaled quickly, and the military model was therefore an attractive one. The newly formed Soviet Union, for example, saw time as of the essence: threatened by outside forces, its leaders felt development had to be imposed from above at rapid speed—and, as it turned out, at great cost.

There has been regrettably little work done to define the circumstances under which hierarchical decision-making may be more effective than decentralized market mechanisms. The available evidence suggests, however, that while market mechanisms may work more efficiently in the long run, there may be short-term circumstances—often entailing dramatic changes in the direction of resource allocation, such as when a country goes to war—in which they are either too slow or unreliable. Cer-

---

[15] See Wolfensohn (1997) for a discussion of the importance of inclusion in the development process.

[16] The time-limited effectiveness of "military" methods was conveyed by Talleyrand's quip that one can "do anything with a bayonet except sit on it."

tainly, the experience of extended periods of unemployment and under-utilization of capacity, as illustrated by the Great Depression and by the financial crises that have plagued the world's economies over the past 25 years, suggests that market mechanisms do not always work sufficiently quickly.[17]

The use of open, participatory processes can be slow. Demography changes and accelerating productivity made it apparent more than 20 years ago that the U.S. social insurance system was not financially viable, for example. Despite this early discovery, it is only recently that the political processes have found it possible to begin to address the underlying problems. This is true even in areas where the experts are in general agreement on the solution, such as on the need to correct the bias in the cost-of-living adjustment.

Slow though open political processes may be, it is not clear that processes entailing less participation are any faster. While an autocratic government may have the capability to quickly address insolvency in the banking system, for example, fears of losing the support of the financial sector leadership may see it instead use public funds to keep the system afloat. Real reform would inevitably become imperative later. It is not inconceivable that a participatory political system, representing depositors and taxpayers as well as moneyed interests, would mobilize more quickly to confront the same problem.[18]

Participation and Political Sustainability

Openness and participation have their own costs—slowness of action may be one—but these costs are overwhelmingly defrayed by the advantages they confer. One advantage that has perhaps received too little attention is that when democratic processes work well they entail a process of consensus-building. Once a policy is agreed and adopted, it can thus better survive the vicissitudes of the political process.[19] For example, India's economic reforms of the past decade were not imposed from the outside, but were adopted from within, and in a way that has engendered broad support for their basic tenets. As a result, most of the

---

[17] While such crises have marked capitalism from its origins, crises appear to be more frequent and deeper. See Caprio and Klingebiel (1996) and Lindgren, Garcia, and Saal (1996).

[18] I am indebted to Phil Keefer for this example.

[19] In Japanese management practice, the slower but more effective process of participatory decisionmaking is likened to careful transplantation. "It is a time-honored Japanese gardening technique to prepare a tree for transplanting by slowly and carefully binding the roots over a period of time, bit by bit, to prepare the tree for the shock of the change it is about to experience. This process, called *nemawashi*, takes time and patience, but it rewards you, if it is done properly, with a healthy transplanted tree." (Morita 1986, 158)

key reforms have been sustained even as governments have changed. More generally, when a society adopts reforms after a process of consensus-building, the political debate can move on to other issues, unburdened by the urge to constantly revisit prior decisions. In contrast, when there is a perception that the reforms were imposed from outside, the reforms themselves can become the subject of debate.

ECONOMIC AND SOCIAL DEVELOPMENT

Too often, development is interpreted as synonymous with economic development—the increase in per capita GDP. Increases in per capita income are clearly helpful for improving services such as health and education, and it is true that countries with higher per capita incomes tend also to have higher social indicators. The correlation is far from perfect, however: Sri Lanka, Costa Rica, and Kerala have pursued pro-poor social policies that have produced social indicators that are far better than the norm for their per capita income, and Korea has long educated its children to levels that do not simplistically correlate to its income. Unfortunately, other examples also illustrate the opposite case, with some countries showing health and education levels far below what might be expected, given their per capita income.

We need to broaden our objectives beyond that of increasing in per capita GDP to include sustainable and equitable development. Social development—the ability of a society to peacefully resolve conflicts and to amicably debate differences of opinion—is an essential prerequisite for the attainment of many of these objectives. Societies in which there is a high level of violence, either within the family or the community, would in these terms be marked by a low level of social development. Similarly, societies that suffer an extended gridlock, with important issues neglected because conflicting positions cannot be resolved, would be marked down. More broadly, social development entails raising levels of trust and responsibility, increasing social capital, and improving the "internalization" of important externalities, such as those associated with the environment.[20]

Little need be said about the direct value of social development; for example, its contribution to lower crime levels. The costs of violence in socially less-developed societies go far beyond the hard cash spent on anticrime measures; the threat of violence also gives rise to anxiety and uncertainty, neither of which can be assigned a price tag.

---

[20] See for example, Coleman (1988), Dasgupta (1997), Putnam (1993), Fukuyama (1995), and Stiglitz (1997a).

Social Development Promotes Economic Development

Social enforcement mechanisms, such as the value of a good reputation, are typically more efficient than are legal enforcement mechanisms. For example, business transactions that take place in an environment of trust would seem to be more cost-effective than those that depend on the intervention of the courts to see the contract through. Recent growth research bears out this contention at the economy-wide level, showing that trust and abidance by shared civic norms are associated with better economic performance.[21] Now that the development of financial institutions is widely recognized as an essential ingredient in a development strategy, a credit culture—that is, a socially developed culture that expects the repayment of debts without redress to legal enforcement—is increasingly being recognized as contributing to financial depth. Similarly, both foreign and domestic business people will shy away from investing in an economy with a high level of crime, corruption, and violence,[22] all of which are symptoms of low levels of social development.

The process of economic development, however, often causes social development to regress. Social sanctions that work well within a close community lose their potency when labor becomes more mobile or if the community itself becomes fragile. Social capital may deteriorate before a country in the throes of adjustment is able to establish the kind of less personalized social capital that is associated with advanced industrialized countries.

Poorly designed policies can exacerbate this tendency. The rise in unemployment that typically accompanies adjustment is a particular problem: workers who are deprived of the opportunity to participate meaningfully in their community commonly lose self-esteem, for example. Welfare is no substitute for work, and the lack of an adequate social safety net in many developing countries means the consequences of unemployment can be truly dire.

In addition to impoverishment, unemployment can give rise to other social ills, notably an increase in crime. As the Nobel Prize-winning economist Gary Becker has pointed out, crime stems at least in part from the expectation of economic gain.[23] That expectation increases and the threat of punishment diminishes for a person who has no other means of making a living. Despair and lost opportunity can tear at the social fabric and reduce the incentive to abide by the laws; and as crime rises, so too do its

---

[21] Knack and Keefer (1997).

[22] See, for example, World Bank (1997).

[23] See Becker (1968).

economic and psychic costs. It is essential that policymakers take these costs into account when developing contractionary adjustment policies.

Participatory Processes and the Restoration of Social Capital

Open, transparent, and participatory processes can play an important role in preserving or, if necessary, reestablishing social capital. Participation can help create a sense of community, a sine qua non for a high level of social capital. If individuals believe that they have had meaningful participation in the decisions that are affecting them, they will be more willing to accept those changes. But if they believe that change has been imposed on them by outsiders, or by a government that has not taken their concerns into account, resentment is likely to mount and subsequently to cause social harm.

For a minimal sense of community, those that are most disadvantaged, particularly those who face starvation or severe health problems, must at least be taken care of. Amartya Sen has stressed that democratic societies simply do not allow famines to occur.[24] Perhaps this is a low bar for a community to hurdle, but it is a crucial one nonetheless. In times of potentially disruptive change, it is the community that does not allow famine that will be trusted by its workers ahead of the one that does not appear to care.

Open dialogue through a free, unbiased, and vigorous press, including television, is essential for the development of this sense of community. Without open dialogue, there will always be the suspicion that decisions do not have the community's interests at heart but are made on the basis of special interests. Often these suspicions are justified.

Economic Development Can Promote Social Development

Economic development in the past has often undermined social development, but this is not to say that social regression is a necessary condition of economic development. Better education and better communications should be seen as essential ingredients of economic development. Better communications enable the timely dissemination of information to the individual, and better education enables the individual to understand and make the fullest use of that information.

Well-designed education systems, which can both contribute to and be financed by economic development, have also served an important role in building social cohesion. Korea's education system is an excellent exam-

---

[24] See Sen and Drèze (1990).

ple. Although Korea has recognized the need to reform certain features of that system in the 1990s, over the past several decades the system has done much to reinforce social cohesion. The availability of mass education and the meritocratic principles underlying the system have strengthened confidence in the equity of social outcomes, in the process deflating any tendency toward social envy and dissent. Conversely, poorly designed education systems that reinforce social stratification may well undermine a broad sense of social cohesion and impede social development.

SOCIAL COHESION, ECONOMIC POLICY, AND THE COMPREHENSIVE DEVELOPMENT PARADIGM

The central argument of this paper is that open, transparent, and participatory processes are important ingredients in the development transformation—important both for sustainable economic development and for social development. The latter should be viewed as an end in itself but also as a means to more rapid economic growth.

Nowhere are such processes more important than in economic policy-making. While there are policies that make everybody worse off or everybody better off, in the real world many of the most important policy decisions entail tradeoffs between policies: not only do some people gain more than others, but some actually lose.

Many have remarked at the increase in social tensions that followed the Latin American crisis of the 1980s. In many cases, education expenditures were cut back, and inequality and unemployment increased. All too often, the process by which the decisions were made did not comport well with open, transparent, and participatory principles: the negotiations that led to adjustment were typically conducted in secret, and the outcomes sometimes were not fully disclosed.

It is widely perceived that the adjustment packages of the 1980s did not fully take into account the social and economic consequences that the adjustments would have on the poor. In the East Asian crisis, these concerns have been compounded by another perception: that the adjustment packages actually went beyond what was necessary to deal with the crisis. (Whether correct or not, this view has drawn enormous attention. Martin Feldstein, in his highly influential Foreign Affairs article last year, argued that the conditions on adjustment packages went not only beyond matters of direct concern to the crisis, but also into concerns that were more properly political than economic. In his view, these questions clearly should have been decided through participatory political processes.[25])

---

[25] See Feldstein (1998).

The perception that economic decision-making on certain key questions is less than fully participatory has been reinforced by the secrecy in which negotiations often occur. The adverse consequences of secret negotiations are clear: there will always be a suspicion that moneyed and vested interests, not common welfare, dictate the solutions. This problem is exacerbated when top decisionmakers do not even go through the motions of weighing the various plausible alternatives. Instead, when decision-making is shielded from the public view, the recommended action is often adopted as if it were the only appropriate and feasible action—even though it is perfectly transparent to most citizens that this is not the case.[26]

Whether we like it or not, and whether it is justified or not, there is now in much of the world an atmosphere of suspicion and doubt. Opponents see in development conditionality an echo of the colonial bonds that their countries may have thrown off only one or two generations ago. And while conditionality is at least widely perceived to have undermined transparency and participation, there is little evidence that it has achieved much in terms of better policies.[27] The results should perhaps not be that surprising, given that policies imposed through conditionality are seldom politically sustainable. Indeed, in many cases the policies are at least perceived to have contributed to the country's problems, to have undermined meaningful participation, and to have led to further breakdown of social cohesion. For example, privatization in Russia has not resulted in an effective market economy; instead, it has increased inequality without providing any compensatory increase in productivity or growth. Rather than providing incentives for wealth creation, it provided incentives for asset-stripping, resulting in huge movements of "private" capital abroad. The way that privatization was carried out additionally resulted in media concentrations that undermined the viability of broad, informed public participation.

---

[26] Even if it were, a dialogue behind closed doors would certainly not convince them otherwise.

[27] See Chibber, Dailami, de Melo, and Thomas (1995). Much of the conditionality concerns "timing"—certain actions (for example, the privatization of a particular company) are required to occur within a particular time horizon. Even if conditionality increased the speed of privatization slightly, the benefits of doing so may well not be worth the cost: The economic losses from a slight delay may be small compared to the gain from allowing the process of democratic decisionmaking to work its course. And indeed, in many cases, by encouraging excessive speed, the manner in which privatization has been conducted has been far from ideal. Governments have received far less than they would have in a more orderly process, and the magnitude of economic restructuring associated with privatization (and therefore the gains in efficiency) has been far smaller than it might have been. In several countries, the privatization process has resulted in undermining, rather than strengthening, confidence in market processes.

These failures of Russian privatization were of course not a goal of the recommendations, but conditionality may have done little to forestall them. While privatization was often a condition that was both explicit and highly visible, far less emphasis was placed on the institutional arrangements that might have mitigated these problems. Had a more broadly participatory process arrived at a homegrown privatization scheme that was then carried out on a schedule determined by domestic concerns, perhaps the combined wisdom and knowledge of the citizenry could have headed off the more egregious failures of privatization.

Those who provide funds, including those of us at the World Bank, must recognize that we have a fiduciary and moral responsibility to make sure that the funds are well spent. Future generations in the borrowing country will be obligated to pay back the loans, and unless the returns on the borrowed funds are sufficient, borrowing today will impoverish future generations rather than enrich them. The funds cannot be allowed to finance capital flight at overvalued exchange rates, for example—which fact supports the argument that it is not so much whether conditions are attached to the funds that matters, but what those conditions are, and how they are arrived at.

These are among the concerns that have motivated the World Bank to seek new ways of working with developing countries. In his annual speech, James Wolfensohn proposed a new approach to development assistance within the outline of a comprehensive development framework. This approach emphasizes the holistic nature of the development process, but also strives to create a new process, one that would entail a new set of relationships between the Bank and the country, between the country and all donor agencies, and within the country itself. Central to the approach is the notion that the "country, not just the government, must be in the driver's seat."

Two of the important results emerging from recent research on aid are that not only is conditionality ineffective, but that aid is highly effective in good policy environments. We need to recognize that funds are fungible: in effect, that money goes to overall budgetary support. It makes sense therefore to give assistance to countries that have adopted good policies, and a comprehensive development framework enhances the likelihood that a country will adopt and sustain such policies. The emphasis on fungibility does not mean an end to project lending: budgetary assistance needs to be complemented with knowledge and technical assistance, and project lending is often the most effective way to combine the two. We must, however, take into account the overall framework for that lending. In developing their strategies, countries may not approach matters exactly as international bureaucrats—unfettered by political constraints—would do. I am not sure on whose judgment I would more often rely, particularly if my objective is the long-run political sustainability of reforms. Those within a country may be in a better position to make the difficult judgments on how best to create a sustainable consensus behind reforms. No decisions are more important than those that affect the economy. Clearly, citizens need to be informed of the likely consequences of those choices—and on these consequences, there is often debate, even among the so-called experts. No institution, whether domestic or international, has a monopoly on wisdom, and it is imperative that there be full articulation of the evidence concerning the consequences of alternative policies.

CONCLUDING REMARKS

I have here discussed mainly general principles, but these principles translate into concrete actions. I have also stressed the importance of the processes by which decisions are made—how consensus-building, open dialogue, and the promotion of an active civil society increase the likelihood of arriving at politically sustainable economic policies and of spurring the development transformation.[28]

There are many other examples of how these principles can guide development action. In some cases, the perspectives put forth here reinforce arguments central to development policy in recent years: the importance of education, and, in particular, the education of women; the need for better communications, which can best be promoted by encouraging a competitive telecommunications sector; the central role of "good government" (inducing a lack of corruption); and the importance of the rule of law and of reducing the scope for discretionary actions in a strategy to reduce corruption.

The view that I have offered here, with its emphasis on the simultaneous pursuit of social and economic development, stresses the need for governments to pursue policies that maintain full employment. There are many dimensions to this, including the need to avoid crises—which necessitates strong governmental regulation of financial institutions and the pursuit of sound macroeconomic policies—and the need to respond to crises in ways that minimize the length and depth of unemployment.

This approach also places a renewed emphasis on the importance of competition policy. The origins of competition policy lie not only in the concern for promoting efficiency, but also in the desire to avoid the concentrations of economic power that can corrode transparency and partic-

---

[28] My immediate predecessor at the World Bank, Michael Bruno (1993), also argued that such processes have been effective means of addressing issues of macro stability.

ipatory processes. Nowhere are these concerns more important than in the media.

The comprehensive approach to development also raises new concerns: the structure of education systems, for instance, may lead to or perpetuate social stratification, undermining social cohesion, or it can be a key ingredient in nation building. More than just efficiency in the delivery of services is at stake. Given the importance of consensus formation, capacity building—creating the capacity for those within a country to forge their own development strategies and to have an active debate about the central tenets of those strategies—needs to move more toward the center.

Though democracy has a long tradition—in the West, it dates back at least to the Greek city-states—it has been slow to evolve and remains highly fragile. It was only in the century just closed that universal suffrage became the norm. Many countries have been slow to grant those basic rights that I believe to be so necessary for an effective participatory system: the right to a free press, free speech, and the right to organize to pursue common objectives, both in general and for workers in particular. Many governments continue not to recognize the people's fundamental right to know, pursuing secrecy well beyond the domain where national security requires it.

Democracy, and participatory processes more generally, is also fragile. Repeatedly, we have seen high levels of social disorder lead to calls for strong (read antidemocratic) government to restore the basic foundations of law and order. We have seen how economic policies, and the manner in which they are adopted, can contribute either to social cohesion or to social disorder. Countries that have experienced hyperinflation are well aware of the economic and social disruption to which failure of the basic market mechanisms can give rise. But too often the wrong lesson has been read from these experiences: that hyperinflation is the underlying problem, and that it should therefore be avoided at all costs. The real problem is the huge disruptions in the social and economic order that result from hyperinflation; if policies designed to prevent inflation at the same time contribute directly to social and economic disorder, the consequences will be disastrous. Keynes, in *The Economic Consequences of the Peace* (1920), in fact predicted the adverse consequences of the terms of the Versailles Treaty well before those consequences became manifest.

The world has experienced financial and currency crises of increasing frequency and severity,[29] with widespread economic and social reper-

---

[29] Caprio and Klingebiel (1996).

cussions. There is a growing consensus about the causes of these crises, and about the policies that must be adopted to reduce their frequency and severity and to mitigate their consequences (developing stronger safety nets, for example).[30] But no safety net can fully replace the security provided by an economy running at full employment. No welfare system will ever restore the dignity that comes from work. It is imperative that countries not only implement policies that prevent crises and minimize their depth and adverse consequences, but also that they respond to these crises in ways that maintain as high a level of employment as possible.

Globalization and economic change provide new challenges for sustainable comprehensive development, but they also offer new opportunities and have made open, participatory, transparent processes essential for long-term success. This is as true for the private sector as for the public. At this start of the twenty-first century, there is much we can learn from the failures of the century just closed. We cannot shut our eyes to the disasters brought on by totalitarian regimes: similar disasters must be avoided at all costs. Nor can we ignore the link between these failures and the economic and social disorder that preceded them.

We now know more about how to manage an economy than we did 75 years ago. We must hope that in the coming decades we will make use of this knowledge, of our broad understanding of the development process, and of the new opportunities afforded by the changing economy to strengthen and extend development through comprehensive strategies. In this vision, these development strategies will incorporate social as well as economic development, arrived at through open, transparent, and participatory processes, that extend the fruits of development in a sustainable way to all the citizens of the developing world.

REFERENCES

Bagehot, W. 1948 (1869). *Physics and Politics*. New York: Knopf.

Barker, E. 1967 (1942). *Reflections on Government*. London: Oxford University Press.

Becker, G.S. 1968. "Crime and Punishment: An Economic Approach." *The Journal of Political Economy* 76(2), 169–217.

Bruno, M. 1993. *Crisis, Stabilization, and Economic Reform: Therapy by Consensus*. Oxford: Oxford University Press and Clarendon Press.

---

[30] See, for example, Stiglitz (1998b).

Bryce, J. 1959 (1888). *The American Commonwealth*. New York: G. P. Putnam's Sons.

Coleman, J. 1988. "Social Capital and the Creation of Human Capital." *American Journal of Sociology* 94 (Suppl.), S95–S120.

Caprio, G., and D. Klingebiel. 1996. "Bank Insolvencies: Cross-Country Experience." Policy Research Working Paper 1620. Washington, D.C.: World Bank.

Chibber, A., M. Dailami, J. de Melo, and V. Thomas. 1995. *Restructuring Economies in Distress: Policy Reform and the World Bank*. World Bank and Oxford University Press.

Clague, C., P. Keefer, S. Knack, and M. Olson. 1996. "Property and Contract Rights in Autocracies and Democracies." *Journal of Economic Growth* 1(2): 243–76.

Dasgupta, P. 1997. "Social Capital and Economic Performance." Paper presented at World Bank conference, *Social Capital: Integrating the Economist's and the Sociologist's Perspective*. April.

Dewey, J. 1927. *The Public and Its Problems*. Chicago: Swallow Press.

———. 1939. *Freedom and Culture*. New York: Capricorn.

Department for Trade and Industry. 1998a. *Our Competitive Future: Building the Knowledge-Driven Economy*. London: Cm 4176.

———. 1998b. *Our Competitive Future: Building the Knowledge-Driven Economy: Analytical Background*.
HTTP://www.dti.gov.uk/comp/competitive/an_reprt.htm.

Feldstein, M. 1998. "Refocusing the IMF (International Monetary Fund)." *Foreign Affairs* 77: 20–33, March-April.

Fukuyama, F. 1995. *Trust: The Social Virtues and the Creation of Prosperity*. New York: Free Press.

Hirschman, A.O. 1958. *The Strategy of Economic Development*. New Haven, CT: Yale University Press.

————. 1970. *Exit, Voice, and Loyalty: Responses to Decline in Firms, Organizations, and States.* Cambridge, MA: Harvard University Press.

Isham, J., D. Narayan, and L. Pritchett. 1995. "Does Participation Improve Performance? Establishing Causality with Subjective Data." *World Bank Economic Review* 9(2).

————. 1997. "Civil Liberties, Democracy, and the Performance of Government Projects." *World Bank Economic Review* 11(2): 219–42.

Keynes, J.M. 1920. *The Economic Consequences of the Peace.* New York: Harcourt, Brace and Howe.

Knack, S., and P. Keefer. 1995. "Institutions and Economic Performance: Cross-Country Tests Using Alternative Institutional Measures." *Economics and Politics* 7(3), 207–27.

————. 1997. "Does Social Capital Have an Economic Payoff? A Cross-Country Investigation." *Quarterly Journal of Economics* 112(4): 1251–88.

Knight, F. 1947. *Freedom and Reform.* New York: Harper & Row.

Lindblom, C. 1990. *Inquiry and Change.* New Haven, CT: Yale University Press.

Lindgren, C.-J., G. Garcia, and M. Saal. 1996. *Banking Soundness and Macroeconomic Policy.* Washington: International Monetary Fund.

Luther, M. 1942 (1523). "Concerning Secular Authority." In F. W. Coker, ed., *Readings in Political Philosophy.* New York: Macmillan, 306–29.

Mill, J. S. 1972 (1859). "On Liberty." In H.B. Acton, ed. *J.S. Mill: Utilitarianism, On Liberty and Considerations on Representative Government.* London: J.M. Dent & Sons.

Morita, A. 1986. *Made in Japan.* New York: E.P. Dutton.

Przeworski, A., and F. Limongi. 1993. "Political Regimes and Economic Growth." *Journal of Economic Perspectives* 7(3): 51–69.

Putnam, R. 1993. "The Prosperous Community: Social Capital and Economic Growth". *Current*. October.

Ross, S. 1973. "The Economic Theory of Agency: The Principal's Problem" *American Economic Review* 63: 134–139.

Sah, R., and Stiglitz, J.E. 1986. "The Architecture of Economic Systems: Hierarchies and Polyarchies." *The American Economic Review* 76(4), 716–727.

————. 1991. "The Quality of Managers in Centralized Versus Decentralized Organizations." *Quarterly Journal of Economics* 106(1): 289–25.

Sen, A., and J. Drèze. 1990. *The Political Economy of Hunger*. Oxford: Clarendon Press.

Stiglitz, J.E. 1975. "Incentives, Risk and Information: Notes towards a Theory of Hierarchy." *Bell Journal of Economics* 6(2): pp. 552–579. (Presented at Berlin Symposium on Planning, August 1973.)

————. 1997a. "Remarks on Social Capital: Integrating the Economist's and the Sociologist's Perspectives." World Bank Conference, April 28.

————. 1997b. "The Economic Recovery of the 1990s: Restoring Sustainable Growth." Paper presented to the Macroeconomics Seminar at Georgetown University, Washington, D.C., September 4, 1997.

————. 1997c. "The Long Boom? Business Cycles in the 1980s and 1990s." Paper presented to the Center for Economic Policy Research, Stanford University, California, September 5, 1997.

————. 1998a. "Towards a New Paradigm for Development: Strategies, Policies, and Processes." Paper given as Prebisch Lecture at UNCTAD (United Nations Conference on Trade and Development). Geneva, October 19. Forthcoming publication 1999.

————. 1998b. "Must Financial Crises Be This Frequent and This Painful?" Given as 1998 University of Pittsburgh McKay Lecture. Internet access: http://www.worldbank.org/html/extdr/ extme/js-092398/index.htm

————. 1998c. "More Instruments and Broader Goals: Moving toward the Post-Washington Consensus." Wider Annual Lectures 2, January.

————. 1999a. "Public Policy for a Knowledge Economy." Remarks at the Department for Trade and Industry and Center for Economic Policy Research. London, U.K., January 27.

————. 1999b. "On Liberty, the Right to Know and Public Discourse: The Role of Transparency in Public Life." Paper presented as 1999 Oxford Amnesty Lecture. Forthcoming in proceedings volume.

"Symposia: Democracy and Development." 1993. *Journal of Economic Perspectives* 7(3).

Tobin, J. 1970. "On Limiting the Domain of Inequality." *Journal of Law and Economics* 13 (October).

Wolfensohn, J.D. 1997. "Annual Meetings Address: The Challenge of Inclusion." Washington, D.C.: World Bank. Internet access: www.worldbank.org/html/extdr/ am97/jdw_sp/jwsp97e.htm

————. 1998. "The Other Crisis: 1998 Annual Meetings Address." Given at the 1998 World Bank/International Monetary Fund Annual Meetings. Internet access: http://www.worldbank.org/html/extdr/am98/jdw-sp/index.htm

————. 1999. "A Proposal for a Comprehensive Development Framework (A Discussion Draft)." Washington, D.C.: World Bank.

World Bank. 1996. *The World Bank Participation Sourcebook*. Washington, D.C.: World Bank.

————. 1997. "Crime and Violence as Development Issues in Latin America and the Caribbean." Mimeographed. Office of the Chief Economist, Latin America and the Caribbean. Washington, D.C.: World Bank.

————. 1998. "Assessing Aid: What Works, What Doesn't, and Why." Washington, D.C.: World Bank.

5

CORPORATE GOVERNANCE AND ECONOMIC DEVELOPMENT: THE KOREAN EXPERIENCE

Ha-sung Jang

THE CRISIS: OLD SINS EXPOSED

The economic crisis of 1997-98 spread through East Asian countries like an epidemic, in much the same way that economic development had spread rapidly in the previous two decades. Many blame the flight of foreign capital for the crisis, but while such capital may have been a carrier, it was certainly not the virus itself. Foreign capital entered Korea for reasons of mobility and profit motivation—fully aware that corporate governance in Korea was inadequate—and ultimately left for the same reasons. When growth slowed and the risks from poor corporate governance outweighed profitability, foreign investors pulled out.

In Korea, the roots of the crisis were in part nurtured within the domestic economic and political system. This had been effective for economic growth in the 1970s and the 1980s, but became obsolete in the open market environment of the 1990s. Many of the same factors that had contributed to successful economic development in Korea earlier are now identified as fundamental causes of the crisis. Both the public and private sectors continued to operate using the old managerial paradigm that had worked in a closed and protected market. But while the close relationship between business and government had been effective in implementing developmental policies, it had also bred corruption. Government interventions had been justified on the ground of rationing limited capital resources, but had favored the politically-connected *chaebols*. The lack of government supervision allowed financial institutions to continue to provide loans to the already debt-ridden *chaebols*, which in turn carried out reckless investments, resulting in huge non-performing assets. Protection from foreign competition allowed the *chaebols* to monopolize the domestic market in order to provide a foundation for exports—but when the domestic market was finally opened to imports, the *chaebols* found themselves unprepared and uncompetitive.

The uncontested controlling power of *chaebol* chairmen had also enabled them to make swift and flexible investment decisions, but many of those investments were made in high-risk areas. Diversification into dozens of different business lines, supported by dubious transactions across affiliated companies, prevented the *chaebols* from focusing on their core competencies. Excessive debt financing—a source of quick funds and a means to protect the chairman's control without raising new equity capital—eroded profitability. And cross-debt guarantees that made it easy for the *chaebols* to enter into new business without first conducting prudent evaluations induced a series of sequential failures among affiliated companies. Equity capital, which had been regarded as free capital, became a scarce and costly financial resource.

The lack of adequate governance in the private sector gave management near-total freedom, but became the source of many of the problems mentioned above. It also made it impossible for the government, the financial sector, and the *chaebols* to adapt themselves to the new, competitive open market economy.

In the new open economy, many of the protective measures that local companies had enjoyed during the developmental era were removed. Consequently, there was a sudden flood of imports, which increased trade deficits and degraded the profitability of local companies. Korea had recorded a trade surplus for four consecutive years from 1986 to 1989, but returned a deficit in 1990. The establishment of the World Trade Organization (WTO) in 1994 formalized the arrival of the open economy, and by 1996 Korea's trade deficit had grown to a record high of $14.9 billion.[1] In addition to the opening of the product market, the liberalization of the financial and capital markets had also been accelerated. Starting in the early 1990s, regulations on the local banking industry and on foreign exchange transactions were relaxed; and in January 1992, the Korean stock market was opened to direct foreign investment.[2] Foreign capital inflow increased dramatically: Korea's financial account recorded a net capital outflow of $19.8 billion during 1985–89; through 1990–94, it recorded a net inflow of $30.6 billion. For the period 1995–97, net capital inflow increased to $47.2 billion. A large proportion of this capital inflow comprised short-term loans invested into long-term, high-risk projects.

---

[1] After the crisis, Korea had achieved a drastic turnover to trade surplus of $40 billion in 1998 from deficits of $7.4 billion and $6.8 billion in 1996 and 1997, respectively. This sudden drastic change in the trade balance into a surplus of US$40 billion is mostly due to a decrease in imports. The exports virtually remained the same.

[2] For details of financial market liberalization and opening, refer to Chapter 6 of Park (1998).

The government, however, failed to provide adequate financial regulations and supervision of this inflow.[3]

The planning system was clearly ineffective in the new open economy, and it became imperative that a new system be introduced. In 1994, the Korean government officially abandoned the system, abolishing the practice of five-year economic plans that had been the backbone of development policy since the 1960s. It also abolished the Economic Planning Board, a gigantic ministry that had been responsible for the five-year plans as well as all other economic policies, replacing it with the new Ministry of Finance and Economy. But although the government structure changed, the bureaucrats continued to intervene in bank management. The necessary distance between the bureaucrats, politicians, and chaebols had not been achieved.

The corporate sector also tried to adjust to the open economy by internationalizing its business. Many of the chaebols invested overseas, and globalization became the new management theme. The drive toward globalization was neither propitious nor practical, however. The chaebols did not change the management strategies they had been practicing for more than 30 years: they continued to seek growth regardless of profitability; they maintained a financial structure characterized by high debt-to-equity ratios and cross-debt guarantees among affiliated companies; and they persisted in their octopus-style strategy of engaging in all businesses from A to Z. Above all, they failed to institute any semblance of corporate governance.

The chaebols had grown up in a bureaucrat-controlled market where their main concern was rent-seeking activities and the rule of the game was "survival of the crony" or "survival of the biggest." Survival of the fittest was an alien concept. Even in the midst of economic crisis, the "too-big-to-fail" philosophy persists among the top five chaebols, with some justification. The huge debts of the chaebols mean the local commercial banks are afraid of cutting their credit lines, even though they are losing money on loans to the chaebols and their credit line from foreign banks has been cut off. If a company belonging to one of the five main chaebols were to fail, it would precipitate a series of bankruptcies that in turn would cause the lending bank's own failure. The classical moral hazard

---

[3] In January of 1997, the government had formed the Financial Reform Committee. The committee had proposed a financial reform law that includes an independent supervisory agency. The Ministry of Finance and Economy and the Bank of Korea had been battling over who would have a supervisory power while the committee proposed to create an independent agency. The current Financial Supervisory Commission, which is independent from both institutions, was created in December 1997 after the International Monetary Fund (IMF) has asked to pass the financial reform law as it was proposed by the committee.

of "fail me if you dare" is pervasive. When interest rates soared over 30 percent in the spring of 1998, the top five *chaebols* became a safe haven for the banks, which believed that the government would not permit them to fail. The *chaebols* enjoyed interest rates significantly lower than the ones applied to other large independent corporations and to small and medium-sized companies. They also monopolized the new capital, sucking in about 80 percent of total corporate bonds and more than 30 percent of bank loans.[4]

The government and the private sector thus share responsibility for the crisis. Bad decisions by the private sector must take most of the blame, however. As Joseph Stiglitz has said:

"The roots of the crisis are not in government profligacy, but in the private sector decisions that made the economies vulnerable to a sudden withdrawal of confidence. The biggest problems were the misallocation of investment, most notably to speculative real estate, and the risky form of financing, especially borrowings short-term debt on international markets and also, at least in Korea, the very high levels of debt relative to equity."

At the center of the problem lie the *chaebols* that had been the center of growth. Many had assumed their dominance to be neither healthy nor tenable, but few foresaw the spectacular collapse that their sins would trigger.

DEVELOPMENT AND THE ECONOMIC RIGHTS OF THE INDIVIDUAL

In many Asian countries, economic development had been propelled not by competitive market operation but by authoritarian or dictatorial regimes. Social stability had been maintained at the expense of people's political and economic rights, and while economic growth had increased trade surpluses it had also widened inequalities between the haves and the have-nots. In a capitalist economy, economic development is sustainable only when it is supported by the market and only when the eco-

---

[4] The following table shows new capital raised in the first half of 1998 for the top five *chaebols*.

(billion won, percent)

	New Equity	Corporate Bond	Bank Loan	Total
Top Five Chaebols (A)	1,448.4	11,656.5	6,350.3	19,455.2
All Listed Companies (B)	5,136.9	14,756.6	19,920.4	39,813.9
A/B	28.2%	78.9%	31.9%	48.9%

Source: Korea Stock Exchange.

nomic freedom and rights of the individual are protected and preserved. This is especially significant given that inequality in the distribution of outcomes is an intrinsic element of capitalism. Additionally, social stability that is maintained by the suppression of individual rights is susceptible to collapse should the government lose control or should its influence weaken.

To support sustainable and equitable development, the market should be competitive, orderly, and fair to all participants. As Thurow has said, "If anyone believes the outcome of the process is unfair and goes looking for a justification for not accepting the outcome of that process, it is always possible to find some place where the process is not in accordance with the theories of competitive markets."[5] If the market process is not viewed as fair and just, those who think that they are getting less than their fair share will certainly not accept their outcomes and may even defy the process itself. Notwithstanding the fact that outcomes will most likely not be equal to everyone, it is essential that a fair and rightful market process be maintained. It is equally essential to build the social consensus that everyone is treated in a fair and rightful manner through a competitive market process, and that no one's right is influenced by the size of his or her own wealth.

A bigger risk of market economics lies in the possibility that a person or a group of people will become endowed with both political and economic powers. Again, Thurow notes that "in democratic-capitalistic societies, power comes from two sources—wealth and political position." and that "capitalism and democracy are very incongruent when it comes to their assumptions about right distribution of power."[6] Placing political and economic power in the hands of a small number of people could threaten democracy as well as the market system. Purchasing power alone is linear to the size of wealth, but the combination of political power and economic power is nonlinear and has a compounding effect on a far greater scale than wealth. There are numerous examples worldwide of cases in which this risk has been realized.

Concerns about such concentration of power are well founded. Many analysts attribute the current economic crisis to crony capitalism, and there is abundant evidence on the moral hazard problems that stemmed from the close relationship between industrial conglomerates and politicians in East Asia (see, for example, Pomerleano, 1998). The Korean *chaebols* are an obvious example. The *chaebols* exercise both wealth and political leverage, and few in Korea are free from their influence. They provide a striking illustration of why the market must be fair and right-

---

[5] Thurow (1997) p.242.
[6] Thurow (1997) p.248.

ful to its participants, and why it must defend people's economic rights
against the abuse of power by the dominant market players.

People's Economic Rights

The economic rights of the individual can be defined using the following
basic identity of national income and product accounts. The left-hand
side of the identity measures GNP by expenditures in final products, and
the right-hand side measures how the income earned in production is
spent:

$$C + S + T = Y = C + I + G + (X\text{-}M)$$

At a micro-level, this identity can be interpreted to represent people's
economic activities: work to earn income (Y), consumption (C), investment (I) and/or savings (S), and the payment of tax (T). Each of these economic activities is associated with individual rights. The identity can
therefore be said to represent people's economic rights as follows: workers' rights, consumers' rights, investors' and/or depositors' rights, and
taxpayers' rights.

Workers' Rights = Consumers' Rights + Investors' Rights (Depositors'
Rights) + Taxpayers' Rights

Every active member of an economy carries and is entitled to these
rights. There are markets for the first three economic activities: the labor
market, product market, and the financial and capital markets. Paying tax
is an obligation to the state and there is no market for it. In any economic
system, capitalist or socialist, the most fundamental economic activity is
working to earn a living, making the right to work the most fundamental
economic right of all. Consumption is a primary way of disposing income
earned through working, meaning that consumers' rights are also one of
the fundamental economic rights of any economic system. Workers'
rights and consumers' rights are common to both capitalist and socialist
economies; investors' rights and depositors' rights, however, are unique
to the capitalist market economy. The financial or capital market in which
investors' and depositors' rights are exercised is what makes the capitalist market economy different from the socialist economy.

Each of these rights is protected by laws, by market regulations, and
by organizations that represent those who hold the rights. Workers'
rights are protected by labor laws, by the labor market, and through the
collective bargaining activities of organized labor unions. Providing jobs
is the most basic way of ensuring workers' rights.

There is no market for taxpayers. Instead, taxpayers' rights are protected by democratic political process rather than by the conventional market—taxpayers are represented by their elected members to parliament and fairness of taxation is enshrined by tax laws.

Investors' Rights and the Market

Investors (depositors) and consumers are not organized in the way that workers are organized into trade unions; nor do they have representation in the way that taxpayers are represented by their politicians. Investors' and consumers' rights are therefore by and large left in the hands of the market and the law. Consumers' rights are protected by competition in the product markets and investors' rights are protected by competition in the financial and capital markets. However, the market is not perfect and the sharing of information among investors and between firms and investors is uneven, with the result that the market process alone, without proper regulation and without structured institutions, cannot guarantee fairness. When the functioning of the market fails to protect consumers' and investors' rights, it is imperative that the state intervenes to ensure fair competition. The state must set the rules of the market and enforce them in order to guarantee a fair and proper market process.

The importance of financial market development to general economic development imbues investors' rights with added significance. Rajan and Zingales (1998) defined the services of the financial market as "an essential catalyst of economic growth," operating by "reallocating capital to the highest value use without substantial risk of loss through moral hazard, adverse selection, or transaction costs."[7] They additionally found that "the ex-ante development of financial markets facilitates the ex-post growth of sectors dependent on external financing."[8] In developing economies, firms tend to have greater need of external capital to sustain growth, but these economies typically are unable to provide adequate protection for investors through a developed and well-functioning financial market. In underdeveloped financial and capital markets, there is a greater probability of moral hazard and adverse selection, and investors are frequently exposed to risk.

In Korea, the protection of investors' rights is also essential to the protection of taxpayers' rights, since taxpayer money is to be used to recapitalize the failed commercial banks. According to government estimates,

---

[7] Rajan and Zingales (1998).

[8] There are various theoretical arguments and empirical evidences on relationship between the financial market development and growth. See Levine (1997) and Levine and Zervos (1998).

64 trillion won (about US$79 billion) will be needed to fix defaulted loans in the financial sector. The entire government budget for 1999 was only 85 trillion won.

Protecting peoples' economic rights, especially investors' rights, is necessary for sound and sustainable economic development. Protecting investors' rights is best achieved through proper corporate governance.

CORPORATE GOVERNANCE IN KOREA

Corporate governance has been variously defined. John and Senbet (1998) define it as the "mechanism by which stakeholders of a corporation exercise control over insiders and management such that their interest is protected." Prowse (1998) describes it as "rules, standards, and organizations in an economy that govern the behavior of corporate owners, directors, and managers." Shleifer and Vishny (1997) provide the much narrower definition of: "ways in which suppliers of finance to corporations assure themselves of getting a return on their investment."[9] Providing another perspective, the guidelines of the Organisation for Economic Co-operation and Development (OECD) for corporate governance address five areas: the rights and responsibilities of shareholders; the role of stakeholders; the equitable treatment of shareholders; disclosure and transparency; and the duties and responsibilities of the board.

Corporate governance is a mechanism that resolves the agency problems of corporation stakeholders, including the shareholders, creditors, management, employees, consumers, and the community to which the company belongs. Proper corporate governance is necessary to establish a competitive and fair market, and is also necessary as the system that ensures fair distribution of ex-post surplus as described in ex-ante contracts, particularly when the contracts among stakeholders are incomplete.[10]

In Korea, the lack of transparency, unreliable disclosure, unaccountable management, and the lack of proper supervision of financial institutions—all of which are the results of inadequate corporate governance—have combined to infringe investors' rights. Poor corporate

---

[9] Definition of corporate governance depends on the how the firm is defined." OECD (1998) defines corporate governance as "The structure through which shareholders, directors and managers set of the board objective of the company, the means of attaining those objectives and monitoring performance." Zingales (1997) defines corporate governance as "the complex set of constraints that shape the ex ante bargaining over the quasi-rents generated by a firm."

[10] Zingales (1997) defines corporate governance in the context of incomplete contracts. This is more appropriate for entrepreneurial firms, not for large publicly traded companies.

governance not only inflated uncertainty but also hampered the application of appropriate remedies for the crisis. Corporate governance is the market mechanism most effective in protecting investors' rights; it is also necessary to secure a stable supply of long-term capital essential for sustained growth.

Corporate Governance of the Chaebols

Chaebol reform has emerged as the central need of private sector reform in Korea since the crisis. Although some have argued that *chaebols* have been pivotal within the Korean economy for the past 30 years and should therefore remain essentially intact in order to support future growth, others contend that the *chaebol* structure is no longer effective in an open market economy.

There are three structural aspects that now characterize the *chaebols*. The first is their octopus-like business structure, reaching into dozens of different business lines.[11] The second is their debt-ridden financial structure, typified by high debt-to-equity ratios and cross-debt guarantees between affiliated companies.[12] The third and most important is their ownership and governance structure. For all practical purposes, the Korean *chaebols* do not have any corporate governance mechanisms, either internal or external. All decisions are made by the chairman, who exercises absolute and unquestioned authority. No chairman of a *chaebol* has ever taken responsibility for a failed investment or for an illegal activity. Accounting manipulation and improprieties are standard practice, and many political contributions have been brazenly made using company money issued in the chairman's name. Internal mechanisms such as the board and auditors exist but have apparently never acted to control a *chaebol*'s activities. Externally, the markets were powerless to exercise corporate control, and legal protection of shareholder's rights was extremely limited. More than one Korean government historically recognized the problem of corporate governance of the *chaebols*, but all efforts to bring changes bore little fruit.

---

[11] As of April 1998, the average number of affiliated companies for the top 30 *chaebols* is 26.8 and the average number of business lines is 20. Samsung Group has 61 affiliated companies over 30 different business lines, and Hyundai group has 62 affiliated companies over 37 different business lines.

[12] As of April 1998, the average debt-to-equity ratio for top 30 *chaebols* is 519 percent (excluding financial firms). Among the top 30 *chaebols*, there are four *chaebols* whose debt-to-equity ratio exceeded 1,000 percent. As of April 1998, the average debt guarantee-to-equity ratio for the top 30 *chaebols* is 93.1 percent.

Entrenchment of Management

Management of public companies affiliated to the *chaebols* is controlled by the *chaebol* chairmen through a complex arrangement of cross or circular shareholdings. The bizarre situation exists whereby the chairman of the *chaebol* is able to run as if they were his own private companies dozens of affiliated public companies, despite holding only a small fraction of the available shares. In December 1997, for all listed affiliate companies of the top 30 *chaebols*,[13] the average proportion of internally controlled shares was 29.6 percent, including 3.3 percent held by the chairmen and an additional 3.3 percent held by their families and associates. Such a small holding would not normally be sufficient to give the chairman stable control of the affiliate; however, the affiliated companies in 1997 also held 23.1 percent of each other's shares. These cross shareholdings were enough to enable the chairmen to maintain control over the entire group with only minor shares of their own.

For example, the Samsung Group, one of the largest *chaebols*, comprises 61 affiliated companies engaged in 30 different businesses. Its asset value is estimated at more than 101 trillion won (US$125 billion). Chairman Lee Kun-hee and his family own 2.9 percent of shares, and the affiliated companies own 40.8 percent. In the case of Samsung Electronics, the Lee family owns 4.1 percent, and the affiliated companies own 7.0 percent, meaning only 11.1 percent of shares are internally controlled. Daewoo Motors provides a more extreme example. Chairman Kim Woo-joong and his family owned only 0.04 percent of the outstanding shares, but Kim was able to exercise complete management control through the 94.5 percent of shares held by the group's affiliated companies.

It is clear that the chairmen and the management of the *chaebols* use cross shareholding as a means to entrench themselves at the expense of minority shareholders. Compounding the problem, management control of the *chaebols*, without exception, descends from father to son—even if those companies are public firms whose shares are widely held by minority shareholders. Jinro, Hanbo, Newcore, and Hanwha are all recent examples of *chaebols* that have collapsed under the failed management of a son and heir.

This entrenchment of authority, coupled with the lack of transparency, means it is impossible to make *chaebol* management accountable for failure or inefficiency. It is also a serious obstacle to the development of a market for mergers and acquisitions.

---

[13] The Fair Trade and Anti-monopoly Law defines the *chaebol*, and the Fair Trade Commission announces the list of *chaebols* in April in each year.

Accountability and Transparency

A fundamental principle of corporate governance is that shareholders should elect the board of directors, and the board of directors should select top management. It is common practice, however, for the board to be elected by shareholders from a shortlist approved by top management, with the board charged with the responsibility of carrying out the monitoring function on behalf of the shareholders. For these reasons, it is essential for sound corporate governance that the board be independent from the company management. In Korean corporations, however, prior to 1998 "board of directors" was just another name for the management: all board members were executive officers and until a new listing requirement was passed in 1998, there would be no non-executive or outside directors on the board.[14] The corporate monarchy of the *chaebols* was such that there was no separation even of the chairman from the board.

In a situation where there is no efficient market for corporate control, such as the mergers and acquisitions market, the role of the board of directors in monitoring management is particularly important.[15] This is the case in many developing economies, including Korea, where the stock market is thin and deficient of liquidity and where the concentration of ownership by management is high. Firms tend to depend on the banks for capital, and the capital market is not mature enough to maintain a monitoring function. The role of the board—the center of the internal governance mechanism—is unusually important in this situation. Accountability is the most effective measure to prevent management from misusing corporate resources and to bring managerial efficiency, but even where the liability of directors was clearly defined by the law it was not until 1997 that a case alleging negligence was first made against the management of a Korean company. The company was the Korea First Bank, and the case was brought by a citizen's action group.[16]

Individual shareholders generally have little incentive to pursue monitoring or corrective actions, for the reasons that they bear all the costs of such actions but stand to receive only a fraction of the benefits. This fact

---

[14] A new listing requirement of the Korean Stock Exchange adopted in February of 1998 requires that at least one-fourth of the board should be outside directors.

[15] For a theoretical model of this argument, refer to Hirshleifer and Thakor (1994), and for empirical evidence refer to Cotter, Shivdasani, and Zenner (1997), and Brickley and James (1987).

[16] A citizen's rights advocate group (People's Solidarity for Participatory Democracy) filed a derivative lawsuit against four former executives of the Korea First Bank in June 1997. This is the first and the only minority shareholder lawsuit against the board members in Korea. The lower court awarded 40 billion won to minority shareholders and it is now pending at the higher court.

would justify the requirement for independent audits, but within the *chaebols* there is no such thing as an independent auditor or independent audit committee. There has never been a liability case brought against management, nor has an auditor ever been held liable for manipulating the accounts. The problems of lack of transparency extend to corporate audits, with cosmetic accounting normal practice among the *chaebols*. Many companies in fact routinely file several different—and fictitious— reports: one for shareholders, one for the banks, and one for tax purposes.[17]

Lack of transparency has also contributed to the agency problem of debts, with the chairman taking upside benefits but assuming only limited downside liability. For example, *chaebol* management would invest in long-term, high-risk projects using funds raised through short-term foreign debts—this despite holding a minor equity stake. The unreliability of auditors' reports has proven so profound that the financial supervisory agency has been unable to figure out the exact amount of debts generated in this way.

Intra-group Transactions

The practice of using transfer pricing is a normal part of the *chaebols'* business strategies. The *chaebols* in fact use a number of innovative ways to subsidize their failing affiliated companies, including the following: [18]

- purchasing goods and services above the market price
- investing in subordinate bonds issued by the affiliated company, paying more than market value
- making deposits at financial institutions, which would then divert the deposit as a loan to the affiliated company
- issuing convertible bonds or bonds with warrants to the chairman's family or to affiliated companies, at lower than market prices
- using affiliated financial companies as a channel to transfer subsidies

---

[17] Kia Motors bankruptcy, which had contributed to igniting the current economic crisis, cost taxpayers 7.3 trillion won in writing off bad loans. It turned out that Kia had manipulated profit figure persistently over six years before it went bankrupt. It had ballooned its profit by 4.6 trillion won, and it was not known until the Parliamentary Special Hearing Committee for Cause of Economics Crisis revealed it in January of 1999. The accounting firm, which had audited Kia Motors, has not been held liable yet.

[18] The Fair Trade Commission investigated 18 companies that belong to top 5 *chaebol* in the spring of 1998. They reported that 80 affiliated companies were providing financial subsidies to 35 affiliated companies, and the amount of capital subsidy was 4 trillion won. The Fair Trade Commission levied a fine of 72.2 billion won against those 80 companies.

- executing bond or equity-carrying bond swaps between two different *chaebols* to circumvent regulations
- establishing a shell company overseas to invest in the affiliated company
- granting a put option to a third party that invests in the affiliated company.

These methods all serve to keep failing companies alive at the expense of the shareholders of the subsidizing company,[19] and amount to little more than acts of theft of company money. They impair not only the competitiveness and the profitability of the companies that provide the subsidies, but also that of the national economy—in particular, by making it difficult for small and medium-sized independent companies to compete.

Disregard of Shareholder Value

The debt-financed growth of the *chaebols* degraded their profitability. In April 1998, the average debt-to-equity ratio was 519 percent for all companies (excluding financial firms) that belonged to the 30 largest *chaebols*. Four of the top 30 *chaebols* had ratios in excess of 1,000 percent. For listed companies, the debt-to-equity ratio was 449 percent. Cross-debt guarantees between affiliated companies increase their level of financial risk, with the danger that the bankruptcy of one company in the group would cause a chain reaction of bankruptcies among its affiliates. For the top 30 *chaebols*, the debt guarantee-to-equity ratio peaked at 470 percent in 1993; government controls subsequently managed to reduce the ratio to 93 percent by 1998. Inevitably, such huge debts and guarantees degraded profitability and suppressed share value. The absence of any kind of governance permitted management to pursue the *chaebol* obsession with growth rather than profitability, however, and the question of share value was largely ignored.

Shareholders' rights were also violated, and important information was not disclosed to them. Company employees would typically occupy the seats at shareholder meetings to discourage the participation of minority shareholders, and bogus "shareholders" would even be hired to support the management and to interrupt when private shareholders tried to speak. Shareholders were also precluded from the process of

---

[19] The Fair Trade Commission investigation showed that 25 companies out of 35 that receive subsidies recorded net loss at least one of past three years, and 9 of them have been in the state of capital encroachment.

selecting board members. Finally, any attempts by outside shareholders to execute a merger or acquisition would be routinely foiled by the implicit or explicit alliance of a group of *chaebols*.[20]

REFORMS TO OVERCOME THE CRISIS

Since the economic crisis began in December 1997, the Korean government has undertaken various reform measures to address problems in both the financial and the private sectors. The Bank of Korea attained autonomy of money supply and became independent from its feudal rival, the Ministry of Finance and Economy. The laws to regulate the financial industry have been revised and a new financial supervisory agency established—the Financial Supervisory Committee, which has independent supervisory power over banks, insurance companies, and security companies. The committee has already proven effective in implementing reforms of the financial sector.

A number of unprofitable financial institutions have additionally gone out of business. Sixteen merchant banks were closed and several other commercial banks were guided to merge with others to create larger banks. The two most troubled commercial banks were put up for sale: one has been sold to a foreign institution and negotiations for the sale of the other are underway. Six security brokerage companies, four insurance companies, two investment trust companies, and 18 mutual credit companies have also closed. The Korea Asset Management Company has assumed the management of bad assets from troubled financial institutions—the government has spent more than 7 trillion won (US$8.6 billion) to take over the non-performing loans of the two most troubled commercial banks alone. Regulations have also been introduced that require that at least 70 percent of the directors on bank boards should be drawn from the population of minority shareholders. Finally, the foreign ownership limit on security brokerage companies has been removed and the limit on ownership of commercial banks has been raised.

Since its inauguration in 1988, the current government has additionally taken many reform measures aimed at improving the corporate governance of the *chaebols*. The leading 30 *chaebols* were required to sign a "financial structure improvement agreement" with their main banks that

---

[20] In the spring of 1997, a group of minority shareholders tried to take over Midopa Department Store Inc., which belongs to Daenong Group. This was the first hostile takeover attempt in Korea. However, three *chaebol* groups, Hyundai, Samsung, and LG, foiled the attempt by purchasing bonds with warrants issued by Daenong even if it was an unworthy investment since the company was on the verge of bankruptcy. The Daenong Group went bankrupt in June of 1997.

specified they would lower their average debt-to-equity ratio to less than 200 percent by the end of 1999. Interest payments on debt in excess of 500 percent of the debt-to-equity ratio will no longer be recognized as a tax-deductible expense. The top 30 *chaebols* are prohibited from entering into new cross-debt guarantee agreements, and all existing guarantees must be cleared by March 2000.

The bankruptcy laws have been revised to expedite the bankruptcy process and to provide easier exits for failed companies. Limits on foreign investments have been erased, and regulations that previously suppressed hostile takeovers have been either eased or abolished. The *chaebols* have been officially discouraged from engaging in excessive diversification, with business swaps instead encouraged to facilitate specialization and new tax laws introduced as incentives to encourage the sale of assets during restructuring. A restructuring fund of 1.5 trillion won (US$1.85 billion) has been set up exclusively to aid small and medium-sized companies and independent large corporations.

The Korean government has also taken several steps to enhance transparency and to strengthen management responsibility. The top 30 *chaebols* have been required to disclose their consolidated statements from 1999; listed companies are required to institute an auditor selection committee; and penalties for deliberately manipulating accounting information have been stiffened. The regulations on accountability have also been reinforced, notably by making controlling shareholders—including the chairmen of the *chaebols*—legally liable for their decisions. Listing requirements additionally now require listed companies to include at least 25 percent of independent outside directors on their board.

The commercial codes and security exchange laws have been revised to strengthen the rights of minority shareholders. Restrictions on institutional investors' voting rights have been removed, and the required number of shares to file a derivative lawsuit against management has been reduced significantly from 1 percent to 0.01 percent of outstanding shares. The number of shares required to inspect the financial books of a listed company has also been reduced, from 3 percent to 1 percent. The introduction of a cumulative voting system means that minority shareholders now have the ability to elect directors to represent them, and shareholders have been granted the right to propose agendas to the management of unlisted companies. [21]

---

[21] The following table shows the changes in the minimum proportion of shares required for each minority shareholder's right. The minority shareholders' right to file a derivative suit, which is a legal mean to bring a personal liability against the management on an illegal activity or on a serious breach of due diligence, had been improved twice in a year.

(*Continues on the following page.*)

New laws and regulations alone will not make the market function, however. It is important that external forces are nurtured to work in the areas where government cannot or should not intervene. This is particularly true for the private sector. In Korea, the first of these external forces are starting to emerge, in the shape of minority shareholder activism.

A citizens' rights group, the People's Solidarity for Participatory Democracy (PSPD) group, has been active since January 1997, scoring small but significant successes. Most notably, the PSPD joined with a group of minority shareholders to bring a derivative and ultimately successful lawsuit against the former management of the failing Korea First Bank. The bank had made illegal and reckless loans to Hanbo Steel, which went bankrupt, leaving default loans of more than 5 trillion won (US$6.2 billion). The PSPD has also filed a lawsuit to nullify the convertible bonds that Samsung Electronics issued to a son of the chairman. The minority shareholders claim that the issue was made without following board procedures and that the convertible bonds were issued at a price far lower than their market value, effectively transferring company money—shareholder money—to the chairman's family. The court decision is yet to come. In a third case, the PSPD joined with foreign minority shareholders to enforce a significant improvement in accountability and transparency on the part of SK Telecom. This campaign saw the election to the board of three independent outside directors and one outside

[21] (continued)	Security Exchange Law (applicable for listed company) percent				Commercial Code (applicable for unlisted company) percent	
Minority shareholders right	Revised April 1997	Revised Feb. 1988	Revised May 1998	As of April 2001	Before Revision	Revised Dec. 1998
Derivative Suit	1 (0.5)	0.05	0.01	0.001	5	1
Request to Remove Directors	1 (0.5)	0.5 (0.25)	0.5 (0.25)	0.25 (0.125)	5	1
Opening Financial Books	3 (1.5)	1 (0.5)	1 (0.5)	0.1 (0.05)	5	3
Shareholder Proposal	1 (0.5)	1 (0.5)	1 (0.5)	0.5 (0.25)	—	3

The numbers in the parentheses are for a company with a paid-in-capital over 100 billion won.

auditor, all of whom had been proposed at the general shareholders meeting. It also successfully instituted an internal mechanism to prevent unfair intra-group transactions, by establishing new procedures in the articles of incorporation of SK Telecom.

Although thus far limited in scope to a few companies, these advances in minority shareholder activism are an important step forward for corporate governance in Korea. Shareholder activism has stirred up considerable interest among management, government, and shareholders—particularly foreign shareholders. It is the first real legal threat to management, and specifically to the management of the *chaebols*, and while the government is unable to explicitly welcome it, it appears to be offering silent support. The activism fills a vacuum: Local institutional shareholders, many of which are either affiliated with *chaebols* or under their influence, are constrained by their position to remain neutral. The reaction of foreign institutional shareholders has been one of pleasant surprise; many have been encouraged to see a citizen's group rally with foreigners against the "invincible" *chaebols* to correct poor governance and put it on the right track.

Further Needed Reforms

There are legitimate concerns that while corporate governance has been improved in law, the same is not true in practice. *Chaebol* reform has yet to be carried out. The government has achieved some significant results in restructuring the financial and business structure of the *chaebols*, but while the laws guiding corporate governance have changed, there has in practice been little improvement. The *chaebol* chairmen are still exercising absolute and uncontested authority.

For sustainable and equitable development in Korea, there need to be more changes in corporate governance. Circular and pyramidal shareholding, which had been deregulated at the beginning of the crisis to expedite private sector restructuring, needs to be re-regulated, and in a stricter manner than before. The *chaebols* must not be permitted to exploit this opportunity to further entrench their management, particularly as entrenchment is the single greatest obstacle in the way of better corporate governance.

Inheritance and gift tax laws need to be revised to prevent the *chaebol* chairmen from transferring company wealth to themselves and their families. Intra-group transactions should also be more closely regulated for the same reason. Such transactions have additionally been used in the past as an innovative way to avoid inheritance and gift taxes.

Minority shareholder's rights need to be strengthened. Any shareholder should have the right to file derivative suits against management as in the United States and other developed countries. Class action suits should additionally be introduced in order to convince company management and auditing firms of their legal liability to shareholders. This is also important for the reason that *chaebols* are allowed to establish a holding company while holding only 30 percent of the shares of their subsidiaries. The threat of personal liability lawsuits may be the most effective means of deterring management from illegal activities and misdemeanors, and class actions in particular are important because of the greater incentive they offer to the minority shareholders who file the suit. Derivative suits do not provide personal benefit to the shareholders who file the suit.

Regulations governing the procedures through which minority shareholders exercise their rights also need to be enhanced. The current regulations require the shareholder to obtain a share certificate from the Security Depository Agency as proof that he or she actually owns shares. This certificate has to be submitted to the company or to the court in the case of a dispute, and the sale of any portion of the shareholding is prohibited until the matter is settled. This procedure clearly takes away the freedom of transaction from the shareholder, and given the rapidity with which share prices fluctuate can act as a deterrent to the exercise of shareholder rights.

A further essential change pertains to the composition of the board of directors. The board must have independence from management, which means increasing the number of outside directors and ensuring that they have no relationship with the members of management. Listing requirements and the security exchange law, which applies only to listed companies, need to be revised and expanded to institute proper procedures for the selection of outside directors.

The cumulative voting system should also be made a listing requirement so that management cannot arbitrarily eliminate it by amending the company's articles of incorporation—as has occurred even in cases where the system was introduced as a part of the government's current reforms. Cumulative voting system is the only way to give minority shareholders a chance to elect outside directors of their own choice. It is particularly true where ownership and management are not separated as in Korea, and where the management entrenches their control through cross and circular shareholding among affiliated companies.

The regulations on proxy voting need to be completely rewritten. The current procedure makes it almost impossible to vote by proxy: the law requires minority shareholders to file a shareholders' proposal six weeks prior to a shareholders' meeting, but it requires the company to give no more than two weeks' notice of the same meeting. And in instances where proposals have been properly filed ahead of time, some companies have foiled the proposal by shifting the meeting to an earlier date. Two weeks is in any case insufficient time for many institutional investors, especially foreign institutions, to complete the necessary internal and external compliance procedures. The regulations should be amended to require the company to give at least one month's notice of the meeting and also to permit votes by mail *in absentia*.

The internal compliance rule that governs intra-group transactions needs to be extended to all listed companies and their affiliates. The Fair Trade Commission's efforts to prevent and to monitor unfair intra-group transactions have greatly improved, but compliance could be monitored much more effectively via internal mechanisms, such as by independent outside directors or audit committees.

The independent audit committee should also be introduced for all listed companies, and should comprise a large majority of independent outsiders. Its responsibilities could also be extended to include the evaluation of executives, review of executive salaries, internal monitoring of executives, and the selection of an audit accounting firm.

The Korea Stock Exchange should take a more active role in monitoring insider transactions and stock price manipulation. Stock manipulation by a group of insiders or by employees of security and investment firms is known to be widespread, but no one has ever been heavily penalized for a transgression of this nature. The Financial Supervisory Board should focus a large part of its monitoring efforts on the Exchange in order to catch price manipulation as and where it happens. Surveillance would be much more effectively executed at the Exchange than from a desk at the Financial Supervisory Board.

Institutional investors—including investment trust companies, insurance companies, and banks—should be required to disclose their votes on all agenda at shareholders' meeting so that the private depositors and investors of those institutions can know whether or not the institution is fulfilling its fiduciary duty to them.

The judicial system also needs to be more effective in its efforts to protect minority shareholders' rights. It also needs to operate with greater impartiality. It is the obligation of the judicial authorities to evenly enforce the law when they deal with corruption committed by *chaebols*, but this will require anticorruption laws to eradicate bribery and illegal political donations. It is also important that the close relationships among the *chaebols*, bureaucrats, and politicians be severed. Judges generally must be more proactive on the issue of corporate governance.

REFERENCES

Brickley, J., and C. James. 1987. "The Takeover Market, Corporate Board Composition, and Ownership Structure: The Case of Banking." *Journal of Law and Economics*: 161–181.

Cotter, J., A. Shivdasani, and M. Zenner. 1997. "Do Independent Directors Enhance Target Shareholder Wealth during Tender Offers?" *Journal of Financial Economics* 43: 195–218.

Giddens, Anthony. 1998. *The Third Way: The Renewal of Social Democracy.* Polity Press.

Hershleifer, D., and A. Thakor. 1994. "Managerial Performance, Board of Directors, and Takeover Bidding." *Journal of Corporate Finance* 1: 63–90.

John, K., and L. Senbet. 1998. "Corporate Governance and Board Effectiveness." *Journal of Banking and Finance* 22: 371–403.

King, R., and R. Levine. 1993. "Finance and Growth: Shumpeter Might be Right." *Quarterly Journal of Economics* 108 (August): 717–38.

Leipziger, D. 1998. "Public and Private Interests in Korea: Views on Moral Hazard and Crisis Resolution." EDI (Economic Development Institute) Discussion paper. Washington, D.C.: World Bank.

Levine, R. 1997. "Financial Development and Economic Growth: Views and Agenda." *Journal of Economic Literature* (June): 688–726.

———. 1998 "The Legal Environment, Bank, and Long-Run Economic Growth." *Journal of Money Credit and Banking* (August): 596–620.

Levine, R., and S. Zervos. 1998. "Stock Market, Banks, and Economic Growth." *American Economic Review*: 537–558.

Organisation for Economic Co-operation and Development (OECD). 1998. *OECD Corporate Governance Guidelines.*

Park, Sang Yong. 1999. "Reforming Board Governance of Korea Companies: International Investors Survey." Preliminary report, Yonsei University.

Park, Yung Chul. 1998. *Financial Liberalization and Opening in East Asia.* Korea Institute of Finance.

Pomerleano, M.. 1998. "The East Asia Crisis and Corporate Finances: The Untold Micro Story." Working paper. Washington, D.C.: World Bank.

Porta, R., F. Lopez-de-Silanes, and A. Schleifer. 1998. "Corporate Ownership around the World." *Journal of Finance.* Forthcoming.

Porta, P., F. Lopez-de-Silanes, A. Schleifer, and R.Vishny. 1998. "Law and Finance." *Journal of Political Economy* 106: 1131–1150.

Prowse, S. 1998. "Corporate Governance: Emerging Issues and Lessons from East Asia." Working paper. Washington, D.C.: World Bank.

Rajan, R., and L. Zingales. 1998. "Financial Dependence and Growth." *American Economic Review.*

Shleifer, A., and R. Vishny. 1997. "A Survey of Corporate Governance." *Journal of Finance* 52 (June): 737–84.

Stiglitz, J. 1998a. "Sound Finance and Sustainable Development in Asia." Keynote address to the Asia Development Forum.

———. 1998b. "Redefining the Role of the State." March. Presented on the tenth anniversary of MITI (Ministry of International Trade and Industry, Japan) Research Institute.

———. 1998c. "Responding to Economic Crisis: Policy Alternatives for Equitable Recovery and Development." September. Washington, D.C.: World Bank.

Thurow, L. 1996. *The Future of Capitalism: How Today's Economic Forces Shape Tomorrow's World.* Penguin Books.

Wolfensohn, J. 1998. "The Other Crisis: Address to the Board of Governors." World Bank Annual Meetings. Washington, D.C.: World Bank.

———. 1999. "Sound Corporation is a Foundation for Social Development." (In Korean). *Hankook Economic Daily,* January 15.

World Bank. 1998. *Corporate Governance Reform: A Key Component of Strengthening the International Financial Architecture.* Private Sector Development Department. Washington, D.C.: The World Bank Group.

———. 1999. *Corporate Governance Reform in East Asia.* Private Sector Development Department. Washington, D.C.: The World Bank Group.

Zingales, L. 1997. "Corporate Governance." Working paper. University of Chicago.

6

ECONOMIC ADJUSTMENT, EQUITY, AND WORKERS' SUPPORT

William A. Douglas

OVER THE PAST TWO DECADES, governments in developing countries have often produced economic adjustment plans that, in both their stabilization and restructuring aspects, have been unacceptable to the workers who produce the goods and services. Given the importance of public acceptance to the success of any adjustment effort,[1] it is imperative that governments cease proposing unacceptable programs and learn to devise programs that the public will accept. To be acceptable to the workers, adjustment programs must be shown to be:

- *Necessary*. To accept the austerity that stabilization efforts often require and the disruption that restructuring entails, the workers must be persuaded that the economy is dangerously unstable, and that its present structure is inadequate.
- *Desirable*. The proposed new economic structure must be viewed as beneficial to the workers.
- *Effective*. The proposed policies must appear to have a good chance of achieving stabilization and of installing a new, more beneficial economic structure.
- *Fair*. The workers must be assured that they will pay no more than their fair share of the costs and that they will receive at least their fair share of the benefits.
- *Consensual*. All major economic sectors, including the workers, must have participated in the design of the adjustment program.

---

[1] See, for example, Joan M. Nelson, "How Market Reforms and Democratic Consolidation Affect Each Other," in Joan M. Nelson, ed., *Intricate Links: Democratization and Market Reforms in Latin America and Eastern Europe* (New Brunswick: Transaction Publishers, 1994), pp.16–18, 35. See also Dani Rodrik, "The New Global Economy and the Developing Countries: Making Openness Work," (Washington, D.C. Overseas Development Council, 1999), pp. 17–18, 90–94, 148–150.

It is because many adjustment programs have failed to meet one or more of these requirements that they have been opposed, rather than accepted, by the workers.

NECESSITY

The necessity for stabilization results from a society living beyond its means. One example of this might be a government printing money to finance a large budget deficit. In cases like this, high inflation often ensues and the need for stabilization is obvious. The problem of inflation has such widespread effects and such high visibility that governments that have successfully controlled it have on occasion achieved reelection even after imposing severe austerity measures.[2] In a second example of a society living beyond its means, importing more than it exports and borrowing money abroad to cover its trade deficit, the need for stabilization may be less apparent to the workers. In cases such as this, the government may be obliged to engage in a campaign of consultation with leaders of key social sectors in order to highlight the problem of external debt. Those leaders can in turn alert their constituents to the need for stabilization.

The necessity for restructuring is not always apparent. The need is most obvious in cases of corrupt "crony capitalism," when favoritism and sometimes outright thievery is so blatant that the whole of society is well aware that it is being robbed. Workers in Indonesia, for example, were fully aware of the depredations of the Suharto family and its allied cronies.

If a call for restructuring is based on the alleged obsolescence of an existing economic model, the need for change may be less obvious, given that virtually every type of economic structure has enjoyed some success in recent history. Protectionist policies served Japan and Korea well in the early stages of their economic expansion in the 1960s and 1970s, for example. Import-substitution industrialization (ISI) led Latin America to impressive economic growth in the same period, and while the fashionable neoliberal model is still too new to have much of a track record, it is often said to have had great success in Chile under President Pinochet. There is in fact no consensus, even among development economists, as to which model works best.[3] To earn public support for restructuring, governments must therefore take a persua-

---

[2] For a Bolivian example, see Joan M. Nelson, "Labor and Business Roles in Dual Transitions: Building Blocks or Stumbling Blocks," in Joan M. Nelson, ed., *Intricate Links, op. cit.,* p. 168.

[3] See Rodrik, *op. cit.,* pp. 54–55.

sive case to the people. This applies not only to convincing the public of the need to change models, but also to the timing of the change. Most observers, for example, concurred on the need to reform the *chaebol*-based crony capitalism of Korea, but not all agreed that the effort should have been launched in the midst of the country's financial crisis of 1997–98.[4]

Desirability

The desirability of the neoliberal economic model, in the eyes of workers in industrialized and developing countries alike, has been nil. With the economic model of state ownership and state planning having fallen into disrepute, there is considerable consensus that the least-bad general economic structure is one in which most economic enterprises are privately owned and in which most economic decisions are based on market forces. There are three main types of private enterprise/market economy (PE/ME) model today. One, which is disapproved of by everyone but which is unfortunately by far the most common, is that of crony capitalism, or mercantilism.[5] Under mercantilism, most enterprises are privately owned and most economic decisions determined by the market, but that market is largely closed to new entrants by government barriers, imposed with the support of the people who profit from the oligopoly.

The other two kinds of PE/MEs—the neoliberal model and the social market economy—feature markets that are open to new entrants and within which there is therefore a high degree of competition. These models in principle favor the most efficient firms, and should therefore engender a pattern of production that strives for efficiency. These two open, competitive PE/MEs differ sharply on a number of key issues of economic organization, as follows:

The Government's Economic Role

The neoliberals take a laissez-faire approach, desiring only a minimum of government regulation of the economy and of government planning that would modify the results that market forces produce. The social market economy model favors much more extensive government regulation, and often favors a planned industrial policy.

---

[4] *Ibid.*, p. 114.

[5] See, for example, the view of Martin Feldstein, "Refocusing the IMF," *Foreign Affairs*, March/April, 1998, p. 25.

Income Distribution

The neoliberals see the concentration of income as promoting capital formation and investment. Supporters of the social market economy prefer to distribute income more widely in order to create demand in the domestic market, and seek to encourage workers and small farmers in the processes of savings and capital formation.

The Role of Exports

Neoliberals call for export-led development, aiming industrial production mainly at foreign markets and basing the competitiveness of exports on low-wage/high-productivity labor. In contrast, the social market economy would aim industrial production mainly at the domestic market, trading exports for imports of intermediate products, capital goods, and technology; in other words, pursuing export-facilitated development. Export competitiveness under a social market economy would be based on the economic advantages of efficiency, design, and quality, as opposed to being based on lower wages for labor of the same productivity.

Wage Determination

The neoliberal model would allow market forces to set wages, even if this were to result in insufficient mass purchasing power to buy the goods that mass production creates. Under the social market economy and in accordance with the recognition that labor is not a commodity, government would exercise policies to modify the effects on wages of market forces, with the goal of maintaining one of the key aspects of macroeconomic equilibrium: a balance between production and purchasing power.

Ownership of the Means of Production

Neoliberals favor strictly private forms of ownership, be they joint-stock corporations for large enterprises or individual proprietorships for small ones. They are unconcerned by the concentration of ownership. The social market economy model is open to a variety of forms of ownership, including production cooperatives and joint state-private enterprises. Based on the belief that there can be no justice in human affairs without a balance of power, this model seeks a society in which citizens are both workers and owners.

At the beginning of the 1990s, most workers and the labor movements representing them, both in the less-developing countries (LDCs) and in the G-7 nations, suspected the neoliberal model of being devised by rich people in rich countries such that they might benefit at the expense of poorer people in poorer countries. They noted that neoliberalism was devised in business-supported research centers and popularized by Ronald Reagan and Margaret Thatcher, both of whom were leaders of conservative, pro-business parties. The doctrine was adopted by the international financial institutions (IFIs) at a time when six of the seven industrialized democracies, representing 47 percent of the votes in the International Monetary Fund (IMF), were under conservative govern-ments. Labor movements in developing and industrialized countries rejected neoliberalism and supported the social market economy model (also known as the social democratic model in unions associated with political parties affiliated with the Socialist International).

Given their strong suspicion of the neoliberal economic model, work-ers naturally found unacceptable those adjustment programs that aimed at a transition to that model. In response to this opposition to their pro-posed economic reforms, the IFIs began to view trade unions generally as obstacles to reform, in apparent disregard of the fact that unions can be key supporters of reforms aimed at the social market economy model.[6]

Economies and Polities

In addition to these economic reasons, labor movements also favor the social market economy model because it provides for the wider distribu-tion of political power. Trade unions need a pluralistic democratic politi-cal setting if they are to effectively represent workers' interests: they need respect for the human rights to freedom of association, assembly, and expression, and they need governments to respect the autonomy of the units of a pluralistic civil society—including trade unions.

Concentrated economic power and concentrated political power go together, as do more widely distributed forms of each. It is no surprise that authoritarian dictatorships such as those of Marcos in the Philippines and Suharto in Indonesia are associated with crony capitalism.

In nations with democratic polities, if the PE/ME model is of the mer-cantilist variety, with markets characterized by oligopoly rather than by free competition, the democratic system is likely to be characterized by the concentration of political power. It is unlikely that all social strata are represented within the political party spectrum, and within the parties that do exist, power is likely to be concentrated in the hands of a leader-ship that controls the selection of the nominees for public office. In addi-

---

[6] See Joan M. Nelson, "How Market Reforms and Democratic Consolidation Affect Each Other," in Joan M. Nelson, ed., op. cit., pp. 19–20.

tion, interest groups may lack autonomy, with their activities "coordi-
nated" by the governing party in a corporatist system. This kind of concentrated power does not provide a political setting that is propitious for
effective trade unionism.

What workers and their unions need are democratic polities in which
political power is more widely distributed among parties, within parties,
and in the relations between parties—especially governing parties—and
interest groups. Distributed political power of this sort is most commonly
found in democracies with the open, competitive version of a PE/ME,
such as many of the nations of North America and Western Europe. Of
the two open PE/ME models, it is clearly the social market economy
model that offers the greatest distribution of economic power. Within this
model, income is more widely distributed, as is ownership of the means
of production. Power is balanced between private economic enterprises
and the regulatory agencies of the state, rather than being concentrated in
the hands of large corporations.

The social market economy model also has much greater affinity with
pluralistic democracy, as evidenced by its approach to exports, which
bases international competitiveness on efficiency, design, and quality
rather than on low-wage/high-productivity labor. The neoliberal model,
in contrast, views low-wage labor as a comparative advantage that
should be put to full use by developing nations. To maintain this advantage, however, wages must be kept low, and this is facilitated by keeping
trade unions weak or non-existent. It is unsurprising therefore that the
world's labor movements should view the social market economy as
more supportive of pluralistic democracy than is the neoliberal economic
model.

EFFECTIVENESS

Trade unionists will question the underlying motives for adjustment programs; they will also question the effectiveness of the methods that those
programs propose. In the same way that the goal of the program—a
social market economy or a neoliberal economy—will invite analysis and
criticism, so too will the means to achieving that goal: the social market
route, or the neoliberal route. This is true both of the route taken to stabilization and of the route to restructuring.

Stabilization

When the economic instability of a nation trying to live beyond its means
is evidenced by inflation, the neoliberal adjustment model recommends
the use of an induced recession as an anti-inflation tool. The doubts of

trade unionists about this tool are less about its effectiveness—induced recession can work, as shown by the 1982 Reagan/Volcker recession in the United States—than are they about whether or not recession is the most appropriate means available.

When too much money is chasing too few goods, it seems counterintuitive to deliberately reduce production, as this initially increases the gap between purchasing power and production. The goal ultimately is to close that gap. Although recession will often bring purchasing power down until it is in balance with production, decreasing production tends to strike workers as an indirect way of fighting inflation. Would it not be more effective to attack the problem directly, by reducing purchasing power while maintaining high levels of production? After all, the more goods that are produced, the less will the money chasing them have to be reduced in order to achieve a stable balance. Perhaps, as Keynes suggested, a temporary anti-inflationary surtax could be imposed on incomes, to reduce purchasing power,[7] or a temporary, compulsory savings plan could be imposed, obliging citizens to purchase shares in mutual funds devoted to investment in new productive facilities? Either approach would cut purchasing power in the short term and increase production in the longer term, thereby attacking the inflationary gap from both directions.

Inducing a recession is also a potential solution when a society's efforts to live beyond its means results in an unsustainable trade deficit. Recession reduces the domestic ability to purchase imports, and if foreign buyers continue to purchase exports at an undiminished rate the result will be an improvement in the trade deficit. Once again, however, an apparently more direct and less drastic solution presents itself to workers: in this case, the imposition of temporary limits on borrowing from abroad.[8] In theory, this would reduce the nation's ability to import more than it exports. The trade deficit would diminish, and the unsustainable growth of the country's external debt would be curbed.

Another doubt that labor movements have held about the feasibility of some neoliberal methods of stabilization surfaced in Latin America during the external debt crisis of the 1980s. Until the Brady Plan began

---

[7] See Guy Standing, "Structural Adjustment and Labour Market Policies: Towards Social Adjustment?" in Guy Standing and Victor Tokman, eds., *Towards Social Adjustment* (Geneva: International Labour Office, 1991), p. 7. See also John K. Galbraith, *A Journey through Economic Time*, (Boston: Houghton Mifflin Co., 1994), p. 103.

[8] The government of South Korea strictly regulated foreign borrowing, even by private firms, during its many years of successful economic take-off. See Yoon Je Cho and Joon-Kyung Kim, "Credit Policies and the Industrialization of Korea," World Bank Discussion Papers no. 286 (Washington, D.C.: The World Bank, 1995).

to finally reduce the proportions of the unpayable debt in the early 1990s, Latin America was devoting as much as 32 percent of its export earnings to debt servicing. Economists had long had a rough guideline of about 20 percent as the maximum that a nation could pay without crippling its economy.[9] Sure enough, the guideline proved accurate, as Latin America suffered through the "lost decade," with standards of education, public health, and sanitation declining, culminating in the return of cholera. With Latin America producing less, the region had fewer resources with which to pay its debts and the external debt actually increased. As labor had foreseen, the tools used in the efforts at stabilization did not work,[10] and eventually partial debt forgiveness had to be used to alleviate the crisis.

Restructuring: Distributing Economic Power

Labor movements tend also to be skeptical about the effectiveness of some of the means commonly used to attempt restructuring. For example, the method favored by neoliberals to reduce the excessive concentration of economic power in the state is privatization of state-owned enterprises (SOEs). To workers, the privatization process risks simply transferring the concentration of economic power from the state to private monopolies or oligopolies, instead of achieving the objective of diluting the concentration of power. In addition, the fear exists that privatization might be used as a tool to break the unions, by creating union-free privately owned firms. Quite the opposite of distributing economic power, this would serve to further concentrate power in the hands of the employers. Where privatization in this way becomes cartelization, labor movements will of course oppose the process.

Labor movements will typically propose that privatizations contain a worker-ownership component, such that workers gain some ownership of the means of production.[11] Where privatizations have taken this social market economy approach, trade unions have often supported and participated in the process.

---

[9] Economic Commission for Latin America and the Caribbean, "Economic Panorama of Latin America," 1995 (ECLAC, Washington, D.C., 1996).

[10] See William C. Doherty, "The External Debt and the Workers of Latin America," presentation to the ICFTU/ORIT Trade Union Conference on the External Debt and Development, Buenos Aires, September 24–26, 1986, AIFLD Report (American Institute for Free Labor Development: Washington, D.C.), March-September, 1986.

[11] See John J. Heberle, "The Challenge to Labor from Privatization," presentation to a World Bank-sponsored Seminar on Telecommunications, held in Abidjan, Ivory Coast, March 6, 1996.

Opening Up to Trade

Labor movements also question the effectiveness of some of the methods used to increase foreign trade. On the export side, the goal is to build efficient firms whose products are competitive in a free international market. However, the use of export processing zones (EPZs) can often produce firms whose competitiveness depends on state protectionism, exoneration from taxes and environmental regulations, and subsidized port and warehouse infrastructure.[12] Worse, in the view of labor, is the virtually universal guarantee, tacit or explicit, that EPZ workers will not be allowed to organize or to bargain collectively. That the overwhelming majority of the workers in many EPZs are young women, characterized to potential foreign investors as more docile than men and less prone to protests and union organization, makes restrictions on freedom of association particularly galling to labor movements.

On the import side of the process, one aspect that often worries trade unionists is the timing of tariff reductions and of the removal of other import barriers. The neoliberal approach to opening up domestic markets to competition is sometimes to make this a sink-or-swim process, entailing the abrupt removal of state protection and subsidies. The inevitability that some firms will sink, leaving their workers unemployed at a time when the rigors of adjustment have made jobs scarce, naturally invites the opposition of the labor unions. One irony of this situation is that workers of threatened industries can find themselves allied with employers who oppose the adjustment program, creating a potent coalition against adjustment of two economic actors who were previously adversaries. Forcing such an alliance is not smart politics on the part of economic reformers.

The social market economy approach to opening the domestic market to competition from imports would operate more gradually, giving formerly coddled and therefore inefficient firms swimming lessons before throwing them into the competitive waters of the international market. Firms would be given time and resources to prepare for the transition to free competition, including retraining, reorganization, and retooling. The less the danger that firms will collapse, the less the danger that employers and workers will campaign against adjustment.

Dismantling Mercantilism

Where domestic markets were characterized by oligopoly, opening up the market to competition from imports is only part of the restructuring

---

[12] See Peter G. Warr, "Export Processing Zones: The Economics of Enclave Manufacturing," *World Bank Research Observer*, January 1989, pp. 65–88.

required to change a mercantilist economy into one of free competition. The excessive licensing requirements, exorbitant registration fees, and other controls used by the state to maintain the oligopoly must also be removed. For labor movements, this again raises the issue of the speed at which the change is effected.[13] A staged and orderly transition will be met with greater worker cooperation and less resistance than an approach that calls for the abrupt removal of state protection and support.

Another concern of workers is how firms will be allowed to compete in the newly competitive domestic market. A sweeping approach to the removal of the barriers that protected the oligopoly that also threatens the removal of fair labor standards or the repeal of social legislation protecting workers would again meet with trade unionist resistance. Adjustment measures should provide for an orderly phase-in of competition and the enforcement of fair labor standards. Restructuring under the social market economy model would address both of these requirements.

Labor-Market Flexibilization

An economy that can quickly and smoothly move workers, with a minimum of social disruption, from one product to another or from one industry to the next, in response to changing demand or to accelerating technological change, has a great competitive advantage in the global marketplace. Again, workers are critical of the neoliberal approach to achieving this type of labor market flexibility, seeing in it a motive to disrupt labor relations. Neoliberal reforms are suspected of seeking the diminishment or even repeal of job security regulations and entitlements to severance pay, and employers suspected of viewing workers as expendable.

The social market economy approach to increasing labor market flexibility begins with the recognition of the fundamental desire of workers for job security. This truism is particularly relevant in a developing nation with high unemployment and a large informal sector. But as Organisation for Economic Co-operation and Development (OECD) Secretary General Jean-Claude Paye noted in 1986, "there is no necessary contradiction between flexibility and security. Indeed, reducing uncertainty can contribute usefully to improving flexibility."[14] The Trade Union Advisory Committee (TUAC) to the OECD shares M. Paye's belief, and has proposed "an alternative agenda for achieving adaptability of workers and

---

[13] See Joan M. Nelson, "Labor and Business Roles in Dual Transitions, in Joan M. Nelson," ed., *Intricate Links, op. cit.*, pp. 152, 161.

[14] Trade Union Advisory Committee to the OECD, "Adaptability Versus Flexibility" (Paris: TUAC, 1995), p. 8.

labor markets" that it says "will work."[15] TUAC's proposals center on retraining programs, supported by workforce reductions achieved through attrition and early retirement programs. TUAC cites examples in which unions and management, negotiating as "social partners," have agreed on innovative ways to maintain job security while providing management with the labor flexibility it needs.[16]

Further supporting evidence comes in the form of a study produced by the Communication Workers Union (CWU) in Britain. The study notes that in the downsizing of British Telecom (BT), "full union consultation ensured no compulsory redundancy. The union negotiated terms for voluntary redundancy..."[17] The study concludes with suggestions to government, business, and labor on how to combine "a flexible and effective use of labor with secure and fair terms of employment." For labor's part, the CWU said that " trade unions need to be willing to look open-mindedly at new, more flexible methods of working, provided that these are introduced by negotiation and have positive benefits to the staff concerned."[18]

The employer should bear the responsibility of helping workers move to other jobs should the firm no longer need them in the positions to which they were originally hired. To spread the costs and risks to individual firms, however, the responsibility for ensuring job security might conceivably be transferred to the industry level. The textile industry, for example, could develop lifetime retraining systems, job-placement services, and early retirement programs to help textile workers made redundant by shifts in the market or by the application of new technology. Funding for such programs could be provided through contributions by employers and workers within the specific industry sector, with employee contributions justified by the security the program would provide. It is through mechanisms such as this, which engage the support of the workers they affect, that labor markets and labor relations systems can be adapted to the new requirements of the global economy.

Liberalization of Capital Markets

The skepticism of many trade unionists regarding the effectiveness of allowing an unrestricted flow of capital across national boundaries has been proven well founded by the events of the late 1990s.[19] By not differ-

---

[15] *Ibid.* p. 5.

[16] *Ibid.*, pp. 17–23.

[17] Communication Workers Union, "Making a Good Job of Employment Policy," April 28, 1998, available on the website of the Postal, Telegraph, and Telephone International: http://www.ptti.ch/cwuemploy.htm, p. 17

[18] *Ibid.*, pp. 4, 34.

[19] See Dani Rodrik, *op. cit.*, p. 149.

entiating between the flow of long-term investment capital and of short-term, speculative "hot money," the removal of controls on the movement of capital made it all too easy for developing nations to rely excessively on short-term borrowing and to thus become susceptible to sudden financial crises. What happened to Mexico in late 1994 was just a preview of the 1997 crisis that threw the economies of Thailand, Indonesia, Malaysia, and the Republic of Korea into financial turmoil and economic depression. Chile's policy of discouraging the inflow of speculative capital by requiring a deposit is now seen to have been well conceived. Investment capital came in for the long term and paid the deposit. Hot money stayed away, and Chile attained both economic growth and financial stability.

The economic collapses in East Asia provided dramatic vindication of the international labor movement's concern that many of the neoliberal adjustment policies would not work. In many cases, these policies were grown out of the intellectual fad for relying on the free play of market forces, and were unsupported by the evidence of economic history. What neoliberals viewed as "rigidities" in need of reform had often been put into place to solve real problems. They were not, as the neoliberal doctrine would have it, designed to fill the pockets of "rent seekers"—a pejorative term that embraced, among others, the organized workforce.

FAIRNESS

Even if a clearly necessary adjustment program aims at an economic model that workers support, and even if it appears that the methods it employs have a good chance of working, it risks rejection by the workers if they suspect that they will bear the costs of adjustment. The first principle of equitable burden-sharing is that those most capable of bearing the burden—the upper-income groups—should make a greater proportional contribution than the lower-income groups. By how much more depends on what share of the national income the wealthier group receives. For example, in Brazil, the richest fifth of the population receives two-thirds of the national income. An aggregate 10 percent reduction of national income could be borne by a fall in income of this upper quintile of 13 percent, of the second quintile by 5 percent, the third quintile 4 percent, and the fourth quintile 2 percent. The poorest quintile need suffer no reduction in standard of living.

It follows from this principle that a country's workers should suffer a drop in their living standards no greater than the decline for the nation as a whole. Even the organized workers in the formal sector, so often demonized by development economists as a "labor aristocracy," are more accurately characterized as the least poor of the poor. Most organized workers

born and raised in developing countries are shorter than their counterparts in the proletariats of rich nations. The difference is not merely
genetic—it is in part attributable to the inadequate nutrition of these
"labor aristocrats" during childhood. Organized workers in the LDCs
certainly do not feel that they are part of their nation's elite—or of the
"dominant classes," as they are known.

Another principle of equitable burden sharing is that no one should be
made destitute by economic adjustment measures. This principle applies
even to those poorest nations in which destitution is widespread before
the adjustment process begins. Deprivation caused by economic adjustment is not only unfair, it is political dynamite, especially when middle-
income groups are cast into destitution. The abrupt pauperization of
middle-income people has been repeatedly demonstrated to create a
spawning ground for fascism.

The austerity programs that stabilization requires and the disruptions
that restructuring inevitably causes all too often result in the exact opposite of what the principles of fairness require, however. The upper-
income groups usually suffer a smaller drop in their living standards
than the middle- and lower-income groups endure, and the organized
workers in the formal sector see a decline in their real incomes far greater
than that of the nation as a whole. What happens to unorganized workers in the formal sector and to those in the informal sector is presumably
even worse. In Mexico, for example, per capita consumption dropped
11.1 percent during the economic crisis of 1983–88, but workers' real
wages dropped 41.5 percent. After the peso devaluation of 1994, Mexican
output fell 6 percent in 1995 but real manufacturing wages fell by more
than double that amount.[20] In the first year of the recent economic crisis
in Korea, the 12.4 percent drop in real wages was 1.8 times greater than
the 7 percent decline in the overall Gross Domestic Product (GDP).[21]

Where economic adjustment causes destitution, the hardest hit are the
workers who lose their jobs. The problem is especially severe in countries
with inadequate social safety nets. Privatization often involves the dis-
missal of many of those who worked for former state-owned enterprises.
The use of recession as a stabilization method also raises unemployment:
as production output declines, fewer workers are needed. Their loss of
income is perversely a major factor in bringing purchasing power into
balance with production. And the abrupt opening of oligopolistic domes-

---

[20] Nora Lustig, *Mexico—The Remaking of an Economy*, 2nd edition (Washington, D.C.: The
Brookings Institution, 1998), pp. 71, 190, 210.

[21] M.G. Sri-Ram Aiyer, "Korea: A Year After the Crisis," p. 17; Park Se-il, "Labor Market
Reform and the Social Safety Net in Korea," pp. 9–10. These papers were presented at the
Ninth U.S.-Korea Academic Symposium, Washington, D.C., November 13–14, 1998.

tic markets to imports and to domestic competition also causes some firms to fail, putting workers out of their jobs.

Workers quite reasonably will not accept adjustment programs that will cause them to suffer proportionately greater declines in real income than those borne by the "dominant classes," or that will cause them to be cast into unemployment and destitution. And it is unfortunately true that if a nation undertakes austerity and restructuring measures and simply leaves the results to the workings of market forces, the costs of adjustment will be unfairly borne by the workers.

A social market economy approach would incorporate policy measures to address these patterns of sacrifice. For example, a "fairness surtax" might be imposed on upper-income groups to bring their degree of sacrifice into line with the principles of equity. The resulting revenue might be appropriately used to create a compensation fund to help finance a social safety net—to enhance unemployment compensation, to provide employment in public works, to subsidize staples such as rice and kerosene, and to expand child nutrition programs, for example. This style of approach would be much more likely to obtain worker support than one prepared to simply let the chips fall where they may.

BUILDING CONSENSUS

Human nature being what it is, when adjustment programs are being designed, the designers will direct the program at creating the economic model they prefer, will choose the adjustment methods best suited to their own interests, and will apportion the benefits of adjustment to themselves and the risks and costs to someone else. This is why workers must be at the table when these programs are designed. Their participation is critical to ensuring that workers' interests are taken into consideration, and also to reassuring workers that they have been considered. Their participation gives the process credibility. Adjustment programs designed behind closed doors by finance ministers and IFI representatives and then handed down as *diktats* to the public have little chance of gaining the acceptance that is so important to their chances of success.[22]

Like so much else in adjustment, arranging effective worker participation in the design process is both essential and very difficult. The method most often attempted, with varying degrees of success, is the tripartite negotiation of a "social pact" involving labor, government, and business. This approach has become so widely used in Latin America that the Spanish word for it—*concertacion*—has now been taken into English as

---

[22] See Dani Rodrik, *op. cit.*, p. 97.

"concertation." The following examples of attempts at concertation yield some useful lessons for the future:

In South Africa, the national parliament in 1994 created the National Economic Development and Labour Council (Nedlac) as a permanent forum for social dialogue through which to seek consensus on major economic, social, and development policies before they are submitted to Parliament. Nedlac is unusual in that it embraces four sectors: government, business, labor, and the community. Both of the nation's main trade union confederations participate in the labor sector; the community sector includes representation from youth organizations, rural areas, civic groups, disabled persons, and the Women's National Coalition. Nedlac's work is divided among four chambers, dealing with issues concerning the labor market, trade and industry, public finance and monetary policy, and development.[23]

Through Nedlac, South Africa's social partners can deal with issues of economic adjustment as they arise. For example, as South Africa has sought to open its economy to foreign trade, it has become involved in negotiations for trade agreements, both multilateral, through the World Trade Organization (WTO), and bilateral. In June 1996, Nedlac's trade and industry chamber produced the Framework Agreement on the Social Clause. The social clause is a controversial issue that affects the WTO as well as negotiations for regional trade agreements such as the Mercosur and the proposed Free Trade Agreement of the Americas. The Nedlac agreement adopted, with the support of business, the labor sector's proposal that "a social clause linking market access to respect for labor standards be included in all South Africa's bilateral and multilateral trade agreements, including those with countries in southern Africa and in the World Trade Organization."[24]

On the issue of opening South Africa's domestic market to freer competition and the related issue of reducing oligopolies, the Nedlac process went less smoothly. As with the agreement on the social clause, the negotiations were conducted under the auspices of the trade and industry chamber. The chamber issued in mid-1998 the *Report on Competition Policy*, which detailed the discussions on what forms of vertical and horizontal restrictive practices among business firms would be considered unacceptable limitations on the free competition that the Nedlac sectors agreed is necessary "for the efficiency, adaptability, and development of the economy." The report listed the points of agreement among the four

---

[23] This information is taken from the National Economic Development and Labour Council's web page: http://www.nedlac.org.za, sections on Background and Overview.

[24] See http://www.nedlac.org.za, section on Agreements and Reports, article on The Social Clause.

sectors and the points on which labor and business disagreed.[25] In general, the Nedlac process is considered by many observers, within and outside South Africa, to have contributed much to the success of the nation's efforts at democratization and economic reform.

The concertation process begun in early 1998 in Korea following the onset of the economic crisis has a more checkered history. The process crisis coincided with the inauguration of Kim Dae-jung, the first freely elected opposition candidate to become president of the nation. President Kim brokered the creation in January 1998 of a tripartite commission drawing together representatives from business, labor, government, and the nation's political parties. Both of Korea's major labor confederations, the Federation of Korean Trade Unions (FKTU) and the Korean Confederation of Trade Unions (KCTU), participated.[26]

On January 20, 1998, the commission agreed on a broad agenda that addressed most areas of economic adjustment, including "enhancing the transparent management of business," "maintaining wage stabilization," and "promoting labor market flexibility." In early February, the commission issued the *Tripartite Joint Statement on Fair Burden-Sharing as a Means of Overcoming the Economic Crisis* as well as a second statement detailing its major points of agreement on measures to deal with the crisis.[27] This second statement indicated that labor's representatives on the commission had agreed to a new Employment Adjustment Law that would modify the situation of permanently employed workers to enable employers to exercise dismissals for reasons of "urgent managerial necessity"—in other words, to avoid bankruptcy. At labor's behest, the adjustment carried a number of conditions, including that "employers must consult in good faith with the representatives of the workers regarding layoff avoidance efforts and selection criteria 60 days before the layoff will come into effect."

Giving up the employment security that about half of Korea's workers had enjoyed was a major concession by the labor sector, and an acknowledgement that drastic action was necessary to resolve the economic crisis.[28] The KCTU was unable to deliver the support of its membership for this change, however, particularly after many employers implemented mass dismissals without the 60-day prior consultation period required by the agreement. The KCTU confederation's leadership was replaced, and

[25] See http://www.nedlac.org.za, section on Agreements and Reports, report on Competition Policy.

[26] "Social Agreement by the Tripartite Commission," document available from the Korean Embassy's Economic Section, pp. 1–2.

[27] *Ibid*, p. 7.

[28] See Park Se-il, *op. cit.*, pp. 8, 11.

the new leadership withdrew from the tripartite commission. Governmental pressure and public opinion saw the new leadership return the KCTU to the commission in August 1998, but at the end of the year they again withdrew in protest against continuing mass dismissals.[29]

Mexico provides several examples of the use of tripartite social pacts involving the participation of the labor movement. In late 1987, during the latter part of Latin America's "lost decade," Mexico went through an economic crisis that involved a fall of the stock market, capital flight, inflation, and a currency devaluation. In December, the labor confederations associated with the governing PRI party threatened to call a general strike to support their demands for compensatory wage increases. In response, President Miguel De La Madrid called for negotiations between the business, government, labor, and peasant sectors. The ensuing talks produced an economic solidarity pact (PSE) that sought to control inflation through income policies, price agreements on utilities such as electricity, and a fixed exchange rate. Workers received some compensatory wage increases under the policies adopted under the PSE and inflation declined, but even so, real wages still lagged behind price increases after the pact was signed.[30]

A series of pacts was also negotiated during the 1988–94 administration of President Carlos Salinas, again involving labor, business, the government, and the peasant sector. These pacts dealt primarily with wages, prices, and exchange rate policy, although the 1992 National Agreement for the Promotion of Quality and Productivity (ANEPC) additionally sought to increase the international competitiveness of Mexico's products by raising labor productivity.[31]

When Mexico suffered another serious economic crisis in December 1994, "pactism" was again employed to try to achieve consensus on policies to deal with the emergency. In January 1995 the new administration of President Ernesto Zedillo signed with business and labor the Unitary Agreement to Overcome the Economic Emergency (AUSE). Again, some

---

[29] *Ibid.*, pp. 11–12; see also the web page of the Korean Confederation of Trade Unions, http.//kctu.org, section on Documents, "Labor on the Second Tripartite Commission," pp. 2–3; see also the web page of the International Confederation of Free Trade Unions, http://www.icftu.org, January 5, 1999, "What Happened During the Break," South Korea.

[30] On the PSE, see Kevin J. Middlebrook, "The Sounds of Silence: Organized Labor's Response to the Economic Crisis in Mexico," *The Journal of Latin American Studies and World Affairs*, 1989 (winter), pp. 206–208; M. Victoria Murillo, "A Strained Alliance: Continuity and Change in Mexican Labour Politics," pp. 55–57, in Monica Serrano, ed., *Mexico: Assessing Neoliberal Reform* (London: The Institute of Latin American Studies, University of London, 1997); Nora Lustig, *Mexico: The Remaking of an Economy*, 2nd edition (Washington, D.C.: Brookings Institution Press, 1998), pp. 50–54.

[31] See Murillo, *op. cit.*, pp. 59, 62.

increases in minimum wages were agreed upon, but these were lower than the expected rate of inflation. During the negotiations the labor sector was able to block the desire of business and government to privatize the country's social security system. The economic crisis worsened during 1995, and in September the labor movement threatened to abandon the pact unless the government agreed to wage increases and to index-link wages to inflation. The government responded by opening talks to revise the pact, and a new Agreement for Economic Recovery (APRE) was signed in October. This new pact provided for further increases in the minimum wage and for public employment projects to reduce unemployment.[32]

Mexico's major labor confederations, which participated in these various pacts, form part of the structure of the long-governing PRI political party, in a corporatist arrangement. For decades they have chosen to work within the party, thus gaining a voice in policy formation, and in turn have accepted the policy discipline of the party. Whether or not this political strategy remained appropriate after the government adopted neoliberal economic policies in 1982 is a matter of great controversy among observers of Mexican labor. By participating in the pacts, the unions were able to defend workers' interests by modulating the government's economic adjustment policies, but they were unable to obtain a shift from the neoliberal to a more worker-friendly, social market economic model.

It is impossible to say if Mexico's major labor confederations could have gained more by breaking with the PRI and trying to enter the negotiations as fully autonomous organizations. The costs of economic adjustment in Mexico were heavy and were borne primarily by the workers and peasants, who despite the ameliorating effects of the social pacts saw their real incomes fall substantially as the government struggled to contain the crisis.[33] The pacts did however contribute to social stability, and thus to the eventual success of Mexico's economic adjustment programs.

In addition to the negotiation of tripartite social pacts on broad macroeconomic issues, there are also some interesting examples of how the participation of trade unions in the design of specific aspects of national-level adjustment, or in the negotiation of specific cases of adjustment at the microeconomic level, can facilitate labor's acceptance of the steps taken. Interestingly, some of these cases relate to privatization, an issue to which labor is often stereotyped as being bitterly opposed.

In Argentina, the state telephone system, ENTEL, was privatized in 1990 and control given to two firms, one in the north and the other in the south of the country. The telephone workers' union, FOEESITRA, was

---

[32] Murillo, *ibid.*, pp. 66–68.

[33] Lustig, *op. cit.*, pp. 38, 75, 210–211.

able to continue as the principal representative of the workers in both of the new firms, and the basic terms of the collective agreement with ENTEL were maintained in the union's contract with the new companies. Ten percent of the shares in each firm went to its workers.[34] Bringing labor into the process was not easy, with the Buenos Aires telephone workers notably disagreeing with their colleagues at the provincial level over whether or not to oppose the privatization. Agreement was eventually reached, and the privatization went ahead.

In Mexico, the telephone workers' union participated in the development of a plan under which a consortium of private Mexican and foreign firms in 1990 bought control of Telefonos de Mexico. The union was able to negotiate a very favorable contract with the consortium, extending to the purchase by the workers of 4.4 percent of the shares in the new firm.[35] In Venezuela, the telephone company CANTV was privatized under an agreement with the Venezuelan labor movement that guaranteed the workers 11 percent of the company's stock.[36] Similar arrangements were made for the workers to receive substantial shareholdings in Viasa, the national airline, and in the Astinave shipyard.[37]

In Tunisia, while labor has not been involved in the formation of economic reform policy it was engaged in a "social corporatism" program set up in the early 1990s to deal with wage policy. Tripartite negotiations between labor, business, and government in 1990 and 1993 produced two agreements on wages.[38] During the course of the talks the participants discovered that there was "an important convergence of interests between [business and labor] around two key points: the need for firms to become more efficient and competitive, and the need for moderate wage increases that protect purchasing power without unduly burdening employers."[39] This discovery has been a factor in Tunisian labor's acceptance of economic reforms, in contrast to the opposition stance taken by labor in two of the country's neighbors, Algeria and Morocco.[40]

---

[34] Maria Xelhuantzi-Lopez, "Telecomunicaciones y Estrategicas Sindicales en las Americas," Postal, Telegraph, and Telephone Workers International (PTTI), Mexico, January, 1997, pp. 11–14. For the PTTI's earlier recommendations on how telecommunications workers should structure their participation in shareholding, see Rodolfo Benitez, "Privatization of Telecommunications Services," PTTI, July, 1992, pp. 28–30.

[35] Xelhuantzi-Lopez, *op. cit.*, pp. 155–158.

[36] Benitez, *op. cit.*, p. 19.

[37] "Venezuelan News and Views," Embassy of Venezuela, Washington, D.C., February, 1992, p. 6.

[38] Christopher Alexander, *op. cit.*, pp. 179–180, 192–194.

[39] *Ibid.*, p. 192.

[40] *Ibid.*, p. 196.

These cases and others suggest some guidelines for future efforts to arrange for labor's participation in the design of adjustment policies. First, concertation over adjustment policies works better if a tripartite forum has already been established and has some experience. For example, Nedlac in South Africa works on various economic and social issues, not only on matters of economic adjustment; and in Mexico, the inclusion of labor in the country's corporatist system has been continuing for decades. Rather than wait until economic crisis befalls the nation before setting up the forum, the relative successes of these systems suggest that the process of concertation be started immediately, so that the forum is experienced and ready should crisis come. The tripartite concertation in Korea, improvised on the spot when crisis hit, has gone through some rocky times.

Second, to assuage labor's skepticism about the concertation process, it is worthwhile guaranteeing the unions in advance that if a consensus cannot be reached, the resulting report on the process will state explicitly that labor opposed the conclusions agreed by the other social partners. Trade unions feel they have been misused politically in some instances when governments—or IFIs—have met with them, issued adjustment programs totally contrary to those proposed by labor, and then blandly declared that the programs were a result of "consultation with labor." In the case of Nedlac, for example, when one or more of the sectors disagrees the disagreements are spelled out in detail, as in the 1988 *Report on Competition Policy*.

Third, as common sense suggests, it is easier to engage in a successful concertation on a specific adjustment project at the local level than to achieve agreement on an entire program of macroeconomic stabilization and restructuring. The larger concertation process might best be limited to seeking general agreement on the broad outlines of the economic model at which restructuring is to be aimed, and to defining some basic criteria for choosing the specific adjustment methods and for apportioning the risks, costs, and benefits. The general agreement could then be supplemented by local-level tripartite consultations dealing with the details of each adjustment step on a project-by-project basis.

CONCLUSION

Workers and the trade unions that represent them are not immutably opposed to economic adjustment—they can be brought to acceptance of economic reform, and can be recruited in some aspects of it as active supporters.[41] Workers will not accept reforms that they perceive as self-

---

[41] Joan M. Nelson, "Labor and Business Roles in Dual Transitions," in Joan M. Nelson, ed., *Intricate Links, op. cit.,* pp. 174, 185.

serving for their architects and irrelevant to the resolution of a crisis.[42] Workers will not support restructuring that seeks a transition to an economic model designed by employers and slanted in favor of the employers' interests. Workers will not accept passively the sacrifices required by adjustment measures that appear to have little chance of success or that unfairly impose the costs of change on the workers. Workers will not accept adjustment measures that require sacrifice on their part but little sacrifice by the rich. Adjustment programs designed in secret, without the participation of the workers, will not win the workers' trust or support.

Workers must see reforms as necessary, desirable, effective, fair, and designed by consensus. When crucial decisions on adjustment policy are being made, the workers want their representatives to be at the table.

REFERENCES

Aiyer, M.G. Sri-Ram. 1998. "Korea: A Year After the Crisis." The Ninth U.S.-Korea Academic Symposium. Washington, D.C.

Alexander, Christopher. 1996. "State, Labor, and the New Global Economy in Tunisia." In Dirk Vandewalle, ed., *North Africa: Development and Reform in a Changing Global Economy.* New York: St. Martins Press.

Benitez, Rodolfo. 1992. "Privatization of Telecommunications Services." PTTI. July.

Cho, Yoon Je, and Joon-Kyung Kim. 1995. "Credit Policies and the Industrialization of Korea." World Bank Discussion Paper 286. Washington, D.C.: The World Bank.

Communication Workers Union. 1998. "Making a Good Job of Employment Policy." April 28. Available on the website of the Postal, Telegraph, and Telephone Workers International.

Doherty, William C. 1986. "The External Debt and the Workers of Latin America." Presentation to the ICFTU/ORIT Trade Union Conference on the External Debt and Development, Buenos Aires, September 24–26. AIFLD Report. Washington, D.C.: American Institute for Free Labor Development.

---

[42] Dani Rodrik, *op. cit.,* pp. 145–146.

Douglas, William A. 1992. "Political and Economic Pluralism." *Freedom Review* (July-August).

Economic Commission for Latin America and the Caribbean (ECLAC). 1996. *Economic Panorama of Latin America 1995*. Washington, D.C.: ECLAC.

Embassy of Venezuela. February, 1992. "Venezuelan News and Views." Washington, D.C.

Feldstein, Martin. 1998. "Refocusing the International Monetary Fund (IMF)." *Foreign Affairs* (March/April).

Galbraith, John K. 1994. *A Journey Through Economic Time*. Boston: Houghton Mifflin.

Heberle, John J. 1996. "The Challenge to Labor from Privatization." Presentation to a World Bank–sponsored Seminar on Telecommunications. Abidjan, Côte d'Ivoire.

International Confederation of Free Trade Unions. 1996. *The Global Market—Trade Unionism's Greatest Challenge*. Chapter two. Brussels: ICFTU.

Kevin J, Middlebrook. 1989. "The Sounds of Silence: Organized Labor's Response to the Economic Crisis in Mexico." *The Journal of Latin American Studies and World Affairs* (Winter).

Lustig, Nora. 1998. *Mexico—The Remaking of an Economy*. 2nd ed. Washington, D.C.: The Brookings Institution.

Murillo, M. Victoria. 1997. "A Strained Alliance: Continuity and Change in Mexican Labour Politics." In Monica Serrano, ed., *Mexico: Assessing Neoliberal Reform*. London: The Institute of Latin American Studies, University of London.

Nelson, Joan M. 1994a. "How Market Reforms and Democratic Consolidation Affect Each Other." In Joan M. Nelson, ed., *Intricate Links: Democratization and Market Reforms in Latin America and Eastern Europe*. New Brunswick: Transaction Publishers.

———. 1994b. "Labor and Business Roles in Dual Transitions: Building Blocks or Stumbling Blocks." In Joan M. Nelson, ed., *Intricate Links*. New Brunswick: Transaction Publishers.

Rodrik, Dani. 1999. *The New Global Economy and the Developing Countries: Making Openness Work*. Washington, D.C.: Overseas Development Council.

Se-il, Park. 1998. "Labor Market Reform and the Social Safety Net in Korea." The Ninth U.S.-Korea Academic Symposium, Washington, D.C.

de Soto, Hernando. 1987. *El Otro Sendero* (Mexico: Editorial Diana), Part VII.

Standing, Guy. 1991. "Structural Adjustment and Labour Market Policies: Towards Social Adjustment?" In Guy Standing and Victor Tokman, eds., *Towards Social Adjustment*. Geneva: International Labour Office.

Trade Union Advisory Committee to the Organisation for Economic Co-operation and Development (OECD). 1995. *Adaptability Versus Flexibility*. Paris: TUAC.

Warr, Peter G. 1989. "Export Processing Zones: The Economics of Enclave Manufacturing." *Research Observer*. Washington, D.C.: World Bank.

Xelhuantzi-Lopez, Maria. 1997. "Telecomunicaciones y Estrategicas Sindicales en las Americas." *Postal, Telegraph, and Telephone Workers International (PTTI)*. Mexico, January.

7

POLITICAL ECONOMY OF REFORM: THE CHARACTERISTICS OF JAPANESE INSTITUTIONS

Kuniko Inoguchi

JAPAN IS IN A PROCESS OF TRANSITION. Some of its long-standing institutional characteristics are being questioned and face enormous pressure for change; at the same time, some of the most traditional institutional forces are carrying out some of the most important changes. This apparent contradiction actually illustrates the fact that Japanese institutions have always had a degree of internal capability for innovation and reform—a capability that enabled Japan to become the first non-Atlantic nation of the modern era to become a major economic power. Because these institutional characteristics are endogenous rather than universal, it may be difficult for outsiders to understand and anticipate the shape and speed of the reforms that Japan is trying to achieve. This paper will outline some of Japan's institutional characteristics, explain why they prevail, and discuss their impact on Japan's current political, economic, and social changes. The inequality with which the benefits of reform are shared among the different sectors of society means that reform is not easily achieved. Japan, for example, has been slow to move away from its much-admired role in the postwar reconstruction era, despite major changes in its external and internal circumstances. Gender and age biases in the decision-making group additionally favor the traditional approach to reform, such as construction-based reflation policies.

BUREAUCRACY-LED POSTWAR RECONSTRUCTION AND MODERNIZATION

Japan achieved universal suffrage and full democratization under Allied occupation following the Second World War. After regaining independence in 1952, Japan worked hard to return to full-fledged membership of the international system. A prominent characteristic of this system was a strong statist orientation that charged the modern government with responsibility for leading its nation toward development based on the core values of the postwar international system: economic growth, democracy, financial stability, free trade, and liberalization.

Japan, eager to recover its international status and credibility after the war, strove to adopt the core values advocated by the major victorious powers. The country's democracy was still in its formative stage, however, and struggling to achieve a stable distribution of power, was not strong enough to fulfill the expected goals of the state. Japan's imperative thus became building and maintaining strong technocratic institutions staffed by bureaucrats with the ability to assure that Japan quickly became a strong and responsible state. Two important institutional characteristics emerged from this experience.

First, the bureaucracy learned to play the role of mitigator as it sought to convey the values of the outside world to the Japanese people, for whom the traditional exogenous values remained strong. The inflexible imposition of an alien system of values would have caused politically intolerable social destabilization, and the bureaucrats were well aware of the enormous gap that existed between the universally manifested values and Japan's traditional social culture.

As time went by, Japanese civic culture and expectations gradually converged with the new value system, but the bureaucracy became caught in the archetypical bureaucratic malaise: inertia. To this day, it still tries to play the role of transmitter and gatekeeper of standards and values between the world and the Japanese people, clinging to the memory of the heroic function it played as buffer between international standards and domestic realities.

Japan's bureaucracy must now confront the challenge of how to become what it was initially meant to be—the agent of modernization needed to harmonize Japan with global values and standards. Recent history has shown that Japan is capable of maintaining its traditional integrity in an environment of globalization, and that cultural strength and integrity in fact can be more easily maintained from the position of economic and political power that is achievable only through participation in the global competitive network. Should it fail to come to terms with this reality, the enhancer of Japanese development could become instead the spoiler of Japan's readiness for reform.

A second major component of the legitimacy of the postwar bureaucracy was its reputation for reliability. To maintain this reputation, Japan's ministries and agencies have strictly defined spheres of jurisdiction that are both mutually exclusive and exhaustive. The extent of bureaucratic responsibility is pervasive, but the coordination of powers and joint problem-solving capabilities in areas involving newly emergent issues or the complex conjunction of issues is limited. This results in excessive transaction costs for domestic and overseas actors that undertake consultations or negotiations with Japanese bureaucratic institutions, since the institutions' spheres of authority are segmented and their ability to engage in coordination is limited. Bureaucrats are also unaccustomed to any kind of intrusion into their spheres of power and responsibility, either in the form of interministerial coordination or through deregulation and liberalization.

One of the major points of emphasis of the initiatives for administrative reform advanced by recent governments was the enhancement of interministerial coordination and the flexibility of the Cabinet Secretariat. The goal of the initiatives was to achieve comprehensive coordination by overriding ministerial segmentation, inertia, and vested interests. The recommendations were contained in the final report of the Prime Minister's Committee on Administrative Reform and were enshrined last year in law. Japan will have a newly defined set of bureaucratic institutions and functional formulae in 2001.

PIECEMEAL ADAPTATION VERSUS CONCEPTUAL ARTICULATION

In addition to the bureaucratic characteristics that emerged from Japan's postwar experiences, some other important characteristics influence Japan's capabilities for reform.

Japan is often accused, incorrectly, of never changing in any significant way. In reality, Japan has frequently shown an ability and willingness to adapt to externally defined constraints and roles—few other countries can have gone through such tremendous social and economic changes as Japan has during the last half-century. The country's political and bureaucratic institutions have similarly shown an ability to adapt. What they have not done so well is provide comprehensive explanations and conceptual articulations of their intentions and commitments, and this has often led to confusion and misperceptions.

Japanese institutions are not known for their willingness to forcefully present principles and concepts, but in their defense, in the postwar era they were not in the position to do so. Japanese decisionmakers were obliged to behave more as decisiontakers in international affairs: it was more important for Japan at that time to be adaptive than talkative. The demands from the outside world were not always consistent or constant. Japan has an extraordinary capability to adapt to external forces, as seen in its industrial development, but its adaptation thus tended to be piecemeal and ad hoc rather than systematic. Articulation of these piecemeal changes was difficult.

Japan has failed to grasp how quickly its position has changed from the status of decisiontaker to that of decisionmaker. It does not fully comprehend the fact that the international community is waiting for Japan to make decisions on nonmilitary problems ranging from the East Asian economic crisis and currency stabilization to remedies for poverty and protection of the environment. As Japan gradually assumes the roles of agenda-setter and consensus-former on issues of global governance it must improve its conceptual articulation, so that the world will better understand its intentions and commitments and feel more comfortable about partnership.

LACK OF INCLUSIVITY IN DECISION-MAKING

Japan is not a homogenous country, but is often perceived as one because of strong homogeneity at the decision-making level. At all levels in the national government, local assemblies, private firms, banks, universities, and labor unions, middle-aged men with similar educational backgrounds are the mainstream decisionmakers. Young people and women are conspicuously absent, and this could also be considered a general characteristic of Japanese institutions.

Pronounced gender inequality and generational imbalance at the decision-making levels of most institutions may be the primary cause of Japan's inability to foster well-balanced development. Japan is a major economic power, but the Japanese citizen must contend with the daily hardships of long working hours, long-distance commuting, cramped housing, inadequate child-care services, excessive competition in education, and scarce help for the elderly. The greater involvement of women in the decision-making process could realistically have produced a greater diversity of economic reform and anti-recession policies, conceivably placing more emphasis on the household sector and on welfare services. The greater involvement of younger men and women in boardrooms and ministries might have seen more emphasis on venture capital, the software industry, and conservation projects, and less on the traditional construction project-based recovery plans. If Japanese institutions were to appoint more women to higher positions, it is likely that the Japanese economy would be more resilient, more flexible, and more creative—in fact, more reform-oriented.

SUMMARY OF RECENT POLITICAL AND ECONOMIC REFORMS

Despite these constraints and constraining characteristics, Japan has shown an extraordinary commitment to invigorating its democracy and economy. Some examples of recent political and economic reforms follow:

Administrative Reform of the Central Government

The Headquarters for the Administrative Reform of the Central Government is overseeing the launch of a new set of government organizations, scheduled for 2001. The reorganization will downsize some national government agencies in order to effect an improvement in efficiency: 84 government activities will be transformed into Independent Administrative Institutions (IAI), and the total number of secretariats and bureaus will be reduced from 128 to 96. The staff of the government will be reduced at least 10 percent within 10 years.

While most ministries and agencies will undergo mergers or downsizing under the reorganization, there are two noteworthy exceptions. First, the Environmental Agency will be upgraded to become an independent Ministry of the Environment, representing Japan's strong commitment to addressing national and global environmental problems. Second, a central office to plan, implement, and monitor gender equality issues will be established in the Prime Minister's Cabinet Secretariat. The office will be charged with promoting women's empowerment and with overcoming the traditional division of labor and prejudice against women.

Financial System Reform

Reforms are addressing the continually diversifying needs of investors by expanding the means of asset management, enhancing investment trusts, introducing over-the-counter securities, derivatives, and providing other means of investment. The government also proposes to liberalize security company services and fees, encourage new entries, and engage in other reforms designed to improve access to higher-quality services from financial institutions. The government will eliminate the obligation for member insurers of the rating organizations to use premium rates calculated by the rating organization for fire, automobile, and other insurance products, and will switch from the current licensing system to a system requiring registration only in order to encourage new entries into the securities industry. To promote cross-sectorial entry, the government will enable insurance companies and other financial institutions to participate through their subsidiaries in other business activities. The government will also allow securities companies in Japan to open and operate proprietary trading systems to enable investors to trade online.

While adhering to the principle of self-responsibility, the government will also enhance disclosure requirements and will formulate fair-trading rules. The law has been amended to require consolidated disclosures covering both parent and subsidiary companies when filing securities registration statements and annual reports. A new requirement will additionally be enacted to oblige depository institutions such as banks to make their financial statements, including the amount of bad loans, available on the public record. Measures are also being taken to create a new securities investor protection fund: The legal obligation to manage customer assets separate from company assets will be introduced to protect investors in the event of a securities company failure.

Financial Regulatory System Reforms

The mounting nonperforming loans problems of financial institutions and housing loan companies triggered reforms in the financial regulatory system, as enshrined by the 1997 Law Establishing the Financial Supervisory Agency and other related legislation. The Financial Supervisory Agency, established under the Prime Minister's Office, is invested with the authority to inspect and supervise private financial institutions. This is done with the understanding that separating financial-institution inspection and supervision functions from financial system planning and formulation functions will contribute to the conversion of financial administration to more transparent and fair administration. Institutions covered by the agency include commercial banks, insurance companies, securities companies, nonbank, and other private institutions dealing with financial transactions.

Amendment of the Foreign Exchange and Foreign Trade Control Law

The goals of this amendment are to liberalize Japan's cross-border capital transactions in order to bring them into line with global standards, and to stimulate the Japanese market through complete liberalization of the foreign exchange business. Permission and prior notification requirements were abolished in principle, enabling individuals and companies to make free capital transactions and settlements with foreign individuals and companies. The authorized foreign exchange bank system, the designated securities firm system, and the money exchanger system were all abolished. In order to ensure a proper understanding of market trends and to prepare statistics on the balance of payments, it remains necessary to develop an effective ex-post facto reporting system on cross-border capital transactions.

CONCLUSIONS

The methods and distortions that have dominated Japanese institutional decision-making mean that the pace and patterns of Japanese reform leave much to be desired. It has also been argued that other major factors, including the political-electoral system and the corporate system, restrain reform efforts. Under the current electoral system, for example, rural voters, who are typically conservative, have disproportionate influence, and are keeping medium-income urban dwellers out of the decision-making process. In the corporate sphere, the business-labor partnership, characterized by the lifetime employment system and other related features, has tended to slow down reform because it tenaciously resists the option of unemployment.

The distortions deriving from the electoral system certainly contribute to the problem, but at the same time one cannot help but notice the irony of such a system. Rural conservative voters repeatedly elect experienced and powerful parliamentarians, but the tendencies of these politicians are in reality to focus on major societal reforms rather than on local projects that would serve their rural constituents. Again, while the employment practices of corporations are part of the problem, the recent dismemberment of the lifetime employment system was so clinical that few would now argue that it is a major factor inhibiting reform. The private sector has been more adaptive to the changes in the market environment than the public sector.

8

THE POLITICS OF GOVERNANCE: LESSONS FROM THE EAST ASIAN CRISIS

Stephan Haggard

THE EAST ASIAN CRISIS has provoked yet another round of debate on the institutional foundations of the region's growth. As in the past, recent experience has elicited widely divergent analyses, with widely divergent implications for the improvement of governance in the region.

To some, the crisis is the necessary outcome of misguided interventionism that created inefficiency, moral hazard, and lack of transparency; problems that can only be rectified by more narrowly circumscribing the role of the state. According to this interpretation, good governance requires an increase in bureaucratic efficiency through: liberalization, reducing unnecessary regulation and intervention; reorienting spending priorities around core government functions; privatization; and eliminating waste, fraud, and abuse through reforms of the civil service and systems of financial management.

These prescriptions have not gone unchallenged. A chorus of critics, including some from within the economics profession itself, has argued that the crisis was caused in part by precipitous liberalization of financial markets. To the extent that government failures contributed to the crisis, they took the form of inadequate, rather than overly intrusive, regulation. In this interpretation, improved governance requires expanded state capacity to oversee financial markets, industrial relations, newly privatized utilities, and the environment. The crisis has also exposed a plethora of public goods as well as new distributive problems that are in need of urgent attention: infrastructure; provision of basic services; improving the quality and coverage of education and health care; and addressing problems of unemployment, income distribution, and poverty. This second interpretation sees a role for a more activist state, and is less hasty to break with styles of governance that contributed to— or at least were compatible with—East Asia's success in the past.

This paper also emphasizes a third, broader and more explicitly political conception of governance. Under this account, we must seek the causes of the Asian crisis not simply in various policy failures, but also in political and institutional weaknesses, including autocratic rule, close business–government relations ("cronyism"), and failures in the design of regulatory agencies. Good government requires accountability to citizens, including through legislative and judicial checks on executive power; responsiveness to a wide array of interest groups and citizens; and, somewhat contradictorily, independent government agencies. Good governance should not be measured in purely instrumental terms of efficiency and economic performance, but should also incorporate standards of democratic accountability and participation.

This paper addresses four issues: the role of autocracy and democracy in the crisis; the role of business–government relations; the management of social protest and resistance to reform through the provision of social safety nets; and the reform of the state itself.

In each case, I draw on the growing literature of political economy to look more closely at the politics of governance; the underlying political factors that have shaped how governments in the region got into trouble and how they have managed the crisis to date; and the types of institutional as well as policy reforms that are likely to emerge in the future. In each of these four areas, I make a case for the benefits of greater democratic accountability as a source of reform and renewed growth.

DEMOCRACY, AUTOCRACY, AND GOVERNANCE

The theoretical debate over the effects of regime type on economic performance, or on the capacity to undertake reforms, has been highly inconclusive. The arguments in favor of authoritarianism typically rest on two pillars: the capacity of the government to reconcile, or override, particular interests in the name of overall social welfare; and the ability of the government to adopt a longer time horizon, unconstrained by elections, short-term political pressures, or the myopia of the electorate. However, as Mancur Olson has argued, the case for the advantages of authoritarianism hinges critically on the nature of the authoritarian leadership. A far-sighted leader, even if entirely self-interested, might find it in his interest to provide public goods and protect property rights in order to maximize his income over the long run. If the autocrat's time horizon is limited, if he is myopic, or if he has a misguided model of the world, he may choose to maximize his income through predatory behavior. Without the checks of democratic rule, such predation can persist with disastrous consequences.

The growing body of cross-national empirical work mirrors theory in generally reaching ambiguous results. Some studies suggest that democratic governments perform less well, some argue that democracies perform better. Others have found that long-lived autocracies outperform both short-lived autocracies and short-lived democracies; long-lived democracies perform best of all. However, a wide review of the evidence reaches the conclusion that there is probably no significant relationship between economic performance and regime type one way or the other.

Asia's role in this debate has been quite central. Even if the argument for authoritarianism does not hold generally, it did appear to hold among the first generation of East Asian newly industrializing countries (NICs). Taiwan was a party-dominant state led by the KMT, and Hong Kong until 1997 was a no-party administrative government under British rule. Most interesting are the histories of the Republic of Korea and Singapore, since they suggest how authoritarian governments may do better in terms of economic performance than weak democratic ones. After the fall of Syngman Rhee in Korea in 1960, a weak but reformist democratic government took office (the Second Republic), but it proved unable to pursue a coherent policy course in the face of serious social divisions and political challenges. There is substantial debate over the nature of the reforms associated with the Korean miracle, but both orthodox and heterodox interpretations trace the takeoff to policies launched under the military leadership in 1961 and to the restricted democratic rule that followed under Park Chung-hee in 1964.

Singapore was also a politically polarized society in the second half of the 1950s and early 1960s. The export-oriented strategy based on attracting multinationals emerged following the defeat of the leftist Barisan Socialists and the consolidation of dominant-party rule. In the late 1980s and early 1990s, a number of Chinese intellectuals associated with the government explicitly argued that China was following a similar path of placing priority on economic before political reform.

Subsequent political and economic developments complicate in several ways the conclusions drawn from this earlier history. First, a number of the East Asian NICs made successful transitions to democratic rule, including Korea, Taiwan, and Thailand. These regime changes did influence policymaking (for example, in altering budget priorities) and social behavior (for example, the increase in strike activity visible in Korea and Thailand), but did not have any significant effect on economic performance or overall growth strategy. Democratic transitions during times of high growth are likely to result in policy continuity because incoming democratic governments have little incentive to change course. Even if it is true that their authoritarian governments contributed to earlier growth in a number of the NICs, it does not follow that the transition to democracy would result in diminished performance—assuming that the transition were to occur in a relatively orderly fashion.

Second, authoritarian rule did not always follow the developmentalist pattern seen in the East Asian NICs. The most disastrous economic records in the region are those of autocracies: the Democratic People's Republic of Korea, Cambodia, and Myanmar. Ferdinand Marcos instituted an authoritarian order in the Philippines under political conditions that resembled the 1961 military coup in the Republic of Korea, and even looked to Korea and Taiwan as developmental models. His government, however, degenerated into a highly corrupt political system in which close ties with favored businesses, monopolization of important agricultural markets, manipulation of the banking system, and outright theft contributed to the onset of a serious balance of payments and financial crisis in 1984–85.

The Philippines also demonstrates a third important point: that under certain circumstances, democratization is not neutral in its effects on economic performance, but positively beneficial. In the Philippines, subsequent democratic governments under Corazon Aquino and Fidel Ramos reversed the Marcos legacy and instituted a variety of reforms, including reform of the banking system, that allowed the Philippines to weather the recent crisis with less disruption than its neighbors.

In sum, as time passes, the case for the superiority of Asian-style democracy is weakening. A number of countries have democratized without diminishing their economic performance; the economic record of the authoritarian governments is looking less and less compelling, and democracy has even emerged as an apparent antidote to the weaknesses of authoritarian rule, including corruption, poor protection of property rights, and incoherent policies.

How does this long-term view hold up when we examine the political roots of the crisis of 1997–98? Democratic governments were able to maintain their prior growth rates for a while in Korea and Thailand, but the onset of the crisis raises the question of whether or not democratization is implicated as a causal factor. In both democratic systems, political factors did contribute to market uncertainty. However, the presence of democracy allowed the people of Korea and Thailand to vote their failed governments out of office. In Indonesia, by contrast, authoritarian rule is centrally implicated in the depth and extent of that nation's crisis.

With a fixed term and substantial powers of legislative initiative, the Korean president would appear well positioned to respond aggressively to economic difficulties. However, policymaking in presidential systems depends on whether government is unified or divided; i.e., whether the president's party enjoys a legislative majority or support from a majority coalition, and whether or not the president and party leadership have control over their own party. If divided government pertains, or if the president's party is internally weak, divided, or undisciplined, then presidential systems can produce legislative gridlock.

In 1997, Kim Young-sam enjoyed a legislative majority, but his administration fell victim to divisions within his party and ultimately between the executive and the legislature. The source of these divisions was a no-reelection rule (and resultant lame-duck status for the president); a succession struggle within the party for the presidential nomination; and subsequent efforts of both the presidential candidate and the ruling party in the legislature to differentiate themselves from a failed incumbent. These internal battles influenced the management of important corporate failures, notably the KIA bankruptcy, and the country's approach to the International Monetary Fund (IMF); the mismanagement of these issues, in turn, further weakened investor confidence and made the crisis worse than it would otherwise have been.

If Korea's political system at least allowed for the possibility of decisive executive leadership, Thailand's constitution and electoral system (until the constitutional revision in late 1997) produced serious and recurrent problems for policymaking. The indecisiveness of political leadership in Thailand was a function of the fragmentation of the party system and the tendency to weak coalition governments. With parliamentary majorities constructed from a pool of approximately a dozen parties, each with its own internal weaknesses, cabinet instability was a chronic problem. As leader of the governing coalition, the prime minister was vulnerable to policy blackmail by coalition partners threatening to defect in pursuit of better deals in another coalition; indeed, all democratically elected governments except the Chatichai government, which fell to a military coup, met their end in this fashion.

The institutional root of these problems was Thailand's combination of a parliamentary structure in which government rests on party cohesion and a multimember electoral system, which undermined party cohesion. Thailand's multimember electoral system strongly encouraged candidates to campaign on the basis of individualized strategies rather than on the basis of party label, as they were compelled to differentiate themselves from competitors of the same party. Not only did this create weakly disciplined parties, but the emphasis on candidate-based rather than on party-based electoral strategies ensured that politicians would strive to deliver selective benefits to voters in their electorate in order to differentiate themselves from rivals from the same party. This encouraged vote buying, and placed a premium on politicians being able to generate a flow of cash to cover their costs while in office. These institutional problems contributed directly to the accumulation of economic distortions that underlay the outbreak of the crisis in Thailand, particularly in the way banking problems were handled, and greatly compounded the difficulties of dealing with the crisis once it broke.

But if democratic politics did contribute to the crises in Korea and Thailand, the built-in corrective mechanisms of democracy have also contributed to their resolution. In both Korea and Thailand, the governments responsible for the crisis (Kim Young-sam and Chavalit) were thrown out of office, allowing new reformist governments under Kim Dae-jung and Chuan Leepkai to assume control. In Thailand, the crisis even prompted a constitutional revision designed to lessen the problems of party fragmentation and corruption.

It is also important to examine how the nondemocratic governments in the region fared, particularly those, unlike China and Vietnam, that were responsible for having increased the capital mobility that was a background condition for the crisis. Indonesia's political system under Suharto provided for an extraordinary centralization of decision-making authority in the presidency, and seemed the very model of the economically successful authoritarian regime. Through the pursuit of a consistent macroeconomic policy and the willingness to undertake further reforms in the face of external shocks, Suharto had successfully established his government's credibility with both domestic and foreign investors. However, precisely because political authority was so unusually concentrated and because there were therefore no effective checks on presidential authority, there was always the risk that the president could introduce unwelcome policy measures, reverse existing policy commitments, or pursue erratic policies. Malaysia under Mahathir faced somewhat similar problems.[1] Although Indonesia's initial response to the crisis seemed more decisive than that of Thailand or Malaysia, the pursuit of conflicting objectives by the president in the last three months of 1997 raised serious questions about the government's intentions.

Moreover, the absence of clear mechanisms for succession raised even more fundamental questions of whether or not the regime would survive—and if it didn't, what the subsequent system of politics, property rights, and inter-ethnic relations would look like. As investor confidence collapsed, the remaining elite support for Suharto's rule began to evaporate. The authoritarian nature of the regime enabled him to cling to

---

[1] A question inevitably arises here: If Indonesia's massively centralized political system under Suharto was inimical to investor confidence, how is it that there were 30 years of strong investment and sustained economic growth? Given that the country's political framework was much the same in 1987 and 1977, how can it have suddenly become a critical problem in late 1997? MacIntyre (1998) argues that for much of the past three decades there have been factors in place which mitigated the credibility problem inherent in the political system. Indonesia offered very strong rates of return, had a demonstrated record of reasonably sound macroeconomic management, and imposed a policy constraint on its own behavior in the form of an open capital account. However the nature and the scale of the economic problems that gripped Indonesia from late 1997 were such that these mitigating factors were swept aside and investors were left to contemplate the full consequences of unconstrained executive authority.

power for several more months, during which time the economic damage was greatly compounded by dramatic political and social conflict.[2]

It must be acknowledged that a number of authoritarian governments in the region have been able to overcome credible commitment problems, protect property rights, and institute reforms that promoted long-term growth. On balance, however, the recent historical record casts doubt on the purported advantages of Asian-style democracy. The democratic transitions effected by several countries did not substantially disrupt the economic success initiated by their prior authoritarian leaderships; and if democratic politics did contribute to economic problems in Korea and Thailand, these political systems also had self-correcting mechanisms that authoritarian governments such as Indonesia lacked. The nondemo-cratic governments in Singapore and Hong Kong, which had particularly coherent governments and high levels of administrative capacity, man-aged the crisis effectively. China has to date been untested by the chal-lenges of open financial markets and increased capital mobility. But Indonesia's difficulties can be attributed in part to the country's highly centralized regime, its absence of effective checks on executive authority, and its lack of a succession mechanism.

GOVERNING BUSINESS–GOVERNMENT RELATIONS

For those looking for culprits on whom to blame the economic crisis, the favored political explanation is the role of interest groups, and particu-larly of close political relationships between politicians and business con-stituencies. This argument has several distinctive variants, but I will focus here on the two most often cited strands. The first is that the Asian crisis was the cumulative result of years of misguided industrial policy. Whatever their stated justification, industrial policies typically favored well-connected firms who could socialize risk or gain access to subsidies, preferential credit, protection, and other sorts of rents through the politi-cal process. Government interventions created moral hazard, including excessive risk-taking, inefficient allocation of capital, and the weakening of domestic financial institutions. Weaknesses in the financial system, in turn, were key to the wider economic crises that ensued.

A second line of argument—that crony capitalism and corruption was to blame for the region's difficulties—differs only in that the exchange relationship between business and government is lacking in any social

---

[2] In this, Malaysia exhibits a fundamental difference from Indonesia; even if the succes-sion issue was equally uncertain, as the Anwar case proved, the existence of an organized dominant party provided Mahathir with both means of political control and for the mobi-lization of support that Suharto's weakly institutionalized Golkar lacked.

welfare rationale. Favors are passed out to political allies not because of their presumed positive economic effects, but on purely political grounds or to enhance the wealth of politicians. An increasing body of empirical evidence suggests that such corruption (or at least international business perceptions of corruption) correlates negatively with economic growth over the long run. In the shorter run, corruption can also generate moral hazard and contribute to financial vulnerability.

To what extent are these arguments plausible? If we take industrial policy as the effort by government to promote the development of particular sectors through subsidies, protection, and other instruments, the argument for its significance as a cause of the Asian financial crisis appears weak. The case is most often invoked with respect to Korea. However, industrial policy in Korea peaked during the Heavy and Chemical Industry Plan of the late 1970s and was gradually dismantled over the 1980s and 1990s as the country liberalized. The government continued to intervene in the activities of the newly privatized commercial banks, continuing to appoint their directors, for example, and played a direct role in the financing of a number of large and dubious private projects through the state-owned Korean Development Bank. Government involvement in banking may have sent misleading signals to the private sector about government backing for specific projects, but a number of corporate failures prior to the crisis of 1997–98 showed that firms would indeed be allowed to fail.

In the early 1980s, Malaysia also experimented with a heavy industry push, primarily through the state-owned Heavy Industries Corporation of Malaysia.[3] In the wake of the recession of 1985–86, the government began to reassess this strategic thrust, however, and started to pay more attention to the development of the private sector through privatization and generic supports, such as tax breaks for investment, local sourcing, and investment in R&D, as well as through incentives to export. Indonesia also undertook a number of high-profile industrial policy projects, including the launch of a state-owned steel company and a national car project, and a highly visible effort to develop an indigenous light aircraft industry. Whatever criticisms might be leveled at these efforts, they played no major role in the crisis of 1997–98. Thailand's industrial policy is the subject of some controversy, with some arguing that it was more extensive than previously thought. However, the general consensus is that the country's industrial planning capabilities are limited, and that, as in Malaysia, the recession of the mid-1980s focused attention primarily on the general promotion of exports rather than on the specific targeting of problem sectors.

---

[3] For compact summaries of industrial policy in Southeast Asia, see Jomo et. al. (1997).

Caution is also required with respect to the role of cronyism and corruption as a source of moral hazard, although it did have discernable effects in some cases. In Korea, outright corruption played a role in the Hanbo failure, which first rattled market confidence in Korea's economic management. Even though Hanbo was subsequently allowed to fail, managers might have assumed ex ante that the bribes they paid politicians to influence loan decisions would allow them to be bailed out if investments went bad. Corruption, or politically motivated decision-making, also appears to have played a role in the expansion of the merchant banking sector; licenses were granted liberally to smaller regional institutions with little attention given to their capacity to manage risk. Moreover, the political weakness of the government in 1997 encouraged firms, most notably KIA, to attempt to save themselves through political appeals.

Korea's merchant banks were ultimately allowed to fail, and although the government nationalized KIA, its management was displaced and shareholders took severe losses. Virtually all Korean firms were over-leveraged, but corruption does not appear to play a central role in the other major companies in financial distress. As was subsequently revealed, however, business payments to politicians during the Chun and Roh administrations were massive. There is a larger structural problem in Korea, which is that the very size of the *chaebols* has made governments excessively sensitive to their interests, but it is questionable if this can be classified as a problem of corruption or cronyism.

In Southeast Asia, the significance of cronyism and corruption as a contributor to the crisis is more plausible, although caution is still required. The case of Indonesia is probably the best known. Direct personal contacts between the president and a group of prominent Chinese businessmen had catapulted their business groups into major conglomerates, aided by such policies as officially sanctioned private cartels in cement, glass, plywood, rice, and paper; price controls of cement, sugar, and automobiles; and exclusive licensing of clove marketing and flour milling—not to mention public sector monopolies. In the late 1980s and early 1990s, immediate family members appeared more prominently on the list of the favored. The inefficiencies of these investments did not, by themselves, generate the crisis. But a high degree of uncertainty concerning Suharto's willingness to undertake reforms that would have directly affected their privileges was harmful to confidence. On the one hand, the fact that Suharto appeared willing to go after some of his own cronies unsettled the prospects of those firms, and constituted a reversal of what might be called their "political property rights." On the other hand, the willingness of Suharto to protect some pet projects was unsettling to foreign investors and international financial institutions, which interpreted it as a broader sign of his unwillingness to undertake neces-sary reforms.

The Malaysian case is complex because the government has long maintained ethnic preferences that are by their very nature discrimina-tory. The government has also exercised a substantial degree of discretion in implementing its pro-*bumiputra* policy—procedures for letting govern-ment contracts and privatization have not always been transparent, for example. But the problem is not simply one of ethnic preferences or gov-ernment discretion. The lines between government, party, and private roles are also severely blurred in Malaysia; several prominent govern-ment officials have had a hand in economic decision-making while simul-taneously running party businesses and their own private enterprises. The potential for conflicts of interest is high: the issue of corruption has been a highly contested one within the Malaysian political system and was a contributor to the political crisis of 1998.

The Thai case is more ambiguous. The political structure outlined in the previous section allowed multiple opportunities not only for business to influence politicians, but also for businessmen to enter politics and politicians to enter business. Phongpaichit and Piriyarangsan have docu-mented in some detail the political manipulation of the budget, and bud-get-related scandals were a recurrent feature of Thai politics in the 1990s. But fiscal profligacy was not central to the crisis, and when we turn to problems in the financial sector, the evidence of outright corruption in government—as opposed to private sector malfeasance—is less clear. The mismanagement of the financial difficulties of the Bangkok Bank of Commerce (BBC), the failure to regulate and act aggressively against a number of failing finance companies, the extraordinarily costly efforts to save a number of financial institutions, and a high degree of uncertainty about the government's intentions were important contributors to the cri-sis. But the 1998 Nukul Commission, established by the Chuan govern-ment to investigate the causes of the crisis, does not present evidence that corruption was responsible for these problems of misguided and lax reg-ulation.

In sum, there is ample evidence that weak financial regulation and poor systems of corporate governance were important precursors to the crisis in Southeast Asia. It is also clear that investment booms were fueled by bad private sector investment decisions. But as a general claim for the region as a whole, it is difficult to say that industrial policy was respon-sible for these ills, and claims about the consequences of corruption and crony capitalism—unless defined to include weak regulation—do not hold across all countries with equal force.

Moreover, it is important to recall that close business–government relations are also seen as an important feature of the model that contributed to Asia's growth. As Peter Evans puts it: "Effective government business relations depended on large quantities of high-quality information flowing between government and corporations, and on mutual confidence that predictions and commitments were credible." The World Bank itself endorsed the value of deliberation councils in its 1993 report on the Asian miracle.

Nonetheless, it is clear that corruption does have some role to play in the crisis, that it is harmful to long-term growth, and that it is corrosive of public trust in government. So what can be done about it? In general, the possible solutions fall into three categories. The economists' approach is rooted in the observation that government intervention itself breeds rent-seeking and moral hazard, and thus liberalization, privatization, the market means of resource allocation, and a reduction in the state's discretion provide a political solution to the problem. This idea has its champions among Asian politicians. Corazon Aquino, Kim Dae-jung, and Anwar Ibrahim have all exhibited elements of what might be called "market-friendly populism:" the ideology that overly close business–government relations are responsible for numerous economic as well as social problems, and that a greater dose of market forces will reduce the opportunities for corruption.

The second solution, championed by the international financial institutions, focuses on the incentives facing bureaucrats, who are often assumed to be the focal point of cronyism and corruption. This approach would seek to remove discretion and the manipulation of bureaucratic incentives through the use of carrots (guaranteeing adequate public service pay) and sticks (monitoring and punishment of corrupt behavior). However, as we have seen, the worst corrupt practices frequently involve politicians, not bureaucrats; and even bureaucratic corruption should be understood in the broader political context that politicians have a political or direct financial interest in corruption within their ministries. The emphasis on bureaucratic reform would appear to neglect the needs to monitor the relationships between politicians and the private sector and to make them more transparent.

The third solution places faith in the power of information, and thus emphasizes transparency. As the World Bank argues: "Governments should publish budgets, revenue collection data, statutes and rules, and the proceedings of legislative bodies. . . . Unauthorized secret funds or extra budgetary funds available to chief executives are an invitation to corruption." Outside the government, a vigorous media can act as a check on government by exposing, and by threatening to expose, corruption. Transparency also needs to be extended to relations between business and government. Campos and Root argue that institutionalizing business–government contacts in formal corporatist bodies can have this effect. By providing a forum for open negotiation over rules and over the way that rents are distributed, councils provide incentives for mutual checks among business interests, thereby avoiding the highly individualized patron–client relations and particularism that are central to corruption.

The World Bank also concludes that "information is of little value . . . without mechanisms for using the knowledge gained to influence government behavior." Thus it is crucial that there are formal checks on politicians and business in the form of institutions that have the incentive to root out corruption and punish it. It is sometimes thought that democracy itself can accomplish this goal, but I am skeptical. Certain types of political parties thrive on corruption, and competing political parties may engage in mutual forbearance on the issue rather than compete to expose it. Rather, governments require independent institutions that are beholden to the law rather than to politicians. Primary among these institutions is a judiciary that is independent and that has the power to enforce its rulings. The model of the independent agency capable of checking politicians also extends to other bodies in the government, including anticorruption units and commissions responsible for monitoring and disclosing the political contributions that constitute the basis for most corrupt practices.

Establishing such agencies raises a paradox, however; how can the government be made independent from itself? Who guards the guardians? I turn to this question in the context of the broader issue of reforming the state.

REFORMING THE STATE: SOME PROBLEMS IN THE DESIGN OF REGULATORY INSTITUTIONS

Most analyses of the Asian financial crisis concur that failures of regulation were central to its onset. Financial regulation has received particular attention given the weak standards for capital adequacy, loan classifications, and loan provisioning, and the general lack of information on the part of regulators. Weak rules with respect to corporate governance are additionally at fault for the risky behavior of companies. Governments in the region are also being called on to introduce a variety of other regulatory functions to guarantee that markets work efficiently, including competition policy and oversight of newly privatized utilities, telecommunications, and transportation companies. Public interest groups are furthermore demanding strengthened regulation in areas such as the environment, occupational health and safety, and product liability.

Some of the regulatory failure and weakness in Asian countries stems from the inadequacy of old methods applied to a changed environment.

For example, weak financial regulation incurred lower costs when domestic financial markets were closed than it does now that they are open to rapid, short-term capital movements. However, as suggested in the previous section, regulatory failures may also have political roots, and may spring from the design of the regulatory institutions themselves, particularly where they lack independence from the influence of politicians and their clients. Regulatory reform is therefore not simply an issue of changing incentives in the bureaucracy or of altering policy parameters; rather, it is a political process of rewriting the contract between elected politicians and bureaucrats.

For some democrats, the idea of strengthening the independence of the bureaucracy seems to run counter to democratic principles of accountability. But the process of delegation from legislators (to the executive branch in presidential systems) to ministries and agencies is crucial to the functioning of any democracy: it is a defining characteristic of the modern state. From an efficiency perspective, delegation is the organizational equivalent of the division of labor, since it enables gains through organizational specialization and expertise.

Delegation also plays a crucial role in solving collective action problems among politicians. For example, legislators have a collective interest in effective fiscal management, as this affects overall economic performance and thus their reputations as incumbents. But legislators also have electoral concerns that may tempt them to seek particularistic benefits for their constituents. If all legislators succeed in this strategy, for example through legislative logrolls, then it is easy to see how suboptimal policy might arise; Barbara Geddes has called this the "politician's dilemma." Even if the problem is recognized, it may be difficult for parties or legislators acting collectively to organize appropriate responses because of conflicts over the distribution of benefits: coalitional politics in Thailand provides numerous examples of these difficulties. Delegation to "control committees" within the legislature, to party leaders, to the executive, or to bureaucratic agencies can solve these collective action problems.

If some are wary of the risks of delegation to unaccountable agencies, other diagnoses engage in what I call the technocratic fallacy: the idea that difficult and contentious policy problems can be solved by simply removing them from the hands of politicians, insulating them from interest group pressures, and assigning them to knowledgeable and well-socialized technocrats.[4] This is equally unrealistic. Politicians in a democracy have an interest in delegating for reasons of efficiency, but they also have an interest in controlling and monitoring bureaucratic

---

[4] For similar criticisms see Bresser Pereira, Maravall, and Przeworski (1993).

agents so that they are attentive to the politician's electoral, constituent, and interest group concerns.

There are a number of ways by which politicians seek to accomplish the objective of bureaucratic control. These may be divided into ex ante and ex post, or oversight, mechanisms.

The first and most obvious ex ante means available is through the legislation or statute itself: for example, by specifying the scope of the regulatory decisions that are delegated to agencies and the legal tools that an administrative agency can use. A second ex ante control mechanism entails the screening and selection of personnel. Even if executives and legislators are willing to establish a relatively independent, meritocratic civil service, they are likely to insist on political control or at least veto power over top administrative appointments. Politicians are also likely to exercise ongoing (ex post) oversight over agencies. One way of doing this is through auditing, monitoring, and reporting requirements, but these "police patrol" mechanisms are quite costly and run up against both moral hazard problems and the difficulty of specifying against all future contingencies.

This problem can be overcome by establishing decision-making structures that build institutional or interest group checks (veto points) into the agency decision-making process. For example, politicians may require intra-agency consultation or may empower affected parties directly; for example, by allowing interest groups the opportunity to comment on agency decision-making, by structuring participation in regulatory agencies, by granting constituents standing in quasi-judicial administrative procedures, and by strengthening the judicial process more generally. These "fire alarm" structures are less costly, reveal less biased information, and shift policymaking authority to the bureaucracy. They also allow for the ongoing representation of affected parties even should unexpected contingencies arise.

In sum, the "reform of the state" can be seen as a political process of striking a balance between the efficiency gains to be achieved by delegation, the interests of executives and legislators in controlling bureaucratic agents for political ends, and the need for politicians and bureaucrats to remain responsive to organized interest groups. This balance can be achieved by depoliticizing certain regulatory decisions—removing them from the operation of line ministries into independent regulatory agencies—while at the same time designing mechanisms through which public comment and participation on the part of interested parties can take place.

Perhaps the clearest example of delegation has come in the area of monetary policy. As with the reform of the civil service, economic crisis has served a catalytic role in moving politicians toward granting greater independence to central banks. But such legal autonomy is only a necessary rather than a sufficient condition for the conduct of an independent and stable monetary policy. Cukierman, Webb and Neyapti (1992) found that independence defined in terms of legal rules has an influence on monetary policy in advanced states but not in developing ones, where turnover is higher and political influence operates to a greater degree through informal channels. Other studies of developing countries note that "independent" central banks typically maintain linkages to private sector actors, and that these linkages constitute checks on political manipulation.

These observations on balancing independence with the participation of interested parties extend to a number of different areas. In the case of financial restructuring, for example, political pressures abound. In principle, only viable financial institutions should stay open; restructuring should allocate losses to shareholders and creditors—who tend to be politically powerful; and the process should maintain credit discipline for borrowers, who also may be able to exercise political influence. At the same time, such agencies need to be responsive to the commercial concerns of the most important likely purchasers of distressed assets, namely, foreign institutional investors. To manage these problems, the Thai government delegated the task of assessing the health of the country's financial companies to an independent financial restructuring agency. The agency quickly took the decision that virtually all of the finance companies were insolvent and should be liquidated, gaining the country substantial credibility in the markets. Subsequent efforts to sell these properties by auction ultimately involved negotiations with, and some accommodation to, foreign buyers. In other countries, questions persist over whether or not similar financial restructuring agencies are independent from political pressures and whether or not they would be willing to liquidate assets at market prices to foreigners.

Similar points may be made by looking at an unrelated policy area: the question of how to effectively target the poor. One mechanism for doing this— the creation of social investment funds (SIFs)—grew out of the 1980s crisis in Latin America. Most of these funds use targeting mechanisms based on objective poverty and income criteria to establish who the beneficiaries should be and have clearly specified project criteria; as a result, their operations are relatively transparent. Most of the funds also have a high degree of procedural autonomy that protects them from political interference by politicians or interest groups in the project approval process. A number of exceptions to normal bureaucratic regulations and procedures have made this possible. Probably the most important of these have been the choice of private sector managers to direct the fund operations and a related exemption from public sector rules on staff recruitment and salaries. Glaessner et al. additionally note a variety of other ways in which the funds have gained independence:

No less important has been the exemption of most of the funds from government procurement and disbursement procedures. . . . Perhaps even more important was that, as autonomous entities, the availability of the funds' resources was subject neither to the vagaries of the annual budget cycle and central government cash management nor to the often cumbersome mechanisms for transferring central government funds to local and municipal governments.

The political stability of the funds has not solely been a function of these internal features of their organizational design; it has also been related to the fact that they have been demand-driven and have thus actively engaged their clients. The funds are financial intermediaries rather than implementing agencies. Local and provincial governments and nongovernmental organizations have thus been mobilized to participate in the choice, design, execution, operation, and maintenance of the projects the SIFsfund, which range across the basic services: health care and nutrition, education, water supply, and sanitation.

To summarize, an important component of governance in the post-crisis period will be reform and strengthening of state institutions, particularly with respect to regulation. Delegation to independent regulatory agencies does not mean lack of accountability; a variety of mechanisms exist through which politicians can exercise oversight, but which at the same time limit the direct involvement in agency decision-making of those politicians and which also increase transparency. One means of achieving this goal is through procedures that allow private actors a monitoring function in agency decision-making, through mechanisms that provide for public comment, hearings, and the direct participation of diverse social interests and constituencies in consultative bodies.

MANAGING THE SOCIAL DIMENSIONS OF THE CRISIS: PROTEST AND ACCOMMODATION

Until recently, limited political participation, broadly shared growth, falling poverty, and preexisting family and community support mechanisms combined to limit the extent of government involvement in the provision of social security in East Asia. The country with the most highly developed social safety net—Korea—acquired many of these mechanisms only since its transition to democratic rule in the late 1980s. The wide-ranging consequences of the Asian financial crisis have now called this noninterventionism into question. These consequences include declining incomes, rising poverty, threats to educational and health services, and increased crime and social violence—particularly in Indonesia.

These developments are, of course, problems in their own right, but a subtext of the heightened concern over the social consequences of the crisis is that a backlash may develop against the reform process. The argument, usually implicit, proceeds as follows: a crisis hits, and the government is forced by events or by external agencies to undertake reforms that impose costs on well-organized groups. These groups mobilize against the reforms. Politicians sensitive to interest group pressures, loss of votes, strikes, and other social actions respond by watering down or reversing the reforms, which has the perverse consequence of further slowing the adjustment process and prolonging the return to growth. Interventions to alleviate the effects of the crisis—from temporary measures such as promoting public works or targeted assistance, to the maintenance of health and education expenditure, to reforming labor market practices, and to longer-term pension reform—can thus contribute to the politics of reform by blunting opposition to it.

There are elements of truth in this model to which I will return: social policy is a critical political component of economic reform and of an open economy more generally. However, the model is also flawed in a few subtle but important respects when applied to the Asian crisis. First, it is not necessarily the most seriously affected who are the biggest political impediments to reform. We have already noted that business practices and rent-seeking were at least partly to blame for a number of the practices that made East Asian countries vulnerable to crisis. In terms of other social strata, it is also often the better organized and better off—members of the middle class, workers, and farmers—who are capable of sustained political influence or protest. Although these groups may be badly affected by the crisis, they are not typically the most seriously affected; it is the poor and very poor to whom most attention should be paid, but targeting such groups often proves politically as well as administratively difficult.

Finally, this model assumes that interest group pressures are of necessity narrow and self-serving. In many cases this is no doubt true, but in the Asian crisis the demand for greater fiscal stimulus and government spending is now recognized as precisely the right medicine: greater concern for the social consequences of the crisis was not simply a humanitarian choice but would have also resulted in superior macroeconomic policy.

In addition, as we have suggested with respect to organized business interests, the development of social organizations need not follow the rent-seeking pattern; many nongovernmental organizations (NGOs) are also formed to provide services and information to members. NGOs can serve as a check on the efficiency and quality of government service provision and as a source of information. A growing body of literature is suggesting at the project level that beneficiary involvement positively affects development project performance. An even larger literature suggests theoretically that "social capital"—the density of civic associations—is positively associated with long-term growth and efficiency of government. Cross-national tests of this proposition are still limited and confirmation elusive, however.

The reform model is nonetheless precisely correct in underlining the importance of building political support for reform. This is typically understood to mean building support among "winners," which can be used to offset the political losses associated with the reform process. Somewhat more counterintuitive is the observation that successful reform may be facilitated by additionally developing political relationships with "losers." This point can be illustrated by considering in more detail the issues surrounding the management of urban labor in the adoption of market-oriented policies.

Organized labor typically faces losses in the initial phase of a standard adjustment program. Tight fiscal and monetary policies imply a reduction in aggregate demand and employment, and hit directly at public sector employment and wages—political models of inflation and stabilization often explicitly or implicitly have a labor–business conflict at their core. Trade and exchange rate policy also engage workers' interests: Trade liberalization places pressure on the import-substituting sector and real devaluation hits nontraded goods producers. Privatization also strikes at well-organized public sector workers. More generally, increasing the flexibility of labor markets has been a central component of reforms in some countries, most notably Korea. In a number of policy domains, we would therefore expect that organized labor would be a key player in resisting reform efforts.

If this assessment is correct, getting labor to agree to temporary setbacks is a crucial aspect of managing adjustment. Under authoritarian regimes, labor is typically subject to a variety of controls, and these controls have arguably been one reason for the success of such regimes in implementing stabilization efforts. In some new democracies, such as Turkey and Korea, controls on labor even extended into the democratic period. If democratization is genuine, however, political liberalization is likely to lead to more extensive and active union organization and to greater labor militancy. This happened in Spain, in Turkey after 1987, and in Poland, where labor led the fight against the Communist government.

Other regions with strategically placed unions (Mexico) or where democratization saw resurgent unionism (Spain) provide examples of cases where labor did not constitute a block to structural reform. Studies of Europe have found that corporatist arrangements or close ties with governing social democratic parties integrate labor into the political system in ways that provide a basis for compromise, enhanced policy credibility, and superior economic performance with respect to both inflation and growth. Center-left governments in Spain and Poland were capable of securing labor acquiescence, at least in the short run; so, too, was the Concertacion in Chile, a coalition led by the Christian Democrats but with Socialist participation. By contrast, where labor had weak links with the government but strong ties with class-based leftist or populist parties, as in Turkey both before September 1980 and after 1987, reform proved more difficult.

The reason for the apparently anomalous result of social democratic governments extracting concessions from labor is that they are more likely to enjoy trust, and are thus better positioned to secure short-run restraint for promises of longer-term gain. Institutionalized labor–government relations of this nature can solve both distributional and time horizon problems. By contrast, right-of-center governments are less credible in their promises of long-term improvements for labor. Labor is consequently likely to be more demanding; ironically, the government is more likely to resort in the face of labor pressure to short-run concessions that undermine the adjustment effort, such as wage increases that outstrip productivity or expanded public employment.

These observations have been used to support the claim that adjustment can be facilitated under democratic auspices through the corporatist institutions that provide a consultative forum between political leaders and the major interest groups, such as labor, capital, and ethnic groups. The essence of *concertacion* is that the most important economic actors are capable either of directly negotiating binding agreements on major policy variables, such as wages, investment, and prices, or of providing credible support for bargains struck on key government initiatives, such as macroeconomic and industrial policies. The enthusiasm for this solution grows precisely out of a reading of the experience of the small European states, which have managed to combine social democracy, very open economies, and comparatively good records with respect to both growth and inflation.

The question is whether or not this institutional solution is viable in the new democracies of Asia. The negotiation of binding agreements implies that all of the actors must be internally cohesive. For interest associations, this implies the capacity to speak authoritatively for their memberships and to guarantee compliance. The government itself must be sympathetic to such incorporation of labor; in Europe, social democratic parties led such experiments. In most of the new democracies in Asia, these conditions are lacking—and it is the weakness rather than the strength of interest groups that constitutes the liability. Only in Korea was a tripartite response to the crisis seriously tried, and it did appear to gain some increased labor flexibility for other concessions on social insurance and political rights.

This discussion suggests several broad conclusions about the organization of interest groups in understanding reform in a democratic context. First, the expansion of the number of interest groups typically associated with the democratization process does not necessarily constitute a threat to growth-oriented policies; on the contrary, it may serve to offset rent-seeking interests that gained power through privileged links with authoritarian governments. Second, close government ties to interest groups are not necessarily inimical to reform. The political mobilization of supporting interests is a critical component of moving from one policy equilibrium to another; as the discussion of labor showed, establishing credible ties with "losers" may also be helpful. Third, corporatist arrangements along the lines of the small European democracies are not likely to constitute an option for most developing countries in Asia because of the weakness of interest groups; other representative institutions and a more fragmented NGO sector will have to play this role.

Finally, the broad outlines of the political model described above do appear to be vindicated; i.e., that building support for a more open and market-oriented economy is not undermined but is enhanced by paying close attention to social welfare issues. As Dani Rodrik summarizes:

The provision of social insurance is an important component of market reforms—it cushions the blow of liberalization among those most severely affected, it helps maintain the legitimacy of these reforms, and it averts backlashes against the distributional and social consequences of integration into the world economy.

CONCLUSION

The main points of this paper are easily summarized:

- Democracies proved equal or superior to autocracies in managing the shocks of the Asian financial crisis.
- Close business–government relations and corruption did play a role—although often exaggerated—in the crisis. Market-oriented policies, bureaucratic reform, and transparency are inadequate to reduce corruption; independent institutions within the government must be empowered to prosecute corruption and business–government relations must be made more transparent.
- Good governance rests in part on delegation to independent agencies, checked by participation and oversight to a broad array of interested constituent groups.

- The development of political ties to "losers" and the development of compensatory social policies play an important role in maintaining support not just for economic reform but also for more open economies.

What lessons are here for the international financial institutions (IFIs)? With respect to the role of democracy, the IFIs will probably have to remain circumspect; the norm of sovereignty—although often the shield of rogues—still holds firm sway and there may be more hurt than harm in denying assistance to autocrats in trouble. Nonetheless, it is perfectly appropriate for the IFIs to make assessments of the credibility of policy commitments in making loan decisions, and political structure should play a role in those decisions.

With respect to reducing corruption, the approaches taken by the IFIs to date have been largely indirect, such as changing bureaucratic incentives and reducing government discretion. While important, it is legitimate for the IFIs to monitor the corruption that undermines the credibility and effectiveness of programs and to assist in developing anti-corruption programs. However, given that core actions involve areas, such as the strengthening of the judiciary, where the IFIs do not have a core competence, such programs might be elaborated in conjunction with interested donor governments or political parties.

With respect to regulatory reform, analysis of policy must be supplemented with much more research on the design of regulatory institutions. In particular, more attention needs to be paid to developing constituents for the mission of newly created and strengthened regulatory agencies; for example, by promoting relevant industry associations and public interest groups with standing in agency decisions.

Finally, it is hopeful to note that the IFIs have already been aggressive in addressing the social dimensions of the crisis. There is no shame in acknowledging that the development of social insurance is a critical component of the politics of helping countries become market economies.

REFERENCES

Bresser Pereira, L.C., J.M. Maraval and A. Przeworski. 1993. *Economic Reforms in New Democracies.* New York: Cambridge University Press.

Campos, Edgardo, and Hilton Root. 1996. *The Key to the Asian Miracle: Making Shared Growth Credible.* Washington, D.C.: The Brookings Institution.

Chang, Ha-joon. 1998. "Korea: the Misunderstood Crisis." *World Development* 26: 8.

Cukierman, Alex, Steven B. Webb, and B. Neyapti. 1992. "The Measurement of Central Bank Independence and its Effect on Policy Outcomes," *World Bank Economic Review* 6: 353–398.

Evans, Peter. 1995. *Embedded Autonomy: States and Industrial Transformation*. Princeton: Princeton University Press.

Glaessner, Philip J., Kye Woo Lee, Anna Maria Sant'Anna, and Jacques de St. Antoine. 1994. *Poverty Alleviation and Social Investment Funds: the Latin American Experience*. World Bank Discussion Paper 261. Washington, D.C.

MacIntyre, Andrew. 1998. "Political Parties, Accountability and Economic Governance in Indonesia." In Jean Blondel, Takashi Inoguchi, and Ian Marsh, eds., *Democratization, Political Parties, and Economic Growth in Asia.*

Olson, Mancur. 1993. "Dictatorship, Democracy, and Development." *American Political Science Review* 87(3): 567–76.

Phongpaichit, Pasuk, and Sungsidh Piriyarangsan. 1994. *Corruption and Democracy in Thailand*. Bangkok: Silkworm Books.

Rodrik, Dani. 1997. *Has Liberalization Gone Too Far?* Washington D.C.: Institute for International Economics.

———. 1998. *The New Global Economy and Developing Countries: Making Openness Work*. Washington D.C.: Overseas Development Council.

World Bank. 1993. *The East Asian Miracle: Economic Growth and Public Policy*. New York: Oxford University Press.

———. 1997. *World Development Report 1997: The State in a Changing World*. New York: Oxford University Press.

9

ASIAN VALUES IN THE WAKE OF THE ASIAN CRISIS

Francis Fukuyama

IN THE EARLY 1990s, former Prime Minister Lee Kwan Yew of Singapore and Prime Minister Mahathir bin Mohamad of Malaysia argued that certain Asian cultural values were are the root of Asia's remarkable postwar success. These leaders maintained that in the political sphere, Asian values supported the paternalistic brand of authoritarian government that they both practiced, and in the economic sphere these values provided a work ethic and supported savings, education, and other practices conducive to economic growth.

In light of the recession that gripped Asia in 1997–98, the collapse of the paternalistic Asian authoritarian government in Indonesia, and political instability in Malaysia itself, these arguments now ring hollow. Lee Kwan Yew has publicly backed away from some of his earlier assertions,[1] and many observers now claim that "Asian values," far from explaining Asia's economic success, lie at the root of the cronyism and corruption afflicting countries there.

It is useful to reconsider the role of cultural values in light of what happened in 1997–98. In retrospect, there are two questions that need to be answered: To what extent did Asian values contribute to Asian development over the past two generations; and to what extent were they responsible for the crisis that ended that period of growth in the late 1990s? One further question needs to be posed regarding the future: In what ways will Asian values continue to support distinctive political, economic, and social institutions?

THE ASIAN VALUES ARGUMENT

The idea that Asian cultural values are more hospitable to paternalistic authoritarianism of the sort practiced in Singapore, Malaysia, or Indone-

---

[1] See his interview in Forbes Magazine (March 23, 1998), where he says, "Cronyism and corruption are a debasement of Confucianist values. Confucianist duty to family and loyalty to friends should be discharged from private, not public wealth. Unfortunately, they have degenerated into abuses of public office and undermined the integrity of government."

sia than they are to Western-style democracy has in the past been advanced by politicians like Lee Kwan Yew and Mahathir.[2] In this they have been supported by a number of Western academic observers, including Samuel Huntington, who has argued that there is a broad zone of Confucian civilization that is hostile to democracy:

> Almost no scholarly disagreement exists on the proposition that traditional Confucianism was either undemocratic or antidemocratic. . . . Harmony and cooperation were preferred over disagreement and competition. The maintenance of order and respect for hierarchy were central values.[3]

Thomas Metzger has argued that there is much in China's Confucian-influenced political heritage that suggests a continuing pattern of authoritarian politics.[4] Tu Wei-Ming in a thorough account enumerates areas of difference between Confucian doctrine and Western values.[5]

The case that Asian values constitute an obstacle to democracy can be summarized succinctly. If we take Confucianism as the dominant value system in Asia, we see that it describes an ethical world in which people are born not with rights but with duties to a series of hierarchically arranged authorities, beginning with the family and extending all the way up to the state and emperor. In this world, there is no concept of the individual and individual rights; duties are not derived from rights as they are in Western liberal thought. While there is a concept of reciprocal obligation between ruler and ruled, there is no absolute grounding of government responsibility in either the popular will or in the need to respect and protect an individual's sphere of autonomy.

Apart from Confucianism, Asia's religions do not give particular support to Western democratic principles. Folk religions like Taoism and Shinto are animist and pantheistic. Westerners sometimes forget the importance of the transcendent monotheism of the Judeo-Christian tradition to their political and social lives. The idea that there is an eternal realm of divine law superior to all positive law gives the individual with access to that higher law potential grounds for revolt against all forms of secular authority. It promotes both individualism and the concept of uni-

---

[2] See Fareed Zakaria, "A Conversation with Lee Kuan Yew," *Foreign Affairs*, vol. 73, no. 2, (March-April 1994): 109–127.

[3] Samuel P. Huntington, "Religion and the Third Wave." *National Interest*, vol. 24 (Summer 1991): 29–42.

[4] Thomas A. Metzger, "Sources of Resistance." *Journal of Democracy*, vol. 9 (1998): 18–26.

[5] Tu Wei-Ming, *Confucian Traditions in East Asian Modernity: Moral Education and Economic Culture in Japan and the Four Dragons* (Cambridge, MA: Harvard University Press, 1996.)

versalism. Universalism is the ground not only for the Western concept of human rights that are transferable from one culture to another; it is also the basis for abstraction in the observation of nature and human behavior that is at the basis both for the natural and the social sciences.

On the other hand, there are a number of key values characteristic of many Asian societies that, while having separate roots from their Western counterparts, are quite supportive both of a modern economy and of democratic politics. (Even if they were supportive only of economic modernization, they would still be conducive to democracy because of the link between development and democracy.) Asian religions and ethical systems are remarkably tolerant in a way that monotheistic traditions like Judaism, Christianity, and Islam historically have not been. Confucianism, with its exam system that offers the prospect of social mobility, can be highly meritocratic. It is a highly rational ethical system and does not have the obscurantist tendencies of, say, orthodox Shiism. The Confucian emphasis on education is well adapted to the needs of a modern technological economy, and the Confucian family system provides a certain protected sphere of private life that is relatively free of state intrusion.

BEATING A DEAD HORSE

Since few people today seem to be interested in making the case for Asian values as the basis for distinctive political or economic institutions, criticizing the concept may seem a bit like beating a dead horse. For the sake of clarity, however, it is important to lay out the weaknesses of the original argument as a means of distilling from it those elements that might remain valid.

The first and probably most important problem with the Asian values concept, as anyone who has traveled through Asia knows, is that Asia is a very diverse place, and that values vary considerably from country to country.[6] Lee Kwan Yew sometimes suggested that Asian values were tantamount to Confucian values, but it is not clear how Confucian values could be considered to apply to the Malay populations of Malaysia or Indonesia. Confucianism is, moreover, interpreted very differently in Japan, the Republic of Korea, and China. Mahathir argued that Asians value family more than Westerners. But kinship ties vary in importance throughout Asia: they play a minimal role in Japan and a very important one in southern China, for example. It is not even possible to argue that

---

[6] This point is made by Amartya Sen, in *Human Rights and Asian Values* (New York: Carnegie Council on Ethics and Public Policy, 1997).

Asian families are more stable than their Western counterparts: during the first half of the twentieth century, the divorce rate in peninsular Malaya was well over 50 percent, falling below Western rates some time only in the 1970s.[7] Interestingly, in contrast to that of most Western countries, Malaysia's divorce rate decreased with economic modernization.

The second weakness of the original Asian values argument, which is shared by many cultural explanations of behavior, lies in the fact that values almost never have a direct impact on behavior; they must be mediated through a variety of institutions to make themselves manifest. Asian cultural values existed in something like their present form long before Asian societies began their periods of explosive economic growth. The causes for that growth are much more likely to be found in the institutions that were created in the interim, such as stable governments and systems of property rights and commercial law, as well as by the macro- and sometimes microeconomic policies carried out by those governments. Values and culture nonetheless play important roles in explaining a society's ability to build and operate institutions and policies: were the United States to try to create its own equivalent of Japan's Ministry of International Trade and Industry (MITI) for example, I suspect the result would be much less successful. But to jump immediately to the level of culture without looking at institutions as an intermediate step is a typical mistake made by proponents of cultural interpretations.

With regard to political institutions, it is not at all clear that Asian values, however interpreted, constitute any kind of insuperable bar to modern democracy. There is a correlation between democracy and development: for a variety of function reasons, wealthier societies tend to expand political participation. Since the original elaboration of this correlation by Lipset in 1959,[8] it has been analyzed intensively using data from the Third Wave democracies formed in the 1980–1990 period. With some exceptions, the correlation continues to hold up well. Adam Przeworksi has concluded that there is not a single historical case of a reversal of a democracy in a country that has reached a level of $6,000 per capita in 1992 parity purchasing power terms.[9]

---

[7] See Gavin W. Jones, "Modernization and Divorce: Contrasting Trends in Islamic Southeast Asia and the West," *Population and Development Review*, vol. 23 (1997): 95–114.

[8] Seymour Martin Lipset, "Some Social Requisites of Democracy: Economic Development and Political Legitimacy," *American Political Science Review*, vol. 53 (1959): 69–105; Lipset, "The Social Requisites of Democracy Revisited," *American Sociological Review*, vol. 59 (1994): 1–22; Larry Diamond, "Economic Development and Democracy Reconsidered," *American Behavioral Scientist*, vol. 15 (1992): 450–499, and Michael Coppedge, *Inequality, Democracy, and Economic Development* (Cambridge: Cambridge University Press, 1997).

[9] Adam Przeworski and Michael Alvarez, "What Makes Democracies Endure?" *Journal of Democracy*, vol. 7 (1996): 39–55.

If we presume that modernization creates conditions neither necessary nor sufficient, but nonetheless very helpful to the establishment of stable democracy, the burden of proof then falls on those who argue that Asian values are so exceptional as to undermine the relationship.[10] But the empirical record in Asia is relatively supportive of the democracy–development correlation: the first three Asian countries to industrialize—Japan, Korea, and Taiwan—now have functioning democracies. The fact that two of the highest per capita income entities, Singapore and Hong Kong, are not democratic on the surface would appear to disconfirm the correlation (as well as the fact that the Philippines, although a democracy, has remained one of the region's poorer countries), but these anomalies can be explained by other factors.

If we focus on economic institutions, it is clear that there were some that were unique to the region, and that they probably could not be created in other cultural settings. These included the so-called Japanese development model in which a technocratic elite oversaw sectoral transitions through control over credit; Japan's system of lifetime employment among large corporations and their *keiretsu* networks; the *chaebol* in Korea; and the family-based networks of overseas Chinese businesses in southern China and Southeast Asia. While many of these institutions are clearly dysfunctional today, it is very difficult to know in retrospect the degree to which they either contributed to or constrained development during Asia's high-growth period. The most basic explanation for Asian economic development lies in conventional factors like inputs of capital and labor, combined with political stability and reasonably good government. But as the reaction to Paul Krugman's extreme version of this argument indicates, this view is not entirely satisfactory.[11] Many uniquely Asian institutions violated precepts of Western neoclassical economics by interfering with market mechanisms; even so, their operation coincided with levels of economic growth that had no precedent in the prior economic history of the West. The least one can say in response to this is that (1) they were not as harmful to economic growth as many Western economists asserted in prior decades, but that (2) many have clearly since become obstacles to growth.

Taking account of both the diversity of Asian values and the importance of institutions, the original Asian values argument begins decom-

---

[10] This case has in fact been made: with a limited number of well-known exceptions, virtually all developed democracies are also countries with a Christian cultural heritage. Samuel Huntington has argued that it is that cultural heritage rather than level of development *per se* that is the determinant of stable democracy. See Samuel P. Huntington, *The Third Wave: Democratization in the Late Twentieth Century* (Oklahoma City: University of Oklahoma Press, 1991).

[11] Paul R. Krugman, "The Myth of Asia's Miracle" *Foreign Affairs*, vol. 73 (1994): 62–78.

posing very quickly. The state-centric Japanese development model was never really implemented in Southeast Asia, many of whose societies possessed less stable and less capable governments. There, problems tended to be more ones of under-institutionalization, such as in the case of Thailand, whose financial problems had much to do with an inadequate system of banking regulation. Japan and Korea need to dismantle certain of their state institutions and deregulate; Thailand and Indonesia need to build up many of their state capabilities and implement more modern regulatory systems. In both cases, the central questions concern institutional design and not culture. Culture may have an effect in promoting or constraining the political conditions for institutional change, but it is otherwise relevant only as mediated through institutions.

TO WHAT EXTENT WERE ASIAN VALUES RESPONSIBLE FOR THE ASIAN CRISIS?

Just as explanations for Asian growth lie in the realm of conventional economics rather than culture, so too do explanations for Asia's current crisis. It would seem *prima facie* impossible for a cultural factor, which changes very slowly, to account for a rapid and unexpected development like the loss of foreign currency reserves or the sudden buildup of short-term credit.

There is, however, one cultural theme that has run through current analyses of the crisis: the tendency of many Western observers to lump all countries in Asia together and to blame "crony capitalism" for their serious misallocation of resources. Cronyism has been widely acknowledged in Indonesia, and all countries in Asia have experienced corruption scandals of greater or lesser seriousness over the past decade, including both Japan and Korea. Throughout East Asia, business relations are generally conducted on a more personalistic basis than in North America or Europe, and there are cultural practices like reciprocal gift-giving that are widely practiced and often shade into what many Westerners would label corruption. But to what extent does this lie at the root of the Asian crisis?

Again, an abstraction like "personalism" hides many divergent practices. Levels of corruption vary widely throughout the region. According to Transparency International's rankings of perceived levels of corruption, Singapore ranks number 7, ahead of European countries like the Netherlands, Norway, and Switzerland. Hong Kong is perceived as less corrupt than either Austria or the United States. China, on the other hand, is tied with Zambia at number 52, and Indonesia is close to the bottom at number 80. While the rule of law may not have roots as deep in Asia as in the West, it has been effectively implemented in Japan, Korea, Taiwan,

Singapore, and Hong Kong. It is therefore impossible to make the generalization that Asian societies are somehow more corrupt or more given to cronyism than their Western counterparts.

The opposite case can in fact be made, that cultural factors have contributed to a relatively low rate of corruption in Northeast Asia. One of the interesting features of industrial policy in Japan, Korea, and Taiwan is how little corruption there appears to have been during these countries' high-growth periods, in light of the enormous powers given to planning bureaucrats and the opportunities this created for corrupt or rent-seeking behavior. Prior to the 1990s, the major corruption scandals in Japan all involved politicians rather than bureaucrats in the Finance Ministry or MITI. Most observers credit former Korean president Park Chung-hee for being personally uncorrupt, and for reining in the Philippine-style cronyism that prevailed during his predecessor's administration. And others have gone so far as to level the counter argument that democratization in Korea, post-1987, was in fact responsible for the emergence in the 1990s of a large number of major corruption scandals, as a more inclusive political process posed temptations to a wider variety of politicians.

Japan, Korea, and Taiwan were able to cultivate a high degree of professionalism among their highly educated technocrats, norms that insulated them to some extent from the kinds of problems plaguing officials with similar powers in, say, Latin America. The problem in these countries was therefore not a cultural proclivity toward personalism and corrupt dealings, but rather a lack of institutional checks that could have served to control corrupt behavior.[12]

FUTURE PERCEPTIONS OF ASIAN VALUES

In the short run, the Asian crisis has produced a backlash against the United States, international financial institutions like the International Monetary Fund (IMF), and Western values more generally. The chief example of this is Malaysia's Mahathir, who has blamed his country's troubles on the global economy and on the Western policies that supported it, as well as on individuals like George Soros. Malaysia has since moved away from globalization by reimposing capital controls. The recessions and depressions in Korea, Indonesia, and other parts of Asia have produced a substantial amount of misery, and with it popular resentment against the West that is seen as the major proponent of globalization.

---

[12] This is not to say that institutional checks were lacking. In the case of the Japanese practice of *amakudari*, where a bureaucrat after retiring would go to work for a corporation, there were rules preventing regulators from working directly for his former regulatees.

Assuming that the current crisis does not deepen into a global depression or is otherwise prolonged, however, it seems likely that it will lead to a greater convergence of institutions between East and West, and that it will tend therefore to undermine arguments that there is a distinct set of Asian economic and political values. This is true both on an economic and on a political level.

In terms of economic ideas, the crisis has led to the unconditional defeat of the Japanese economic model of state-led development, which during the 1980s was trumpeted by leaders like Mahathir as an alternative to market-oriented Western modernization strategies. Whatever the past virtues of the Japanese model, seven years of stagnation, punctuated by recession, in Japan have put paid to this alternative. The Japanese themselves, albeit slowly and painfully, are in the process of dismantling many of the regulations and state institutions that set their country apart from the West; lifetime employment and the *keiretsu* system are unlikely to survive the current recession in Japan in anything like their earlier form. Institutions elsewhere in Asia patterned on Japanese practices, such as the Korean *chaebol*, are under similar pressure.

The more important area in which the crisis has undermined the case for Asian values is the political realm. Lee Kwan Yew argued that Western democracies were excessively preoccupied with individual rights rather than communal interests, and that in Asia there was a broad consensus in favor of strong governments that would single-handedly pursue economic growth. But while Lee from time to time tried to argue that traditional Confucian ideology could serve as a source of legitimacy in Singapore and other Asian societies, he never made the case that he or any other Asian leader personally held the mandate of heaven. Rather, legitimacy was built on economic success and the view that authoritarian government was better at producing growth than democracy.

The Asian crisis has, needless to say, demonstrated the weakness of this position. A leader whose legitimacy rests on uninterrupted growth has nothing to fall back on in times of recession or depression. Indonesia and Korea provide an interesting contrast in this regard. Indonesians understood perfectly well that the Suharto family over the past two decades was getting unusually rich, but many were willing to tolerate their evident corruption as long as the country as a whole was prospering. This good will rapidly dried up in the wake of the financial crisis, leading to the fall of the regime and ushering in the current period of instability. Even for a relatively poor country like Indonesia, there was no alternative to democracy as a source of legitimacy. Malaysia has experienced instability as well: the legitimacy of Mahathir's rule has been called into question, and the other great weakness of authoritarian government—its lack of effective mechanisms for bringing about political succession—is now plainly visible.

Korea, in contrast, although faced with a similarly grave economic crisis suffered no similar challenge to the fundamental legitimacy of its political institutions; indeed, Koreans managed to elect a long-time opponent of past military regimes, Kim Dae-jung, in the teeth of this crisis. There is no question that the crisis has posed many severe problems for Korean democracy, as workers and managers struggle with corporate restructuring, downsizing, and recession. The existence of democratic political institutions provides a forum, however imperfect, for these societal forces to try to resolve their differences in a structured way.

As in the economic sphere, Asian values in the wake of the economic crisis do not appear to suggest a serious alternative political model to that of Western democracy. It is possible that a dramatic worsening of the crisis could undermine support for globalization, democracy, and anything remotely connected with the West, but at this point there is no reason to think this is a likely outcome.

THE SOCIAL SPHERE

While Asian values have produced distinct economic and political institutions, their most notable impact is probably social. As noted earlier, values regarding family differ widely across Asia, but there are nonetheless no counterparts anywhere in Asia for Western social patterns—including among the region's most highly developed societies. The Asian members of the Organisation for Economic Co-operation and Development (OECD), Japan and Korea, are quite distinct from Western countries at a similar level of development. In both countries, crime rates are very low relative to Europe and even more so relative to the United States (Figure 9.1). In Japan, most types of crime have actually decreased over the past 40 years. Crime rates in postwar Korea have been higher than in Japan, and increased in 1982 apparently in connection with the Kwangju uprising and the political repression associated with Chun Du-hwan's rule. But even so, levels of crime in Korea have also been remarkably flat. Low crime rates in these two countries *ipso facto* invalidates any general theory that urbanization and industrialization inevitably encourage higher levels of criminal behavior.

It is not clear what is responsible for the low crime rates in these two countries. It is possible that the answers are different in each case: while Japanese society tends to smother deviance in a web of informal communal norms and obligations, the Koreans have been more inclined to use the naked power of the state to keep people in line. Even after Korea's

Figure 9.1. Crime Rates in Japan and Korea, 1970–1994

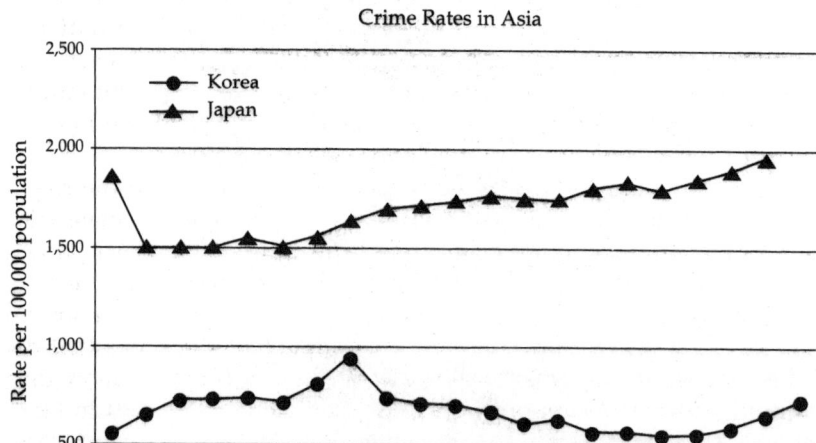

post-1987 democratization, police action has been strong when necessary to maintain public order.

Asian exceptionalism is also apparent in data on family structure.[13] Family structure has changed dramatically in Korea and in other modernizing Asian countries as various extended family systems are replaced with nuclear ones. The number of three-generation households dropped from 22.1 percent of all households in 1970 to 12.2 percent in 1990, and the average size of a household fell from 5.2 persons to 3.7 in the same period.[14]

Modernization has had a very different impact on family structure in Asia than it has in Europe and North America. In the West as in Asia, economic modernization broke down larger extended families, but its effects

---

[13] Other parts of Asia run counter to European patterns of modernization. In peninsular Malaysia and Indonesia, divorce rates have fallen sharply in tandem with economic modernization. See Gavin W. Jones, "Modernization and Divorce: Contrasting Trends in Islamic Southeast Asia and the West." *Population and Development Review*, vol. 23 (1997): 95–114.

[14] *Social Indicators in Korea* (Republic of Korea, National Statistical Office, 1995), p. 228. On changes in Korean family structure, see Yeonoak Baik and Jin Young Chung, "Family Policy in Korea." *Journal of Family and Economic Issues*, vol. 17 (1996): 93–112.

do not stop there. Between 1950 and 1990, the U.S. crude divorce rate moved from 2.6 to 4.7 and the British rate rose from 0.69 to 2.9. Illegitimacy rates have also soared, reaching well over 50 percent in Scandinavia and 32 percent in the United States. And although divorce rates have also been rising slightly in Japan, the problem of poor, single-parent families that is so pronounced in the United States is all but unknown in either Japan or Korea.

The reason for this difference has a great deal to do with the role of women in Western as opposed to Asian societies. While female labor force participation is reasonably high in Korea, Japan, and other parts of Asia, women tend to stop working when they get married and tend to return to the labor market, if ever, only when their children are grown. This tendency is reinforced by labor laws in Japan and Korea that discriminate against women in the workplace and make it much more difficult for them to earn an income sufficient to support themselves and their children over a lifetime.[15] An international survey that posited "Men should work outside the home and women should stay home" found the highest levels of agreement in Japan and Korea (30.6 and 35.9 percent, respectively).[16] The one area where Asian values diverge most strongly from Western ones arguably does not concern attitudes toward economic life or politics, but attitudes to gender relations and the family.

As in the case of Asia's distinctive economic institutions, it is likely that there will also be a convergence with Western practices over the next two generations in the social sphere. Due to its sharply declining fertility rate, Japan has a shrinking labor pool: in the late 1990s, for the first time, the Japanese workforce declined in absolute numbers. As we have seen, absent an unanticipated increase in fertility, Japan's total population will begin to decline early in the next century at a rate of well over 1 percent per year. The aging of Japan's population and the declining ratio of working-age to retired persons creates a huge future social security liability, and one that has already constrained Japan's ability to spend its way out of the 1998 recession. One method of mitigating this situation would be to allow more foreign workers into the country, something that Japan has resisted strongly up to now. The other possibility would be to encourage more women to remain with the workforce throughout their working

---

[15] On Korea, see Insook Han Park and Lee-Jay Cho, "Confucianism and the Korean Family," *Journal of Comparative Family Studies*, vol. 26 (1995): 117–133, and Hyoung Cho, "The Position of Women in the Korean Work Force," in Eui-Young Yu and Earl H. Philips, eds., *Korean Women in Transition* (Los Angeles: Center for Korean-American and Korean Studies, 1987); on Japan, see Eiko Shinotsuka, "Women Workers in Japan: Past, Present, Future," in Joyce Gelb and Marian Lief Palley, eds., *Women of Japan and Korea* (Philadelphia: Temple University Press, 1994), pp. 95–199.

[16] Shinotsuka in Gelb and Palley (1994), p. 102.

lives, as opposed to through the limited years prior to marriage. Of these two possibilities, Japanese policymakers are likely to favor the latter, raising the possibility that the social problems that have plagued Western countries, such as family breakdown and rising crime rates, may come to affect Japan as well.

A NOTE ON KOREAN VALUES

While there is a core of values that Koreans share with other Asians, Korea differs markedly from other Asian societies—and particularly from East Asia's oldest and most developed democracy, Japan—in ways that would seem to have some implications for the quality of democratic politics there. Koreans seem to prize social order less, and are more willing to engage in social and political struggle than other Asians.

This conclusion should be obvious to anyone aware of recent Korean history. Korea has Asia's best-organized and most powerful trade union movement, one that played an important role in bringing down the military dictatorship in 1987 and that has succeeded in extracting large yearly wage increases from Korean employers: over the past decade, labor costs in Korea have risen more than 600 percent. Korea also has Asia's most vocal and in many ways most radical student protest movement, one that also played a key political role during the 1987 events.

Surveys of Asian values, like that of David Hitchcock, show that Asians generally prize social order much more highly than do Americans.[17] This difference appears to be least marked in Korea. Take, for example, the willingness to engage in various forms of political protest. Table 9.1, based on Gallup data, shows the willingness of young people aged 18–29 from Europe, Japan, and Korea to take part in various forms of protest. In all but one category, young Koreans score higher in their willingness to protest than do young Japanese; in all but two categories, they also score higher than young Europeans. It should be noted that there is a clear generational shift at work here, since the table shows that for respondents aged 50 and older, Koreans are generally less willing to participate in protest than their European or Japanese counterparts—particularly for the more serious forms of protest. The willingness to protest of young Koreans sometimes shades into outright cynicism about the law: in another survey, 25–32 percent of the sample expressed a disregard for the law.[18]

---

[17] David Hitchcock, *Factors Affecting East Asian Views of the United States: The Search for Common Ground* (Washington, DC: CSIS, 1997), p. 73.

[18] Aie-Rie Lee, "Values, Government Performance, and Protest in South Korea," *Asian Affairs*, vol. 18 (1992): 240–253.

Table 9.1. Comparative Willingness of Europeans, Japanese, and Koreans to Engage in Protest (percent)

	Ages 18-29			Ages 50 and up		
	Europe	Japan	Korea	Europe	Japan	Korea
Sign a petition	42	54	58	32	23	36
Join in boycotts	44	54	55	17	44	31
Attend lawful demonstrations	44	36	51	23	22	13
Join unofficial strikes	32	25	23	7	8	4

Source: Data is taken from Aie-Rie Lee, "Culture Shift and Popular Protest in South Korea," *Comparative Political Studies,* vol. 26 (1993): 63–80.

The lesser value accorded to social order by Koreans is also borne out in a poll taken of its readers by the *Far Eastern Economic Review*. Koreans stood out for placing greater emphasis on "personal achievement," "achieving financial success," and "individual rights," and less on "orderly society," "respect for authority," "self-reliance," and "accountability" (Table 9.2).

The World Values Survey shows Korean trust level to be approximately comparable to those of a number of Catholic developed countries in Europe; slightly below Japan; and considerably below that of the United States and a number of European Protestant countries. Japan's relatively low trust score seems anomalous, but these findings are otherwise roughly consistent with the view that familism and regionalism, which limit the radius of trust to small groups, continue to be relatively strong factors in Korean culture, as they are in parts of Latin Catholic Europe and Latin America.[19]

I have argued elsewhere that Korea has a relatively low level of generalized social trust between people who do not belong to common families, kinship groups, or other small-scale social structures, an assertion that is

[19] Whatever the levels of social trust compared to other societies, public trust levels in Korea appear to have been improving over the past two decades. This would seem a natural development given the shift from military authoritarianism to democratic government in this period. In Korea, 77 percent of respondents said they approved of the present regime in 1997, compared to 17 percent who said they approved of the previous one. Forty one percent of Korean respondents said they felt "people like me" can have more influence on government in the present than they could under the previous regime, compared to 29 and 23 percent for the Czech Republic and the Russian Federation, two other countries that made the transition to democracy in this same period. Rose and Shin (1997), Figure 9.1 and Table 9.1.

Table 9.2. Relative Importance of Societal Values

	Very Important	Less Important
Honesty	Singapore, Philippines, Malaysia	Korea, Taiwan
Hard work	Singapore, Philippines, Hong Kong	Japan, Korea
Helping others	Thailand, Indonesia, Philippines	Korea
Respect for learning	Singapore, Philippines	Australia
Harmony	Indonesia, Malaysia	Australia, Western expatriates
Self-reliance	Singapore, Philippines, Malaysia	Korea
Orderly society	Singapore, Philippines, Malaysia	Korea
Freedom of expression	Australia, Philippines, Western expatriates	Singapore, Taiwan
Respect for authority	Philippines, Singapore, Malaysia, Indonesia	Korea, Japan, Western expatriates

Source: *Far Eastern Economic Review* (1996), August 1.

generally borne out by the data presented above.[20] In this respect, Korean culture is closer to that of traditional China than Japan, and the problems of inadequate trust should resemble those of the former country. There is no ready counterpart in Korean culture to the Japanese concept of *amae*, the unwillingness to take advantage of other people's weaknesses that is important in establishing bonds of mutual dependence in Japanese society.[21] Many observers have consequently argued that Korean culture is more individualistic—more "Western"—than that of Japan.[22] While this perception is in many ways accurate, true individualism is less prevalent than a certain kind of small-group solidarity within what Koreans call the *uri*, or "we-group," defined by family, friends, neighbors, classmates, military academy graduating class, and the like.[23]

---

[20] See *Trust: The Social Virtues and the Creation of Prosperity* (New York: Free Press, 1995), pp. 127–145.

[21] For a discussion of this point, see Fukuyama (1995), p. 135.

[22] Byong-Nak Song, *Rise of the Korean Economy* (Hong Kong: Oxford University Press, 1990), p. 199.

[23] See Diane Hoffman, "Culture, Self, and 'Uri': Anti-Americanism in Contemporary South Korea." *Journal of Northeast Asian Studies* (1993): 3–20; and Yun-Shik Chang, "The Personalist Ethic and the Market in Korea." *Journal for the Comparative Study of Society and History*, vol. 33 (1991): 106–129.

The problems created by a small radius of trust can affect the quality of governance within a democracy. Strongly familistic societies tend to develop a two-tier system of ethical values, with high standards of behavior reserved for relations within the family or other types of personal relations and lower ones for public life. One consequence of this is a poorly developed sense of civic obligation that in turn engenders a propensity for political corruption. Corruption produces economic inefficiency and, from the standpoint of democratic order, increases citizen cynicism over the political system.

Beyond these obvious and relatively recent sources of social distrust are longer-term cultural patterns of hierarchy and authority. By all accounts, class structure in premodern Korea was more rigid than its Japanese and Chinese counterparts. The gulf between *Yangban* and *Chonmin* was large and for all practical purposes unbridgeable, and the history of dynastic Korea is marked by periodic peasant uprisings. Class cleavages and sharply hierarchical authority persist under the current democratic regime, most notably in the internal structure of large Korean corporations. Most Korean *chaebols* are much more hierarchical than the Japanese *zaibatsu* or postwar *keiretsu* on which they were modeled, though practice varies from one group to another. Additionally, the *chaebols* have never practiced corporate paternalism—for example, by providing extensive in-company welfare and support services—to the extent that Japanese corporations do.

The consequences of this authoritarian business culture are manifest in labor-management relations, which given the current economic crisis will probably be the most significant source of social conflict and perhaps even instability over the next few years. The militancy of Korea's trade union movement was evident in the 1996–97 showdown between the unions on the one hand and the employers and the government party on the other, a confrontation in which neither side acquitted themselves well. The unions, which had been responsible for driving Korean labor costs up to perhaps 70 percent of Japan's by 1996, were for their part uncompromising in the face of employer demands for greater flexibility in wages and hiring. In response, the government, facing intransigence from both the unions and from the opposition party, forced through new labor legislation in a special early-morning session to which only its own members had been invited. It also used the occasion to pass new national security legislation that many observers feared would give the government new powers to restrict individual rights. The economic crisis that Korea now faces can only add further stresses to what is already an uneasy relationship, by increasing unemployment, forcing wage cuts, and dramatically raising the incidence of bankruptcies.

There is, fortunately, an important positive to the all-too-evident divisions within Korean society. To any Western observer, Korean politics looks much more recognizable than does Japanese democracy, despite the latter's greater age and greater degree of institutionalization. What seems strangest about Japan is the fact that the different social actors are so reticent in asserting their interests against various forms of authority. The interests of workers are smothered in a system of corporate unions and lifetime employment, and the long-ruling Liberal Democratic Party is run on a personalistic basis that amalgamates a wide variety of frequently contradictory societal interests; for example, rice farmers and industrialists. Korean interest groups, on the other hand, are not reluctant to challenge authority—and at times do so violently. Workers and managers dislike each other and are prepared to fight for a bigger piece of the pie. In an authoritarian political system, this might be a formula for instability, but if Korea's interest groups learn to use the available democratic political mechanisms to advance their interests, Korean politics might well develop along more European lines. That could see political participation broaden with the development of societal interest groups, and ultimately the emergence of distinctive political parties representing those interests. One of the unfortunate things that Korea has imported from Japan is the concept of a broad, all-embracing majority party that remains in power for extended periods of time, rather than smaller but more focused parties alternating in power. Whether or not the election of Kim Dae-jung will break this mold and force the definition of a multiparty system based on underlying societal interests rather than on personalities remains to be seen.

One further aspect of Korean values that will affect the country's future social stability relates to the traditional cultural preference for sons. Medical technology has given parents the ability to choose the sex of their children, and sex ratios have shifted in favor of boys throughout much of Confucian Asia (with the exception of Japan). According to demographer Nicholas Eberstadt, this has in recent years produced the sex ratio in China of approximately 118 males to 100 females; and in Korea, 122 males for every 100 females.[24] This does not bode well for Korea's future social stability, given the fact that young, unattached males are responsible for the vast majority of crime, violence, and general mayhem in any society. With as much as one-fifth of the male population unable to find Korean brides, there will be strong competition for women, a competition that will spill over into the north if the peninsula is unified by that time.

---

[24] Nick Eberstadt, "Asia Tomorrow, Gray and Male," *National Interest*, no. 53 (1998), pp. 56–65.

CONCLUSIONS

Asian values in all their diversity have played a role in shaping the economic and political institutions of East Asia and in giving Asian societies a very different degree of social order than that of the developed countries of the West. The impact of these factors can be easily overstated, however, both in terms of the degree to which they facilitated Asia's postwar economic growth and in the extent to which they are responsible for the region's current troubles. In the three areas of economics, politics, and society, there are good reasons for thinking that the distinctive institutions and practices fostered by Asia's cultural systems will converge over time with the patterns seen in the West. That is, economic life will be more open and subject to market forces; governance will be increasingly democratic; and social structure (as well as social problems) will come to resemble that of postindustrial Western societies. Far from reinforcing Asian exceptionalism, the current economic crisis will accelerate homogenizing trends in all three areas.

REFERENCES

Baik, Yeonoak, and Jin Young Chung. 1996. "Family Policy in Korea." *Journal of Family and Economic Issues* 17.

Chang, Yun-Shik. 1991. "The Personalist Ethic and the Market in Korea." *Journal for the Comparative Study of Society and History* 33.

Cho, Hyoung. 1987. "The Position of Women in the Korean Work Force." In Eui-Young Yu and Earl H. Philips, eds., *Korean Women in Transition.* Los Angeles: Center for Korean-American and Korean Studies.

Coppedge, Michael. 1997. *Inequality, Democracy, and Economic Development* Cambridge: Cambridge University Press.

Diamond, Larry. 1992. "Economic Development and Democracy Reconsidered." *American Behavioral Scientist* 15.

Eberstadt, Nick. 1998. "Asia Tomorrow, Gray and Male." *National Interest* 53.

Far Eastern Economic Review August 1, 1996.

Fareed, Zakaria. 1994. "A Conversation with Lee Kuan Yew." *Foreign Affairs* 73(2): 109–127.

Hitchcock, David. 1997. *Factors Affecting East Asian Views of the United States: The Search for Common Ground.* Washington, D.C.: CSIS.

Hoffman, Diane. 1993. "Culture, Self, and "Uri": Anti-Americanism in Contemporary South Korea." *Journal of Northeast Asian Studies.*

Huntington, Samuel P. 1991a. *The Third Wave: Democratization in the Late Twentieth Century.* Oklahoma City: University of Oklahoma Press.

———. 1991b. "Religion and the Third Wave." *National Interest* 24 (Summer 1991): 29–42.

Jones, Gavin W. 1997 "Modernization and Divorce: Contrasting Trends in Islamic Southeast Asia and the West." *Population and Development Review* 23.

Krugman, Paul R. 1994. "The Myth of Asia's Miracle." *Foreign Affairs* 73.

Lee, Aie-Rie. 1992 "Values, Government Performance, and Protest in South Korea." *Asian Affairs* 18.

———. 1993. "Culture Shift and Popular Protest in South Korea." *Comparative Political Studies* 26.

Lipset, Seymour Martin.1959. "Some Social Requisites of Democracy: Economic Development and Political Legitimacy." *American Political Science Review* 53.

———. 1994. "The Social Requisites of Democracy Revisited." *American Sociological Review* 59.

Park, Insook Han, and Lee-Jay Cho. 1995. "Confucianism and the Korean Family." *Journal of Comparative Family Studies* 26.

Przeworski, Adam, and Michael Alvarez. 1996. "What Makes Democracies Endure?" *Journal of Democracy* 7.

Republic of Korea. 1995. *Social Indicators in Korea 1995.* National Statistical Office.

Sen, Amartya. 1997. *Human Rights and Asian Values.* New York: Carnegie Council on Ethics and Public Policy.

Shinotsuka, Eiko. 1994. "Women Workers in Japan: Past, Present, Future." In Joyce Gelb and Marian Lief Palley, eds., *Women of Japan and Korea*. Philadelphia: Temple University Press.

Song, Byong-Nak.1990. *Rise of the Korean Economy*. Hong Kong: Oxford University Press.

Wei-Ming, Tu. 1996 *Confucian Traditions in East Asian Modernity: Moral Education and Economic Culture in Japan and the Four Dragons*. Cambridge, MA: Harvard University Press.

10

VALUES, CULTURE, AND DEMOCRACY: A KOREAN PERSPECTIVE

Jong-keun You

THE QUESTION OF WHETHER or not Asian values and culture are compatible with democratic governance, in the public sector as well as in the corporate sector, is one that carries great weight in light of the recent worldwide financial turmoil. In the past, Asian values attracted much attention as a foundation for the region's economic success. These same values and their alleged deficiencies are now being blamed as one of the root causes of the Asian economic crisis and of the spectacular failure of several of the region's high-flying economies.

In the course of the debate on the economic crisis, the so-called Asian values have been oversimplified to mean filial piety, diligence in school and work, respect for one's elders, and so on and so forth. This oversimplification has caused much confusion. The concepts of values from culture are inevitably interrelated, but it is important to distinguish between the two.

Webster's *New Universal Unabridged Dictionary* defines "values" as "the ideals, customs, institutions, etc. of a society toward which the people of the group have an affective regard." "Culture" is defined as "the behavior and beliefs characteristic of a particular social, ethnic, or age group," or "the sum total of ways of living built up by a group of human beings and transmitted from one generation to another."

There is a considerable area of overlap for which "value" and "culture" can be used more or less interchangeably. The two words, however, are not synonymous, and the difference between them is more than simply nuance. For clarity of discussion, I will use the word "value" in reference to the "ideals" of a society toward which the people of the group have an affective regard. "Culture" will be used in reference to the "customs and behaviors" that are characteristic of a particular social or ethnic group.

Asia is a vast region of diverse cultures, and it is inappropriate to talk about Asian values and culture as if the region were homogenous. This paper will focus on the area in which Confucian values and culture exert the predominant influence, with particular emphasis on Korea.

MARKET ECONOMY AND THE RULE OF LAW

The exchange crisis of 1997 turned the miracle economy of Korea into a shambles. In an attempt to explain the crisis, many Western observers decried the Asian economies for "crony capitalism," ridiculing this as an inevitable byproduct of Asian values. Mortimer Zuckerman, for example, wrote that "Asian values have now become Asian liabilities."[1] It is true that cronyism is responsible to a considerable degree for the failure of the Asian economies, and it is also true that cronyism, while not a uniquely Asian phenomenon, is a distinctive shortcoming of Asian societies. But before one characterizes it as an inevitable result of the moral deficiencies of Asian values, one needs to conduct a more thorough analysis of Asia's values, cultures, and institutions.

The explanation most commonly offered for the cause of the Asian financial crisis is moral hazard. The corporations that borrowed money from the financial institutions, and the financial institutions that lent money entrusted to them by their depositors behaved irresponsibly prior to the crisis because of a lack of discipline on the parts of those responsible for financial losses. Rampant moral hazard led to extremely high debt-equity ratios in the corporate sector, excessively risky investments, and the piling up of bad assets by the financial institutions. This created serious structural vulnerabilities in the economy.

Economic theory tells us that moral hazard may arise when the market suffers from information imperfections, but that it may be made manageable through the use of appropriate institutional devices. When moral hazard originates from fundamental defects in legal discipline, however—a discipline that economic theory usually takes for granted—it can bring the entire economic system to the brink of collapse. Many Eastern European countries, in their transition to a market economy, suffered terribly when the breakdown of their legal systems created moral hazard of historic proportions. It is understandable that such confusion could occur in countries that were trying to dismantle one economic system and erect a new one in a matter of a few years. But how could Korea, a seemingly successful market economy, suffer from such a basic institutional defect?

The source of the problem, I believe, is the traditional disregard for the rule of law in Korea. Consider, for example, how legal discipline in finance gradually disintegrated in Korea. After nationalization in 1971, Korea's banks mismanaged their lending practices and accumulated an unhealthy sum of high-risk and ultimately nonperforming loans. Ironically, however, it was when the government engaged in privatizing and

---

[1] Mortimer Zuckerman, "Japan Inc. Unravels: How Asian Values Have Become Asian Liabilities," *U.S. News & World Report*, August 17, 1998.

liberalizing the banking sector in the early 1980s that the problems began to systematically proliferate. Although ownership of the commercial banks was handed over to the private sector, the government continued to intervene in their management. In theory, liberalization should have accompanied privatization; in practice, Korea's politicians and bureaucrats had no intention of actually relinquishing their power. Behind the scenes, they continued to exercise control over the banks, resulting in a growing divergence between what was on the books and what was happening in reality. The rule of law was undermined.

The single most important government intervention in the management of the commercial banks was the appointment of the directors and the CEOs. Despite the fact that the banks were private institutions, everyone took it for granted that the Ministry of Finance and the President would have the final say in selecting the bank directors and their chairmen. Given this environment, it was only natural for bank directors to do what they thought would please the politicians and bureaucrats—even if it meant neglecting profit maximization and proper risk management. The circumvention of rules and regulations became commonplace. Compounding the problem, the financial supervisory bodies were unwilling or unable to step in, as they could not afford to confront the powerful people who were ultimately responsible for the irregularities. Even when irregularities occurred in the absence of pressure from above, the supervisors would turn a blind eye in order to avoid accusations of uneven or unfair enforcement of the rules.

Moral hazard in finance proliferated and discipline in the financial institutions evaporated, not for want of prudential regulations but because of the government's inability to enforce them. This in turn led to the widespread problem of bad lending by the financial market. In an economy where bank loans can be easily arranged using political influence, the worse the financial situation of a firm is, the harder it will try to secure finance through lobbying bureaucrats and politicians. A firm that is technically bankrupt and without any hope for a real turnaround will frequently seek to survive by obtaining additional credits. In Korea, the case of Hanbo Steel is a good example. By offering substantial contributions to the nation's most powerful politicians, Hanbo's founder-chairman Chung Tae-soo managed to secure a total of 5.7 trillion won (about US$7 billion) in bank loans before his empire finally crumbled under the weight of snowballing debts. Nor was Hanbo an exceptional case: almost every major Korean *chaebol* accumulated an unmanageable amount of debts in the same manner.

The rule of law is the foundation of a market economy. Whether competition improves or destroys welfare depends on whether the means of competition is improvement of one's own performance or of sabotaging and cheating one's competitors. The rule of law enables efficient market competition by prohibiting the latter. No matter how fierce competition may be, a market economy must be a place where the rule of law reigns, not the law of the jungle.

Democracy promotes the rule of law through checks and balances on the exercise of power. The democratization process in Korea since 1987 was so limited and distorted, however, that it contributed little to the promotion of the rule of law. Until the presidential election of 1997, the opposition had virtually no chance of winning power: the most basic mechanism of checks and balances therefore remained absent. Pre-1997, the ruling party never expected any change of government and the president, while elected by popular vote, behaved little differently from military dictators in his exercise of power above the law. It seems fair to conclude that the success of the Korean reform drive hinges on establishing the rule of law.

DEMOCRATIC VALUES AND THE RULE OF LAW

It may be argued that the failure of Asian economies is attributable to their failure to practice genuine democracy. Many Koreans who profess to believe in democracy actually want a "benevolent government" by "virtuous men." To many, democratic processes are cumbersome, inefficient, and unnecessary: even 50 years after democracy was first introduced in Korea, there is a lack of a law-abiding spirit and a persistent avoidance of legal procedures. The contradiction between our wish for democratic governance and our daily practices is a tremendous obstacle to our quest to become a modern democratic society.

While the law presides over government, the maintenance of social order, realization of rights and responsibilities, punishment, and societal reform, it also holds a bigger role in the development of society. Specifically, adherence to the rule of law enables society to form a basis for rational and predictable behavior. In a truly democratic society where the rule of law prevails, accountability, fair competition, and transparency are the fundamental principles that govern the management of public affairs. Adherence to these principles annuls the threat of cronyism. As such, the blame for the Asian crisis must be placed on Asia's undemocratic governments, as opposed to undemocratic values. This distinction lies at the heart of an earlier debate over values, culture, and governance between Lee Kwan Yew and Kim Dae-jung.[2]

---

[2] See Lee Kwan Yew, "Culture is Destiny," *Foreign Affairs*, (Spring 1994), and Kim Dae-jung, "Is Culture Destiny?" *Foreign Affairs*, (Winter 1994).

The question of why Asian societies have failed to practice genuine democracy remains unanswered, however. Does the fault lie in Asia's values, in its cultures, or in its systems of governance? What we have learned from the Asian experience is that there is a distinct two-way relationship between the failure to institute democratic principles and cronyism. To answer this question, we need to consider the interrelationship between values, culture, and democracy—or the lack thereof.

Until recently, democracy was predominantly a Western phenomenon, this fact purportedly supporting the conclusion by some observers that Asian or African societies are not suitable for democracy. History simply does not bear this out—to say that Asia lacks a cultural and political heritage suitable for democracy would be as wrong as if one were to say that the West lacked a history susceptible to authoritarianism or dictatorship. It should be remembered that, until after the end of the Second World War, many Americans asserted that Germans are incapable of practicing democracy.

Looking at this issue from another perspective, one can see clear similarities in the political philosophies that guide democratically oriented societies in Asia and in the West. According to John Locke, sovereign rights reside with the people; based upon a contract with the people, leaders are given a mandate to govern, which the people may usurp.[3] Locke's philosophies echo those espoused nearly 2,000 years earlier by the Chinese philosopher Mengtzu (Mencius), who said that heaven bestows upon the king, or "son of heaven," the mandate to provide good and benevolent government. If the king fails to govern righteously, the people have the right to rise up and overthrow his government in the name of heaven.[4]

Where Locke and Mengtzu diverge, however, is on the issue of the mandate. Locke's philosophies frown upon the idea of heavenly or divine mandate, arguing that a leader's right to rule is based solely on a mandate of the people. But while Locke is careful to maintain the separation between church and state, it is Judeo-Christian ideas that provide the foundation for Western societies. One of the key principles in the teaching of Jesus Christ is that to serve men, even the least of them, is to serve God.[5] The connection between the West's "mandate of the people" and

---

[3] See John Locke, "Second Treatise on Government, Concerning Civil Government, Second Essay, An Essay Concerning the True Original Extent and End of Civil Government" (1690).

[4] See D.C. Lau's *Mencius* (New York: Penguin Books, 1970) and Philip Ivanhoe, *Ethics in the Confucian Tradition: The Thought of Mencius and Wang Ying-ming* (Atlanta: Scholars Press, 1990).

[5] The Gospel According to Matthew, 25:31–46.

the idea espoused in Eastern thought, that the "will of the people" is the "will of heaven," is clear.

In terms of the basic values that Western and Eastern societies have sought to realize, there is therefore no fundamental difference. The answer to whether or not democracy and a market economy can work together lies not in the differences in values that divide East and West, but rather in the common values and fundamental principles that connect democratic peoples all over the world.

DEMOCRATIC PRINCIPLES

An affective regard for democratic values does not by itself guarantee the successful realization of those values. Realization of democratic values requires the institutionalization of the fundamental principles of accountability, fair competition, and transparency. Furthermore, successful institutionalization of these principles requires a strict adherence to the principle of the rule of law.

When looking at the causes of the Korean economic crisis, it is evident that the problem can be attributed to the weakness of the Korean financial system, and specifically to the plague of bad debts that followed a succession of corporate bankruptcies. To restructure the banking system, the government has allocated 64 trillion won (US$79 billion)—about 15 percent of gross domestic product (GDP)—to purchase nonperforming loans from financial institutions and to help recapitalize the banks. The significance of this allocation of funds is the enormous sum of nonperforming loans, which was estimated at 120 trillion won (US$147 billion) at the end of March 1999. The loans were originally made predominantly to *chaebols* seeking expansion into high-risk industries, often at the expense of shareholder value. Despite the risks involved, Korea's financial institutions did not restrict their lending to the *chaebols*.

Bad lending practices were not a result of the lack of laws or regulations governing the financial institutions, but the result of a lack of adherence to these rules. The restructuring agenda of the financial sector reveals the need for reforms to increase the legal liability of management. In other words, banks must be effectively supervised to ensure they do not take excessive risks of this nature, and that they maintain the resources to pay back depositors. Furthermore, corporations must follow appropriate rules of governance to ensure that managers, as agents for shareholders, act responsibly. These rules include increasing the transparency of the *chaebols'* operations by requiring consolidated financial statements, by introducing external auditor committees, and by improving auditing standards. Markets will not allocate funds to borrowers unless investors have precise and timely information about the prospective borrower that they are able to effectively use. It is because these elements were not in place in the run-up to the crisis that credits were badly allocated, making the Korean economy vulnerable to a collapse of confidence among firms and investors.

Improving governance of the financial institutions does not necessarily entail setting up a legal system modeled on that of the West. Governance should focus primarily on implementing and, more importantly, enforcing rules that prevent the practice of lending to high-risk borrowers and that prevent corporate managers from exploiting conflicts of interest. In addition, it is important that Korea increase the capacity of its regulatory and judicial bodies to handle disputes over corporate matters.

In a society in which power is overly centralized, such as that in which credence is given to a "heavenly mandate," abuses can spread unchecked by the people—except on the rare occasions when they reach such an extreme that the people rise up in revolt and overthrow their government. The causes of the economic crisis seem to indicate that Asian societies lacked the wisdom of Lord Acton, who wrote that "Power tends to corrupt and absolute power tends to corrupt absolutely."[6] It was because of this understanding of the nature of power that Europe devised what is possibly the greatest contribution to modern democracy: the rule of law coupled with the electoral system.

In many ways, elections are analogous to the market competition that enhances the welfare of consumers. In a monopolistic market, consumers can be—and usually are—exploited. Similarly, one-party rule inevitably results in government arrogance, corruption, and inefficiency, in a political exploitation of the "consumer"—in this case, the constituent. But there is one essential difference between a monopoly in the market for goods and services and a monopoly of power by a political party: In the market, consumers have the option to refrain from making purchases. Citizens subjected to a one-party dictatorship do not have this option.[7]

In contrast, where two or more political parties and candidates compete for votes, the constituents are the sovereign power (or de facto sovereign in a constitutional monarchy), just as the consumers exercise the ultimate power in a competitive market for goods and services. In other words, elections are an effective device to ensure that each candidate or party for public office will strive to come up with better policies than its opponents do. Periodic elections are not only a means by which the views

---

[6] Lord Acton, from letter to Bishop Mandell Creighton, April 1887; see *"The Life and Letters of Mandell Creighton"* (1904).

[7] See You Jong-Keun, "Democracy and the Role of the Media," in *Creating a Dynamic Future: Local to Global Initiatives* (Chonju, Korea: 1998), pp. 9–23.

of constituents are registered, but are also a powerful reminder to incumbents that they serve at the pleasure of the people. In sum, elections are a device to hold elected officials and their parties accountable for what they have or have not accomplished during their tenure. In both the Eastern and Western interpretation, the people have, in principle, the right to replace a malevolent ruler: one by a mandate from heaven; the other, by a mandate of law. In other words, Eastern societies have also traditionally believed in the principle of holding their governments accountable to the people. Without an institutionalized mechanism to do so, however, the difficulty in upholding this principle has been far greater in the East than in the West.

Asia has a historical record of maintaining a level of fair competition and equal opportunity that refutes the myth that it has chronically unfair playing fields. For nearly 1,000 years in China and Korea, even the sons of high-ranking officials could not be appointed to important positions unless they passed civil service examinations. This system guaranteed a level of equal opportunity and social mobility, in sharp contrast to that of the European fiefdoms of the time or even, until recently, to that of the present-day British House of Lords, where bloodlines preserved a seat.

In a society that upholds the principles of accountability and fair competition, honesty and transparency are naturally respected. There is an anecdote that has been passed down in East Asia as an important lesson on maintaining honesty and transparency. During the later Han dynasty in China, a local magistrate was approached by his subordinate in the middle of the night. The latter offered the magistrate a large sum of money and said, "No one knows about this." But the magistrate refused to accept the money and admonished his subordinate by saying, "Heaven and Earth know, and you and I know! How can you say no one knows?"

Eastern societies have not failed to practice democracy because they do not have an affective regard for democratic values. Nor have they failed because they do not understand and care for such democratic principles as accountability, fair competition, and transparency. Why, then, have they failed?

DEMOCRACY AND CULTURE

In Western democracy, Judeo-Christian values underpin the sociopolitical institutions. The implicit goal of the state is the realization of the values expressed in the Lord's Prayer: "Thy kingdom come; thy will be done, on Earth as it is in Heaven." This same idea is expressed in Eastern thought as a "great peace under heaven," which can be realized by obeying the will of heaven—i.e., the will of the people.

The state that seeks the fulfillment and realization of the will of the people as its ultimate goal implicitly seeks "government for the people." In Eastern thought, this goal is implied by Mengtzu's doctrine justifying the overthrow of a government that turns against its people. In Western democracy, the principle is famously enshrined in Abraham Lincoln's Gettysburg Address.[8]

The institutional or methodological settings that promote "government for the people" and that seek to realize "great peace under heaven" diverge between East and West. Western democracies recognize the people as the sovereign ("government of the people") and select their leaders through periodic elections ("government by the people"). In contrast, Confucian thought states that "only when states are well-governed [zhiguo] will there be peace under heaven [pingtianxia]." Good governance requires a class of ruling elite who are well-cultivated (xiushen) and able to keep their families in order (qijia). The condition of "great peace under heaven" is therefore to be realized through a four-step process (xiushen qijia zhiguo pingtianxia) that ultimately relies on the rule of man— albeit of well-cultivated man.[9]

Herein lies one of the major reasons why Korean and other Eastern societies, in spite of their affective regard for democratic values and their acceptance of democratic principles, have failed to realize these ideals. They do not understand the importance of the principle of the rule of law, without which the principles of accountability, fair competition, and transparency can be easily violated. Many contemporary Koreans would still prefer a benevolent dictator ahead of an ineffectual democrat, and many yearn for the days of Park Chung-hee.

There is another reason why Eastern societies have failed to practice democratic principles: the extended family culture. Our ways of thinking and living—our culture—are conditioned by the prevailing socioeconomic structure. As the latter changes, the former also change. But man's thought structure, customs, and behavior cannot be quickly changed. In the West, industrialization and the accompanying changes in socioeconomic structure took place over many generations, and people thus were afforded the time to adjust their thinking and behavior. In Korea, in contrast, the transformation from an agrarian to an industrial society has taken place in a single generation, and people have had little time to make the commensurate adjustment of their thinking and behavior. To compound this problem, we now find ourselves at the

---

[8] Abraham Lincoln, Pres. U.S., 1809–1865, "Lincoln's Gettysburg Address in Translation." See U.S. Library of Congress Cataloging in Publication Data ISBN 0-8444-0018-1.

[9] Attributed to Confucius in prelude to "The Great Learning," paragraph 4–5; see also Confucian Analects, Chapter 1, Section 5.

threshold of an information- and knowledge-driven post-industrial society. The Korean family structure has also changed, to the point that the once-common three-generation household is now almost a rarity. In spite of these dramatic changes, the dominant feature of Korean customs and behavior is the extended family culture of an agrarian society.[10]

An important characteristic of a market economy is that the producer and consumer of a given good or service is seldom the same person. Producers thus compete fiercely for the trust of consumers. This competition is the driving force that helps a market economy grow. At the same time, a market economy features extensive division of labor, and, as a result, strong interdependency between economic agents. Prosperity in a society driven by a competitive market therefore requires not only competitiveness but also trust and cooperation, and these in turn depend on fairness, honesty, and accountability.

An agrarian society is characterized by much less division of labor and interdependency. In addition, personal wealth is more or less proportional to how much land one possesses. In such a society, particularly in one where there is limited arable land relative to the number of people to feed, such as China or Korea, wealth distribution is viewed as a zero-sum game. This is well explained by a Korean proverb that says, "When your cousin buys an additional rice paddy, you get a stomachache [in envy]."

Koreans thus tend to trust the members of the modern-day equivalent of their extended family—for example, clansmen, school alumni, and people hailing from their hometown—and strongly distrust others. Members of the "family" are not held accountable for their actions, as introducing accountability would potentially weaken the family to breach by outsiders. By the same token, the rules of fair competition do not apply within the family as a fair competition could conceivably be won by an outsider. Within the family, it is even acceptable to bend the rules and twist or obscure the facts. Koreans may have in principle accepted the tenets of accountability, fair competition, and transparency, but their overriding concern for "family members" has eclipsed their concern for these principles.

The tendency to distrust outsiders can be found in almost every aspect of Korean society. For example, Korean bureaucracy has a notorious reputation for refusing to share information between departments or divisions. Even when the nation was at the precipice of defaulting on its external financial obligations, senior officials of the Korean government

---

[10] Francis Fukuyama describes Korea as a *"familistic"* society. See his *Trust: The Social Virtues and the Creation of Prosperity* (New York: Free Press, 1995).

were unable to act together and the president was given conflicting information. In the end, it was U.S. President Clinton who warned President Kim Young-sam of Korea's imminent liquidity crisis.

There is another area in which Korea's culture of the extended family exerts a strong influence: corporate structure. Traditionally, Koreans have regarded it a blessing to have a large family and many sons. This may explain why the *chaebols* have been obsessed with expanding their empires, regardless of profitability, and why their subsidiaries support each other with cross-debt guarantees and unlawful intragroup transactions. It is in sharp contrast with the fact that each subsidiary of a Western conglomerate must stand on its own feet, and may again reflect a cultural difference. In the West, siblings are generally expected to compete against each other; in Korea, they are morally obligated to help each other. Rather than sibling rivalry, the *chaebols* tend to practice a corporate version of sibling solidarity in which the weaker subsidiaries are propped up with financial help from the stronger ones.

CONCLUSION

It would be a mistake to blame Asian values for the Asian economic crisis: Asians share basically the same democratic values as their Western counterparts. Realization of these democratic values, however, has been obstructed by a lack of respect for the principle of the rule of law and by the culture of the extended family, in which people tend to trust members of "family" and distrust outsiders. The extended family culture is characteristic of an agrarian society, and is a culture that persists in Korea as people have struggled to adapt to the change, effected in a single generation, from an agrarian to an industrialized society. Industrialization in the West took many generations, in contrast, affording people the time to make the cultural adjustment.

Does this imply that Koreans will be unable to realize their democratic values for generations to come? I do not believe so. Global integration of the markets has changed the nature of competition, putting great pressure on all of us to discard our old ways of thinking. Prior to the onset of the economic crisis at the end of 1997, Koreans regarded foreigners using their typical extended family way of thinking—i.e., with extreme distrust. Foreign investment would have been tantamount to colonization of the national economy. The crisis has forced Koreans to change their way of thinking, however. In a remarkable turnaround, they have quickly embraced foreign investment as beneficial to their national interests. There is now also widespread agreement that accountability, fair competition, and transparency are essential to creating the foundation for the rebuilding of the nation.

The convergence of economic systems and institutions as a result of globalization has additionally created new pressure to harmonize economic policies and government practices. The World Trade Organization (WTO), Organisation for Economic Co-operation and Development (OECD), and APEC are promulgating new rules and policy guidelines for their member nations, and the competitive pressure of the globalized markets makes it imperative that these nations adapt their policies to the new reality.

REFERENCES

Acton, Lord. 1904. Letter to Bishop Mandell Creighton, April, 1887. In *The Life and Letters of Mandell Creighton*.

Dae-jung, Kim. 1994. "Is Culture Destiny?." *Foreign Affairs* (Winter).

Fukuyama, Francis. 1995. *Trust: The Social Virtues and the Creation of Prosperity*. New York: Free Press.

Ivanhoe, Philip. 1990. *Ethics in the Confucian Tradition: The Thought of Mencius and Wang Ying-ming*. Atlanta: Scholars Press.

Jong-Keun, You. 1998. "Democracy and the Role of the Media." In *Creating a Dynamic Future: Local to Global Initiatives*. Chonju, Korea.

Kwan Yew, Lee. 1994. "Culture is Destiny." *Foreign Affairs* (Spring).

Lau, D. C. 1970. *Mencius*. New York: Penguin Books.

Locke, John. 1690. *Second Treatise on Government, Concerning Civil Government, Second Essay, An Essay Concerning the True Original Extent and End of Civil Government*.

Zuckerman, Mortimer, 1998. "Japan Inc. Unravels: How Asian Values Have Become Asian Liabilities." *U.S. News & World Report*, August 17.